Critical Essays on Henry James: The Late Novels

Critical Essays on Henry James: The Late Novels

James W. Gargano

G.K. Hall & Co. • Boston, Massachusetts

Library of Congress Cataloging-in-Publication Data

Critical essays on Henry James: The Late Novels.

(Critical essays on American literature)
Includes index.
1. James, Henry, 1843–1916—Criticism and
interpretation.   I. Gargano, James W.   II. Series.
PS2117.C75   1987   813′.4   86-25686
ISBN 0-8161-8877-7   (alk. paper)
        0-8161-8882-3 (set)

This publication is printed on permanent/durable acid-free paper
MANUFACTURED IN THE UNITED STATES OF AMERICA

CRITICAL ESSAYS ON AMERICAN LITERATURE

This series seeks to anthologize the most important criticism on a wide variety of topics and writers in American literature. Our readers will find in various volumes not only a generous selection of reprinted articles and reviews but original essays, bibliographies, manuscript sections, and other materials brought to public attention for the first time. This volume, the second in a series on Henry James, contains a selection of reprinted reviews and comments by William Dean Howells and Joseph Conrad as well as by William Morton Payne, Harry T. Peck, Richard A. Hocks, Marcia Jacobson, Sallie Sears, and Ruth Bernard Yeazell. In addition to an extensive critical introduction by James W. Gargano, there are original essays by Barton Levi St. Armand and Daniel Mark Fogel. We are confident that this volume will make a permanent and significant contribution to American literary study.

JAMES NAGEL, GENERAL EDITOR

Northeastern University

CONTENTS

INTRODUCTION

Henry James ruefully assessed his literary prospects at the start of 1895 in a confessional letter to William Dean Howells. His sanguine dramatic hopes dashed by the hisses that greeted his appearance on stage after the performances of *Guy Domville* in January 1895, he saw his future as made up of rejection and shrinking opportunities: "what is clear is that periodical publication is practically closed to me—I'm the last hand that the magazines, in this country or in the U.S., seem to want."[1] Resorting to his sovereign remedy in troubled times, he applied himself to the "pale little art of fiction," which a zeal for the stage had led him to patronize and, with creative prodigality, he produced, before the turn of the century, such experimental novels as *The Other House* (*Illustrated London News*, 4 July–26 September 1896); *The Spoils of Poynton*, which appeared in the *Atlantic Monthly* as *The Old Things* (April–October 1896); *What Maisie Knew* (The *Chapbook*, 15 January–1 August 1897); and *The Awkward Age* (*Harper's Weekly*, 1 October 1898–7 January 1899).

What James's pessimism did not immediately envision was the long-term benefit that would result from his abortive theatrical ventures. Extended analyses by Joseph Weisenfarth, Walter Isle, and Michael Egan have demonstrated how much the later fiction is enriched by such dramatic techniques as foreshortening, the presentation of action in scenic units, and authorial objectivity and neutrality. Egan even contends that "Eighteen ninety-five is the pivotal year in James's artistic evolution" because from that time on he was to write under the influence of Henrik Ibsen. Although specific influences may be debatable, it is clear that after 1895 James conceived of every element of his novels—dialogue, action, imagery, and the inner life of his characters—as intensifying dramatic interest.[2]

Unique in the James oeuvre for its violence, *The Other House* throws a histrionic spotlight on an arresting "bad Heroine," Rose Armiger, who unites coldness, passion, and manipulative genius. As sketched in James's *Notebooks*,[3] the novel was conceived as a play tentatively entitled *The Promise*, in which the hero's dying wife exacts a promise that he will not remarry during the lifetime of their child; in the play's original scenario as a comedy, the unnamed "bad Heroine," as James calls her, falls in love

1

with the hero but seeing that he loves someone else decides to poison the child under circumstances that will incriminate the "good Heroine." In the spirit of serious comedy, evil is thwarted, the child lives, and the hero marries his second love. As a novel, *The Other House* retains the scenic structure and the dialogue of a play, but comedy turns to tragedy, Rose Armiger assumes an almost mad malignity, drowns the child of the bland but universally loved Tony Bream, and remains free at the end to live with the evil she has done. In writing *The Other House* for the *Illustrated London News*, James naturally intended to treat his popular audience to melodrama, but he appears to have become more interested in his art than in the graphic depiction of horrors.

Many reviewers of *The Other House* clung to long established biases against James as, in the words of the *Independent*, a manipulator of "thin blooded, muscularly degenerate" characters "wanting in personal magnetism." In describing the novel as an "analytical study," the *New York Tribune* also voiced an old complaint against James's penchant for dissecting his characters to the point of draining them of vitality. The *Literary World* repeated the familiar charges that James wrote with a "cold-blooded lack of moral sense" and with the sham art of a "literary juggler [who] substitutes highly colored impressions for balls"; *Current Literature* avoided harshness but raised the commonplace protest that James concentrated on fictional technique at the expense of subject matter.[4]

Mixed reviews in the *Nation*, the *Academy*, and the *Dial* praised *The Other House* for the sureness of its art, but expressed doubt about the motivation of Rose's crime, the *Dial* even maintaining that the murder degrades the plot to "crude melodrama." But denunciation and lukewarm approval were not universal: the *Chicago Tribune* pronounced the characters strong, individual scenes subtle, and "the game of cross purposes . . . brilliant"; the *New York Times* ranked *The Other House* a "masterpiece" that on the whole rewards the demands it makes upon its readers; the *American* cited it as superior to "all novels in English" for 1896; and the *Critic* hailed the novel as a masterpiece that possessed a decided "grip" rather than James's usual "exquisite sense of touch."[5]

Largely a footnote in early Jamesian scholarship, *The Other House* is called a sham by S. Gorley Putt, is given little attention by F. W. Dupee, and is ignored by many of James's most insightful critics. Leon Edel, who compares it to *Rosmersholm*—calling it "an Ibsen play without Ibsen's morality"—considers it an "outburst of primitive rage" at odds with its efficient dramatic structure and "cultivated dialogue." Only partially satisfied with Edel's view of Ibsen's influence on James, Oscar Cargill sees striking parallels between *The Other House* and Euripides' *Medea:* moreover, in contrast to Edel's autobiographical interpretation, he describes the novel as a "commentary on the hypocrisy of Victorian morality." In a very astute analysis, Walter Wright locates the novel's failure in "the imperfect fusion of reality and romance," but he also argues that *The Other House* creates a convincing microcosm in which all the characters provoke one another's actions and finally recognize their own part in the "corporate guilt." In a searching interpretation of the book's dramatic qualities Walter Isle also demonstrates how Tony Bream's passive acceptance of affection, the dying wife's jealous love for her child, Rose's passion for Tony, and even the heroine's quiet devotion to father and child contribute to the novel's tragic denouement.[6]

The complex issues of *The Spoils of Poynton,* a less sensational and more subtly scenic novel than *The Other House,* spring from what James stigmatizes in the *Notebooks* as the "ugly" English custom of compelling a widowed English mother to surrender her "big house" to her son upon his marriage. Mrs. Gereth, the mother in James's novel, endures the special affront of losing a house she has filled with treasures of art to a son lacking both her aesthetic sense and her acquisitive passion. In fact, Owen Gereth's want of taste is evident in his love for Mona Brigstock, whose family revels in the atrocious architecture of Waterbath, a house they insist on decorating with "trumpery ornament and scrapbook art." With a collector's mania, Mrs. Gereth schemes to prevent Mona's desecration of Poynton by diverting her son's interest to Fleda Vetch, a young friend with fine artistic sensibilities and a finer moral rigor. The mother's illegal removal of her treasures from Poynton succeeds in angering Mona, imperiling the marriage, and waking Owen up to Fleda's attractions. When he proposes to break his engagement to Mona, Fleda struggles with her passion but insists that her pliable lover honor his pledge to his fiancée. Once Mrs. Gereth restores her spoils to Poynton under the illusion that she has saved her son, her possessions, and Fleda, Mona is placated and Owen lapses into a comfortable marriage with her. He does, however, offer Fleda the gift of a Maltese cross, the prize of Mrs. Gereth's collection, but the heroine is denied even this sentimental consolation when fire consumes Poynton's rare museum world.

Critical opinion on *The Spoils* ran the gamut from the *Critic's* exclamatory praise to the *San Francisco Chronicle's* dismissal of it with a barrage of words like "prolix," "artificiality," and "countless mannerisms and affectations." The *Critic* lavished superlatives on the novel as an incomparable "study of the collector's passion" and on the portrait of Fleda as one that made even Isabel Archer's appear "crude and unfinished." The reviewer asserted that one's experience in contemplating "something so fine" finally "becomes almost overwhelming." Far from overwhelmed, the *Independent* appreciated the book as "whey but delicious," the *New York Times* forecast that only one reader in 10,000 would be attracted to it, and the *Athenaeum* found James's language arcane, Mrs. Gereth an "abstraction," and the climactic fire an unnecessary resort to melodrama. Although the *New York Sun* commended James's painstaking art for invigorating characters who never become "mere automata," the *Literary World* regarded the same characters as lifeless. The *Academy* ambivalently generalized that James's works "are a series of exquisite disappointments" and hoped that he would create heroines, unlike Fleda, who are "admirable without being nervous and hesitating." Champions of *The Spoils* were numerous, but many no-tices also reveal a widespread distaste for its author's fascination with psy-chological nuance and refined ethical problems. *Current Literature* rose above the critical controversy in its own pages, convinced that "no one need get into any kind of hurry about any new book [by James]; it is in no hurry itself; it has come to stay."[8]

Despite its disarmingly simple narrative, *The Spoils* has provoked a wide variety of critical response. James's insistence in his preface that his heroine is a "free spirit," has not deterred critics from declaring her renun-ciation of Owen a case of neurotic self-destruction caused by an overrefined conscience. An apologist for Fleda, Laurence B. Holland, concludes that her surrender and loss do not quench her will to live but enable her to possess "the past in the only way finally it can be known and redeemed: in memory and in art." In Holland's view, then, the novel does not end on a note of desolation: Owen's marriage to Mona does not appear to be un-happy; Owen himself has acquired a new sense of values; Mrs. Gereth has constructed another museum out of her modest new possessions; and Fleda has accepted her role in a world that does not totally satisfy her aesthetic and moral sensibilities. Manfred Mackenzie, on the other hand, contends that the almost religious fervor of Fleda's abnegations destroys Mrs. Gereth's hopes and destines Owen to a "sterile marriage." Indeed, according to Mackenzie, Fleda's self-martyrdom denies her the chance to expand a po-tentially rich consciousness: it is as if she herself "has lighted the pyre" that finally consumes Poynton. Defining *The Spoils* as a parody of "the whole convention of romance comedy," Ronald Wallace perceives Fleda as a fe-male Don Quixote, "a parody of the idealistic and virginal romance hero-ine." She thus becomes a woman who entertains beautiful illusions that en-dow all she encounters with qualities they do not inherently possess: she imagines Owen better than he is, attributes beauty to Mona and Owen's marriage, and, in exercizing her moral "scrupulosity" even at her own ex-pense, behaves with a "madness [that] reveals goodness." Wallace further maintains that the novel's structure encourages the reader to hope for Fleda's failure, because only failure will insure her freedom from the worthless Owen. Joseph Weisenfarth accounts for the book's psychological intensity in terms of its dramatic qualities: its economy, the objectivity that James attains by making Fleda his center of consciousness, and the sym-metrical scenes that become more meaningful in contrast with each other.[9]

What Maisie Knew, James's next novel, has an audacity of style and form ideally suited to its dramatic presentation of how a child's expanding consciousness accumulates and learns to interpret experience. It may be said that with *Maisie* its author has become fully Jamesian in showing life as, paradoxically, an irresistible flood of impressions amid recurring stabilit-ies and patterns: the ambiguities and sinuousities of James's style communi-cate the sensations of a child-protagonist reaching into the flow of time, grasping certain objects while others elude her, and seeming simulta-neously immersed in the stream while remaining on the banks.

James places Maisie in an unstable world in which her divorced parents, Ida and Beale Farange, appear to be involved in an endless series of sexual escapades. Soon after their divorce, Beale marries Miss Overmore and Ida marries Sir Claude, but these new arrangements do not prevent Beale from seeking fresh amours and Sir Claude from attaching himself to the second Mrs. Beale, Ida meanwhile entertaining herself with a succession of lovers. Immersed in this licentious atmosphere, Maisie is educated by the comical Mrs. Wix, a semi-literate, conventionally moral, and immensely loyal governess. In fact, the girl is educated by her own powers of observation and by her creative desire and quest for constancy and support. She is attracted by Mrs. Beale's beauty and cleverness and by Sir Claude's good looks and generosity. She feels protected by Mrs. Wix's motherliness and is somewhat bewildered by her anxious zest for "saving" Sir Claude. Finally, after being abandoned by her mother and father, Maisie achieves a measure of maturity when she sees the limitations of all the adults in her world and is compelled, nevertheless, to choose with whom and on what terms she will live.

The reception of *Maisie* proves that many late nineteenth-century critics welcomed James's audacious experimentations in point of view and in style. There was, of course, outrage at James's unsparing picture of the sexual license of Victorian society and some indignation over the trials the novel imposed upon readers accustomed to a good story; the *Literary World*, for example, accused *Maisie* of being "alike repellent to taste and feeling, to law and gospel," and the *New York Times* worried about a technique "productive of Ah's and Oh's." But for every periodical that, like the *Spectator*, declared the novel unedifying and unpleasant, there was one like the *Pall Mall Gazette*, which announced, "we are here dealing with genius." The *Nation's* priggish stand that *Maisie* was a "tale not only without a moral, but without morals" was offset by *Book News's* view that "the author . . . brings purity out of the impure and nobility out of dishonor." While the *Independent* objected to a style that "spread like a fog of phrases," *Book News* cautioned readers that "every word counts."[10]

What remains surprising is the sheer excitement with which many reviewers discovered a novel that even today seems difficult and obscure. The *Critic* greeted *Maisie* as "one of the most astonishing *tours de force* the present generation has been privileged to behold"; it expressed wonder at "the psychological feat Mr. James has performed in inclosing himself in the child's mind and ascertaining her point of view." The critic for the *Academy* confessed, "I have read this book with amazement and delight," and the *Bookman* celebrated the "wonderful dramatic analysis of this marvelous book." Even *Literature*, which did not like "the atmosphere of the Divorce Court" and "the slough of immorality," admitted that *Maisie* "is Mr. James at his best." Despite its few reservations, the *Athenaeum* filled a column and a half with superlatives.[11]

Recent discussion of *Maisie* has inevitably given priority to two things: James's method of rendering the inner life of his child-heroine and the question of whether, in acquiring the wisdom to make choices, she acts with "innocence" or is more or less motivated by the sexual urgencies of her immediate world. In his passing remarks on James's method, F. W. Dupee wonders whether James's style with its "bizarre shifts of pace, unexpected brevities," does not turn the novel into "more of a torment than a pleasure." Other critics, however, have accepted the method as a vehicle that effectively communicates a special sense of the process by which Maisie's understanding grows. Nicola Bradbury, for example, shows how much significance inheres in Maisie's silences, how subtly James employs "future hindsight" to mark the child's storing up of knowledge for later use, and how the novel "can be seen as a model of perceptual development" with "close analogies to the [models] of . . . Jean Piaget."[12] Many studies have pointed out the war and the games imagery that defines the society in which Maisie does her special battle, and others have revealed the skill with which the narrator weaves in and out of Maisie's consciousness, interpreting, dramatizing, and adding metaphorical point to her insights. In short, the critical consensus seems to establish that in few novels are methods and subject so carefully and successfully interrelated.

Nevertheless, critics of *Maisie* have disagreed profoundly about what the heroine learns from her exposure to sexual license and parental irresponsibility. Harris W. Wilson was the first to propose that Maisie is so vitiated by the evil of her guardians that she seeks to resolve her dilemma by offering to become her stepfather's mistress. Sallie Sears, on the other hand, believes that the girl's knowledge is "unaccompanied by (ethical) judgment" and that because of James's "refractions of his material through the media of several consciousnesses," none of them altogether trustworthy, it is impossible to arrive at any "final attitude . . . toward Maisie." Philip Weinstein goes beyond those critics who wish to see the heroine's achievement of a moral sense as the climactic stage of her maturity: he suggests that her repudiation of her self-indulgent stepparents stems from a need for the stable love that her family, with its sexual misalliances and uprooting, has denied her. He concludes, however, that Maisie ultimately retreats from a society which, because of its promiscuities, she perceives as "uninhabitable." Weinstein thus links Maisie with Nanda Brookenham, the heroine of James's next novel, *The Awkward Age*, who also has the misfortune of being too good for her society.[13]

The Awkward Age, published serially in *Harper's Weekly* from October 1898 to January 1899, extends James's unflattering survey of English manners undertaken in such novels as *A London Life, The Other House, The Spoils of Poynton,* and *What Maisie Knew.* The tenous sexual alliances observed and puzzled over by Maisie continue as facts of English life in *The Awkward Age*. Moreover, James establishes a connection between sexual, financial, and social arrangements as he adumbrates the self-interested maneuvering that pervades Mrs. Brookenham's sophisticated inner circle.

James described *The Awkward Age* as a study of what happens when a nineteenth-century mother is compelled to admit her young daughter into the drawingroom where an adult and uninhibited society amuses itself. In his preface to the novel, he states that "the prime propulsive force of *The Awkward Age*" derived from his observation of "the difference made in certain friendly houses . . . by the . . . coming to the forefront of some vague slip of a daughter." James not only reveals the genesis of his idea but also describes his subject: "*The Awkward Age* is precisely . . . an account of the manner in which the resented interference with ancient liberties came to be in a certain instance dealt with."[14] The progress of the novel shows that from the second book, James focuses attention on Mrs. Brook's efforts to deal with her daughter Nanda's entrance into society; in addition, Mrs. Brook's latitude in allowing Nanda to be exposed to a full knowledge of life is contrasted with the Duchess's obduracy in preserving her niece, Little Aggie, from soiling contact with reality; and finally, with Jamesian irony, Aggie turns into a hoydenish married woman while Nanda wrests from her exposure a formidable understanding and tolerance of the world.

James sharpens the issues of his novel by introducing Mr. Longdon, a superannuated outsider from a simpler time and a different social convenant, into the daring Mrs. Brook's "temple of analysis." For him, the new modes of talk and permissive behavior betoken the demise of friendship and a harrowing collapse of moral values. Bewildered by Nanda's precocious initiation into an unwholesome society, he tries to arrange a marriage for her with Vanderbank, a glittering Victorian beau whose relationship with the witty Mrs. Brook is, at the least, intimate. He is exposed to a world in which the Duchess's lover, Lord Petherton, transfers his attention to her niece, Mrs. Brook's son borrows money from her guests, and salacious books are read by young girls like Nanda. When Mrs. Brook, who is anxious to keep Vanderbank for herself, stages a scene designed to show her group at its worst, Longdon retreats with Nanda, whom he adopts, into a refuge where she will be able to breathe pure air.

If its decadent milieu made *The Awkward Age* an unpleasant novel for its generation, its dramatic form and multiple points of view prevented easy reading and seemed to obscure if not destroy the book's narrative. The stream of scintillating dialogue, with its "leaps" and in-group patter and assumptions, conspired with James's authorial neutrality to keep meaning muted. And, although authorial comment was not excluded from the novel, it rarely clarified the characters' motives and relationships.

The Awkward Age impressed most reviewers as finespun artifice and effeminate folderol. In addition, the sexual freedom of the Duchess, Lord Petherton, Lady Fanny, and probably other characters led the *Spectator* to bristle at James's "whispering gallery of ignoble souls," the "smart degenerates" who live in an "atmosphere of mental and moral squalor." The critic for the *Independent* was thoroughly bored, the *Dial* reviewer worried through the book "from a sense of duty," and the *New York Sun's* writer spoofed the characters' inordinate tea drinking, meaningful looks, and allusive small talk. The *Athenaeum* was oppressed by the novel's tedious dialogue, airlessness, and sense of confinement while the *Pall Mall Gazette* lost patience with James's "refined refinements, subtilized subtlety, and suggested suggestions," and the *London Bookman* complained that "everyone has grounds for complaint against 'The Awkward Age.' " For the *New York Tribune*, *The Awkward Age* was made up of "small talk and small motives" that afflicted one with "a headache," The list of objections and accusations could be easily extended: *Literature* mentioned the novel's "relentless longeurs;" the *Chicago Tribune* tagged James a "carver of cherry stones;" and the *New York World* called his latest book "rather flabby and dispiriting."[15]

Among the rare defenders of *The Awkward Age*, the *Critic* and the *London Times* both considered Nanda James's supreme creation while the latter marveled at the elaborate art with which James weaves "innuendo," "a chance phrase," and "a subtly covert warning" into a unified structure. Most interestingly, perhaps, the *Academy* traced James's charged intimations and expressive reticence to the English "national habit of repression" and called his approach to fiction "a new realism, delicate as a silverpoint." Still the approving minority, which included the *Brooklyn Eagle* and the *Detroit Free Press*, could do little to reverse the growing condescension to James.[16]

With the surface sparkle of a "dialogue novel" and what Charles Thomas Samuels calls its "byzantine intricacies" of plot, *The Awkward Age* has managed to alienate, confuse, and delight critics. As early as 1916, Rebecca West summed it up as "incidentally beautiful but devastatingly artificial;" in 1934, Edmund Wilson protested against "the gibbering disembowelled crew who hover around one another with sordid shadowy designs"; an admirer like Pelham Edgar concedes that in the novel James confines himself in a constricting form; and F. R. Leavis balances his admiration for its "marvellously good dialogue" with a demur at James's "disproportionate interest in technique." In his thoroughgoing analysis of the novel's design, however, Walter Isle confidently states: "In *The Awkward Age* James redeemed his dramatic years and wrote his greatest 'scenic' novel." Most recently, Daniel Schneider traces the novel's flaws to the very nature of the "play-novel," in which James refuses to interpret or evaluate and leaves too many issues in doubt.[19]

Other critical disagreements center on James's own moral position and on his attitude toward Mr. Longdon, Mrs. Brook, and her daughter Nanda. Whereas Leavis pronounces the book "robustly, delicately, and clairvoyantly moral," F. W. Dupee discovers in it "a certain relaxation of the moral, or at least magisterial, impulse," and Samuels reads it as a "dispassionate scrutiny of rival claims." For Edgar, Longdon represents, "upon a reduced scale, the *alter ego* of his creator," while Samuels argues that neither Longdon nor any other character deserves our full approbation. In contrast to Dupee, who ranks Mrs. Brook with "the charming rogues of literature," J. A. Ward admits her vitality but stresses her immorality in cold-bloodedly sacrificing her daughter. Little agreement exists even in interpretations of Nanda; she is seen as innocence incarnate, "the moral sense gone bleak" in Dupee's words, or, according to Schneider's view, a "divided" character capable of scheming and playing the social game with less than absolute purity of motive.[18] Finally, *The Awkward Age* has been classified as a comedy, a tragi-comedy, and a tragedy, and accounts of what actually happens in the novel can hardly be brought into harmony.

James sent *The Sacred Fount*, his last novel dealing exclusively with English life, to his literary agent, James B. Pinker, with a description of it as "fanciful, fantastic—but very close and sustained, and calculated to minister to curiosity."[19] When quizzed about it after its publication in 1901, he rewarded curiosity by dismissing it as an "incident of technics, pure and simple."[20] In an illuminating letter to Mrs. Humphrey Ward, however, he first calls it a "mere tormenting trifle" and "a consistent joke," and then, taking it quite seriously, corrects her blatant misreading of certain characters.[21]

Written in what some critics have considered a Jamesian burlesque of his own method, *The Sacred Fount* makes use of a speculative narrator whose tireless imagination transforms life's heterogeneity into theory. During a weekend at Newmarch, an English countryhouse, James's prescient or mad observer sees or thinks he sees the premature aging of youthful Guy Brissenden and the conspicuous rejuvenation of his somewhat older wife. Constructing a psychological hypothesis that in all intimate relations one partner flourishes at the expense of the other, he attempts to explain Gilbert Long's increase in wit and May Server's emotional and social collapse by conjecturing that they are carrying on an affair. His stay at Newmarch dedicated to proving his suspicion, he abandons himself to all the arts of detection: he also spends much of his time in pursuing and elaborating fears and hope, and in trying to validate his researches; he even entertains the notion that he has insanely lost himself in airy, vaporish fabrications.

The narrator's unrelenting cerebration and clairvoyant intuitiveness were easy satirical targets for most reviewers of *The Sacred Fount*. James's old mannerisms, new intricacies of style, and increased reliance on pregnant looks, gestures, and silences to convey meaning also invited attack. Essentially, however, the early critics of *The Sacred Fount* put their fingers on the aspects of the narrative that have remained points of contention to the present. To begin with, many reviewers candidly confessed bewilderment, the *New York Bookman* writing that "James is beyond all question in a bad way" and has slipped into "a chronic state of periphrastic perversity." The *Boston Evening Transcript* summed up the book as "insane," the *Chicago Tribune* had "little or no notion what it is all about," and the critic for the *Times* of London admitted that after three readings he had "the dimmest notion" of what he had read. The reviewers generally agreed in disliking the narrator: he is a "sort of refined Sherlock Holmes with a rat terrier's nose for scandal" (the *Independent*); he is a bore and a vulgarian (the *Athenaeum*); and he is a victim of a "distempered fancy" (the *San Francisco Chronicle*). A majority of the reviewers anticipated twentieth-century critics in believing the narrator's deductions about his fellow guests at Newmarch to be mistaken, and the *Pall Mall Gazette* speculated that "the narrator has been making fun of us all through" the novel. The *Academy* questioned whether "Henry James, in a grimly humorous mood, [turned] his analytic mind on himself." Anticipating some recent readers, the *Times* of London more boldly proposed that James "has gone about to parody himself" and is laughing at the "sham enthusiasts" who accept *The Sacred Fount* as serious. Like modern critics, too, the reviewers differed about the conclusion of the novel, some of them seeming sure that Mrs. Briss "demolishes" the narrator's gossamer web of misinterpretations (the *San Francisco Chronicle* and the *Pall Mall Gazette*), others accepting the narrator's version of events (the *New York Tribune*), and still others suspending judgment as to whether the protagonist is crazy, as Mrs. Briss charges (the *Critic*). Finally, there was almost complete unanimity about the disproportion between James's treatment of his material and the intrinsic merits of the novel: *Current Literature*, feeling that James had out-Jamesed James," derided his concern with "daintily unimportant matters;" *Literature* characterized the book as "hypochrondriacal subtlety run mad;" and the *New York Times*, reflecting the hostility of many other reviews, scoffed at this "niggling work, this humanity writ small."[22]

In 1916, Rebecca West described *The Sacred Fount* as a "small, mean story [that] worries one like a rat nibbling at the wainscot." It continues to worry readers and to give rise to ingenious and perceptive ventures in explication. One of the most judicious approaches to the novel can be found in Leon Edel's introduction to it, in which he grants that "we can never be sure of the purity of our facts" and concludes that the reader must ultimately act as his own "detective" in contending with this "tale of ratiocination." Philip Weinstein speculates, with more amplitude than like-minded critics, that the narrator of *The Sacred Fount* embodies "in his ambiguous and suspect nature . . . a profound, if skeptical, version of the artist himself at work." With his customary thoroughness and insight, Walter Isle presents an analysis of the book's five-part structure and theme of vampirism in terms of the narrator's romantic, subjective attempt to penetrate the opaqueness of the real world: "The subjective is presented in a balanced war with the objective, and the result is a stalemate." Perhaps the most widely accepted view of the narrator, however, is that he creates out of a misguided if not disordered fancy an unsubstantial structure of ideas. But, the search for a "key" to *The Sacred Fount* goes on, many years after Edmund Wilson found the narrator "mystifying, even maddening," and after proposed solutions by Wilson Follett, Oscar Cargill, and Jean Frantz Blackall in her book-length study of the novel.[23]

With *The Ambassadors*, rejected in scenario form by *Harper's* and serialized in the *North American Review* (January-December 1903), Henry

James entered what F. O. Matthiessen has called his "major phase" by returning to his first successful subject, the American experience in Europe. No longer seeing the old world from the youthful perspectives of Rowland Mallett, Christopher Newman, and Isabel Archer, the aging author chooses as his center of consciousness an aging American, Lambert Strether, who has a "vague resemblance" to himself. Along with his American innocence, rectitude, and unexamined moral biases, Strether has the imagination to respond to manners and atmospheres at odds with his own. When he is dispatched to Europe to rescue Chad Newsome from its sexual contaminations, his malleability makes him less than the ideal ambassador to carry out the orders of Chad's mother, a symbol of American Puritanism and capitalist enterprise. Strether speaks for the moral provincialism and business ethic of Woollett, Massachusetts, with too open a mind, too willing a spirit to compromise the values he represents. With the aid of Maria Gostrey, James's most attractive confidante, he succumbs to the sensuous beauty of Paris and tests the very assumptions of Mrs. Newsome's mandate. Further, he approves of and envies Chad's evolution, under Parisian influences, into an accomplished man of the world with a zest for life; he marvels at the Cleopatra-like variety of Madame de Vionnet, who has made Chad into a paragon; and, with little prompting he induces himself to believe that Chad and Marie de Vionnet enjoy a "virtuous attachment." Communicating this implausible deduction to Mrs. Newsome, he is supplanted by a new ambassador, Mrs. Pocock, who interprets her brother's relationship with a narrowness worthy of her mother. In one of the richest episodes in the novel, Strether sees the virtuous attachment turn into an adulterous affair. Later, however, although disabused of his idée fixe, he liberates himself from Woollett's cramping austerity by enjoining Chad to be faithful to his mistress. With an austerity of his own, nevertheless, he returns to America, leaving the loyal Miss Gostrey, who has offered him a haven with her.

In *The Ambassadors*, James achieved near perfection in presenting a multifaceted experience from a single point of view. With disinterested sympathy, he records the full register of Strether's double consciousness: his fear of surrender to sensuous pleasure; his earnest commitment to his mission; his openness to evidence that will defeat his aims; and his naive romanticism and final realism. James's style attempts to give the sense of an active inner life through its qualifications, reticences, hints, resonances, and involutions. The resulting fabric challenges close attention and critical discriminations without assuring complete resolutions.

The *Philadelphia North American* may have taken the measure of James's altered standing in the world of letters when it greeted *The Ambassadors* by commenting, "A new novel by Henry James means scarcely so much nowadays as when *Daisy Miller* first flashed forth upon the literary world." Yet, despite the grumbling of critics who, like the reviewer for the *San Francisco Chronicle*, treated it as a mere "tangle," *The Ambassadors* elicited more sympathetic responses than did *The Wings of the Dove*, which though written later was published earlier. For the *New York Times*, for instance, the novel exhibited a "riper art" and was "more comprehensive" than *Daisy Miller*, *The American*, and *The Portrait of a Lady*. The *Pall Mall Gazette* attempted a serious analysis of James's method, defining it as an evocation that "divulges" rather than "tells" a story, that gradually strips off "the veils which hitherto obscured . . . vision"; James's ideas were metaphorically described as betraying themselves like "peaks of submerged, deep-rooted mountains." Alice Duer Miller in the *Lamp* emphasized James's objectivity by insisting that he does not "moralize" but "present"; she went on to discuss him as the novelist who has discovered the "subconscious" and the "inner everyday life." She also, like the critic for the *Academy*, pointed to James's omnipresent and humane comic sense. James's objectivity struck the *Boston Evening Transcript* as the very thing that caused him to write about people as if he were observing them from some faraway and inaccessible planet." In a singular review in the *Chicago Tribune*, Elia W. Peattie left-handedly complimented *The Ambassadors* as a "masterpiece which lacks to a degree all the elements which go to constitute a noble book." Peattie's criticism of this "so unlovely" and "base" book is full of regret that, in abandoning the United States, James abandoned its values, adopted a cosmopolitan cynicism, and came to look down upon "ideals" as distinctly American and middle-class.[24]

Not surprisingly, other critics condemned the freedom James had taken in dealing with an adulterous relation in *The Ambassadors*, and even the urbane *New York Times* cautioned that the "subject did not invite discussion in tea parties." Most of the adverse criticism of the novel, however, focused on the grammatical inversions of James's style and his ingenious attempts to avoid the obvious (the *Athenaeum*), the pompous verbiage and syntactical dislocations (the *Boston Evening Transcript*), and the pointless reiteration of words and phrases like "prodigious," "splendid," "wonderful," and "there we are" (the *Spectator*). Still, a host of newspapers and magazines agreed with the sentiments of the *Literary World* that "there has been nothing like [*The Ambassadors*] in years."[25]

In praising *The Ambassadors* for its technical perfection, Percy Lubbock declares that James achieves his artistic success by "never pass[ing] outside the circle of his protagonist's thought." E. M. Forster, however, complains that James worked on the "premise" that the complexity and range of human life must be sacrificed to form: *The Ambassadors*, he observes, has relatively few characters and they are so stingily constructed as to be "incapable of fun, of rapid motion, of carnality, and nine-tenths of heroism." F. R. Leavis voices a similar discontent in maintaining that the conscious art of *The Ambassadors* works against rather than intensifies the dramatized life, and even F. O. Matthiessen finds in Strether's final renunciation a symptom of "a certain soft emptiness" in both James and his character. Still, Matthiessen's chapter in *The Major Phase* remains an early classic that celebrates James's cultivation of "the skills of the painter" in his descriptions of Paris, his Renoir-like attention to the play of light in vividly realized scenes, and his emphasis on "seeing" as "living."

Going beyond Matthiessen's reminder that James never abandoned the transcendentalist belief that "seeing" should convert appearance into moral vision, Quentin Anderson converts *The Ambassadors* into a dramatization of Henry James, Sr.'s Swedenborgianism: he thus conceives of Strether as "a Pharisee, righteous to the last," an exemplar of a "church" frozen in formalism. Among other noteworthy critics of the novel, William M. Gibson explores James's use of historical and garden imagery, and the artistic function of the famous balcony scenes; Frederic C. Crews addresses the theme of Strether's expanding consciousness and his movement toward a larger and larger integration of life; John E. Tilford takes issue with Lubbock and demonstrates that James, "the Old Intruder," does not strictly confine himself to Strether's point of view; Christof Wegelin stresses James's "detachment from any one local point of view"; Sister M. Corona Sharp concludes that Maria Gostrey is James's finest *ficelle* "because of her independent existence as a person, and her dramatic part as a foil"; and Sallie Sears argues that although James has a "negative imagination," criticism can find no "aesthetic basis for insisting that a writer feel and write 'positively,' or with tragic grandeur."[27]

James described *The Wings of the Dove*, the second novel of his major phase, as " 'a love story' of a romantic tinge, and touching and conciliatory tone,"[28] but if the male protagonist learns to love the heroine, he does so only after participating in an ugly plot against her. In Milly Theale, his appealing and stricken dove, James created an American heiress, inspired by Minny Temple, whose passion for life is intensified by the fear of imminent death. Introduced to the excitement of English society by the affluent Maud Lauder, a sort of "Britannia of the Market Place," she becomes the friend and later the victim of Kate Croy, Mrs. Louder's dependent niece. Unwilling to be estranged from her aunt by marrying Merton Densher, a poor journalist, Kate encourages her lover to win Milly's affections, marry the dying girl, and thus inherit her money. More a panther than a dove, Kate has the courage to mature her plot by rewarding Densher's occasional importunities with promises, kisses, and a night of lovemaking. When the stratagem shows every sign of succeeding, it is exposed by an aristocratic predator who also aspires to Milly's fortune. The heartbroken girl, who has lived on assurances of love, turns her face to the wall in despair, but before dying summons Densher to a last interview, which leaves him with an elevated sense of redemption. In the novel's denouement, Densher agrees to marry Kate if she will give up the fortune Milly has bequeathed him, but Kate, understanding how the dead girl has intervened in their lives, recognizes that Densher has been converted to something like adoration of the saintlike Milly.

With his allusive style, unpleasant subject, and deliberate avoidance of dramatizing crucial scenes, James braved critical disapprobation and the general reader's consternation. Once again, he eschewed narrative incident in favor of transcribing a shadowy inner realm of psychological compulsions, inchoate emotions that refuse to form and state themselves, and subterranean streams of desire and repulsion.

Most contemporary critics of *The Wings of the Dove* addressed themselves to the stylistic and technical peculiarities of James's late manner, now grown, it was felt, inveterate and alarmingly close to unintelligible. The *Contemporary Review* entertained the notion that James's retirement to Rye had estranged him from reality and made his style more private. The *Independent* was of the opinion that James "has begun to show his age" by lapsing into garrulity and speculative habits which have become "dissolute and irresponsible." The *Spectator* noted in the novel "a veritable passion for evasion," and the *New York Sun* lampooned James's obsession with a special vocabulary. A. Macdonnel announced in the *London Bookman* that James has "provoked us into an agressive Philistinism" and a "dull suspicious anger that we are bamboozled" by his "very refined slang." The *San Francisco Chronicle* condemned the style for producing "vagueness throughout," and F. M. Colby in the *New York Bookman* blamed James for "pottering in nebulous workshops" and for being too "puffed up with his secrets." Although the *Nation* and the *New York Times* betrayed distinct annoyance with the manner of the novel, they managed to take refuge in hackneyed tribute to James's art and virtuosity, and the *Athenaeum* sighed that James had arrived at making "the obscure more obscure."[29]

The *Academy and Literature* went against the current in championing the novel as rising to the "highest level of the author's attainment" in the portraits of "two magnificently designed women." It also praised the "emotional quality" of the style, the "orderly evolution of theme" and the genius that inspired the creation of character.[30] With few supporters, however, James became a convenient whipping boy, someone who stood for all that was effete, sterile, longwinded, and leeringly immoral. Even though the *Academy* scoffed at the *New York Bookman*'s attack on James's "complicated and dissolute Muse," many reviewers suggested that if such works as *Maisie, The Awkward Age,* and *The Dove* were not swathed in protective obscurity, they would be positively revolting.

F. O. Matthiessen's analysis of *The Wings of the Dove* calls attention to the novel's fairy-tale elements, the indirect presentation of its heroine, and the elegiac tone that registers James's lament for the innocent America of his youth. Despite his praise of the novel as a masterwork, however, Matthiessen doubts that Milly Theale "is of sufficient emotional force to carry a great work," and he questions the success of James's reliance on imagery to heighten the atmosphere of his novel. Quentin Anderson, on the other hand, contends that, under the influence of his father's Swedenborgianism, James portrays Milly as a Christ-like figure who "rejects every lure that the world can offer and determines that the best mode of expressing her love for mankind and her forgiveness for its selfishness and greed is to die for it." Without deifying Milly, Dorothea Krook ascribes the hero-ine's vulnerability to the generous trust she reposes in a society "implaca-bly hostile to her very being." One of James's major successes for Krook is the delineation of Densher's gradual emergence from his bondage to Kate and from the deceptions he has practiced upon himself. Charles Thomas Samuels, in contrast, pronounces "virtue" as represented by Milly much less compelling than Kate's "evil"; he further argues that Densher remains a "moral moron" incapable of any real conversion or redemption. Less hard on Densher, Leon Edel nevertheless belittles him as a passive character who "sits back and allows women to be kind, devoted, sacrificial." Daniel Mark Fogel's discussion, noteworthy in challenging Matthiessen's stand on James's imagery and the generally negative views of Densher's atonement and moral growth, compares the novel to *The Tempest* and maintains that James "worked on many levels to show" Densher's conversion "convinc-ingly, most subtly and powerfully . . . through the transformation that the marine images undergo."[31]

In a letter to Edith Wharton, James characterized his last great novel, *The Golden Bowl* (1904), as "the most arduous and thankless task I ever set myself."[32] Perhaps the most involute and inscrutable product of his major phase, its very structure complicates earlier complexities. To begin with, James probes the confusions of the Italian Prince Amerigo on the eve of his marriage to Maggie Verver, the daughter of an American millionaire art collector. Initially concerned about his ability to sound the mysteries of the American consciousness, he is forced to contend with the appearance of Charlotte Stant, a Europeanized American with whom he had once been in love. The increasing intimacy between the married Maggie and her fa-ther, Adam, mystifies the Prince and causes him to wonder about his place in the new menage; an even stranger situation develops when Maggie ef-fects the marriage of her widowed father and Charlotte; and the mystery utterly confounds the Prince when he and the alluring Charlotte are en-couraged to represent the two families on social occasions while the father and daughter commune at home or remain in the nursery with the little Principino.

The second half of *The Golden Bowl* traces with analytical minuteness the history of Maggie's psychological awakening and her strategies to regain her husband's love. The novel becomes a record of her suspicions, firmer and firmer intuitions, and ultimate certainty that her husband and Char-lotte are lovers; her communication of her new knowledge through atti-tude, looks, and shades of conduct rather than through outright condemna-tion; and her management, with the silent collusion of the others, to dissolve the "family" by having her father and stepmother move to Amer-ica. Decorum is preserved as if, during the nightmare of moral and psycho-logical terror, nothing extraordinary has taken place.

James made the meaning of *The Golden Bowl* more difficult to unravel by working into its texture an abundance and variety of images and symbols and an inexhaustible commentary on the action by Fanny Assingham and her patient husband. Narrative has only secondary importance to such images as the bowl itself, the "dazzling curtain of light" that the Prince remembers from reading Poe, and the haunting pagoda that challenges entrance. Moreover, the Prince's eyes resemble "the high windows of a Roman palace," and his "look," like almost everything else about him, "suggested an image;" Adam seems "inscrutably monotonous behind an iridescent cloud"; and the "union" of Maggie and the Prince "resembled a good deal some pleasant public square, in the heart of an old city, into which a great Palladian church, say . . . had suddenly been dropped."

Most reviews of *The Golden Bowl* sounded some of the old notes of ridicule, obligatory praise, and outright disparagement. Habituated to its role as parodist of James, the *New York Sun* derided all the male characters of the novel as Henry Jameses and all the female figures as Henrietta Jameses. After finding great merits in *The Ambassadors*, the *Pall Mall Gazette* exclaimed, "Henry James is almost enough to excuse any amount of blasphemy and desertion to the Philistines." Mary Moss, in the *Atlantic*, squeezed her ambivalence about James and *The Golden Bowl* into a neat sentence: "He is a precious, morbid phenomenon, too exceptional for healthy discipleship," and the *New York Tribune* insisted on James's morbidity and summed him up as a "talent consuming itself in wrongheaded exercizes."[33]

Among the sensitive reviews, that of Claude Bragdon in the *Critic*, surmised that James, like other original geniuses, had become less interested in the externals of life as he matured and now devoted himself to "the reality behind the seeming"; this apparently accounts for his increasing preoccupation with the "inner life," his transplantation of his father's Swedenborgianism (an anticipation of Quentin Anderson?) to "an English hothouse." The *Athenaeum*, with particular sophistication, stressed James's presentation of his characters through "the refracting medium of some person's mind"; the reviewer also singled James out for trying, in his dramatization of thought processes, to do what has "never been attempted before, even by the most 'psychological' of novelists"; and the reviewer showed special insight in remarking that James's main aim was to reveal "the soul developing from within, finding in other persons, circumstances, and happenings nothing but the matter of its thought." Alice Duer Miller in the *Lamp* dealt less favorably with James's intellectual-psychological method, maintaining that *The Golden Bowl* "confines itself solely to the regions of synthesized thought." Interestingly, the *Academy and Literature* discovered "Ibsen-like symbolism" in the novel, but concluded that its intellectuality overpowers its sensuousness and makes it a "flawed masterwork." James's last great novel inspired stereotyped responses to his unpleasant subject, but the *Independent* contended that Maggie and her father "lift the book from degradation," and the *Nation* declared that only James could tell such a disagreeable story "in English without grossness and vulgarity."

Not surprisingly, the reviewers, like later critics, could not agree about a novel in which Robert L. Gale, in his invaluable study of James's "figurative language," counts an extraordinary 1092 images.[34]

The thematic and stylistic ambiguities of *The Golden Bowl* have encouraged brilliant and discordant interpretations; the heroine has been elevated to angelic status or abased to the demonic, the Prince is said to be humanized by love or to remain an accommodating man of the world; and the novel itself has been classified as a tragedy, "the highest kind of romance of adventure," or a comedy. Dorothea Krook calls the work a magnificent "long poem" and again "a great fable—one of the greatest in modern European literature—of the redemption of man by the transforming power of human love"; she recognizes, nevertheless, James's insistence that "the sense of grimness and bitterness of human life inseparably fuses with the sense of its beauty and blessedness." Walter Wright, refusing to see Maggie as either "Divine Grace" or incarnate evil, declares that despite the "flaw" that results from her ignorance of evil she saves herself by her adherence to decorum during her inward struggle and by her imaginative refusal to violate the need of others for self-respect. Naomi Lebowitz investigates the novel's "magic" motifs and traces Maggie's metamorphosis "from dream princess, through disillusionment, to real princess"; this metamorphosis occurs only when Maggie acquires consciousness and attempts to save herself by real exertions in the real world. In an unusual view of *The Golden Bowl*, Ronald Wallace compares it to *A Midsummer-Night's Dream* and finds comic elements in the characters' sexual confusions; he argues that Maggie, anything but a goddess, helps to promote the adultery which causes her grief; he concludes that even though she never understands her own guilt, she succeeds in righting wrongs and creates a new society at the end of the novel. Daniel Schneider also considers Maggie as James's redemptive agent; arguing that evil in James's work can be defined as inertness and passivity, Schneider condemns the "active" Charlotte as fixed or inert in her conformity to the world's values; Maggie, on the other hand, outgrows her passivity and achieves being and freedom.[35]

The debate about *The Golden Bowl* grows more sensitive and acute, and though it sometimes appears to produce only discord, it sheds light on aspects of the novel that once appeared impenetrable. Gone are the days when Rebecca West could write that *The Golden Bowl* "is an ugly and incompletely invented story about some people who are sexually mad." It is hard to believe that fifty years ago Edmund Wilson lumped it with those stories that are filled with "the Jamesian gas instead of with detail and background." To see how far understanding of *The Golden Bowl* has progressed, one need only turn to Laurence B. Holland's authoritative analysis of how stunningly the novel's form is determined by James's management of the bowl and "money" imagery, the characters' "crisis of transformation," and the "redemptive process" effected by Maggie as she accepts the role of scapegoat to validate her love and the family's "sanctity." Or one might turn to Daniel M. Fogel's scrupulous and imaginative study in which "detail" and "background" are shown to be synthesized into a work of exquisite symmetry and profound humanity.[36]

Except for the publication of an insignificant short novel, *The Outcry* (1911), James's career as a writer of long fiction ended with *The Golden Bowl.* Yet, in a sense he continued to exercise his novelistic art with the controversial revisions of a selection of his tales and novels for the famous New York Edition which appeared, along with critical prefaces, in twenty-four volume, between 1907 and 1909. Some of James's revisions, notably those in *Roderick Hudson* and *The American,* drew fire from old admirers and reviewers who complained that, in reworking earlier material in terms of his later style, James violated the freshness of his youthful fiction. The revisions proved to be extensive and time consuming, but James took more pleasure in his task than "I had fondly dreamed." Throughout his application to his task, moreover, he appears to have remained confident that he was improving his works; "I have absolutely no doubt whatever of the benefit I shall have conferred on each of them—and I mean of course benefit not only for myself, but for the public at large."[37] Not all readers, however, were to accept his contention that he had, as he maintained in reference to *Roderick Hudson,* left "substance" unchanged and confined himself to "mere revision of surface and expression."[38]

Not all readers were to agree, either, with James's decision to exclude from the edition such short novels as *The Europeans* and *Washington Square, The Bostonians, The Other House,* and the tantalizing tour de force, *The Sacred Fount.* James had no doubts about the fate of *Washington Square,* which in 1905 he professed himself unable to read, but he tepidly debated the inclusion of *The Bostonians.* In 1905, he did not consider the question of bringing *The Bostonians* into the collection a momentous one, and, as late as 1915, he thanks Edmund Gosse for his "good impression of the *Bostonians,*" but after writing about it with ambivalence, he merely regrets, "I should have liked to write that Preface to the *Bostonians*—which will never be written."[39]

The Ivory Tower and *The Sense of the Past,* two uncompleted novels published in 1917, more than a year after James's death, were perhaps victims of the first World War. In his preface to *The Ivory Tower,* Percy Lubbock states that the three books and one chapter that make up the fragment were written in 1914 and put aside because of James's inability to "work upon a fiction supposed to represent contemporary or recent life."[40] The completed portions of *The Ivory Tower* and James's copious notes to it reveal that before the war he felt himself in possession of a big American subject. In the novel, Gray Fielder, an expatriate American, inherits a fortune from his uncle, who in a death-bed revulsion against his own sordid financial career desires an heir without even a rudimentary knowledge of the ruthless world of high finance. The Europeanized nephew has so little business aptitude and so much kindness and naivete that he invites Horton Vint, a handsome and amoral American friend, to manage his affairs.

James's notes tell the rest of the story in a masterful scenario in which he counsels himself about the proper ages of his characters, invents and then refines upon incidents, and determines which relationships to make explicit and which to keep ambiguous. Both narrative and psychological complications take on Jamesian coloration as Gray Fielder, endowed with a new social aura because of his inheritance, attracts the attention of Cissy Foy, a beautiful but impoverished girl who has had "relations" with and still loves Vint. The notes project a modern American society more concerned with money than refinement, more dedicated to conspicuous consumption than to taste and intellectual pursuits. Against this background of expensive waste and triviality, Fielder's consciousness grasps new truths about himself and others as he detects Vint's predations and discovers Cissy and her lover in intimate relations.

The four books and detailed notes of *The Sense of the Past* tell the phantasmagoric tale of Ralph Pendrel's fading from the modern world of 1910 into the past of 1820 and his ultimate return to his own time.[41] Anything but a Connecticut Yankee, Ralph is a sensitive American writer who has two passions, a love for Aurora Coyne, an American widow, and an obsession with the "sense"—not a second-hand knowledge—of the past. After being rejected by Aurora, he takes possession of an inherited property in England and fantastically exchanges his place in the present for a remote relative's role in the past. His adventure results in psychological complications when he meets the girl that his alter ego is expected to marry but prefers her younger sister. Eventually, as the notes make clear, he feels the horror of being trapped "out" of his more congenial time, and through the efforts of the younger sister and Aurora, he recovers his original identity and is restored to his first love and the twentieth century.

Once again, the notes provide an astounding disclosure of Jame's literary imagination at work on the motivation of his characters, the counterpointing of his scenes, and the resolution of his doubts and worries. He frets, for example, about departing from his established point of view, and he decides to foreshorten his conclusion because he wishes to avoid a "graceless literality." He also states difficulties with a candor based on his confidence of overcoming them. Above all, he reveals an intellectual agility and concentration that give a sense of his complete absorption in the creative process.

The last volume of Leon Edel's *Letters* affords both a panoramic and a detailed view of the later years (1895–1916) of James's life. The letters record his move in 1898 from De Vere Gardens in London to Lamb House, his residence in the picturesque town of Rye, his trip to the United States in 1904–5, during which he visited old scenes and also went as far afield as Chicago, Florida, and California; his horrified response to the outbreak of the first World War; and his adoption of British citizenship in 1915. James's correspondence with Ellen Terry, Rhoda Broughton, Mrs. Humphrey Ward, Edith Wharton, and Isabella Gardner bears testimony to his friendship with some of the interesting women of his time. The affectionate tone of his letters to Hugh Walpole and Jocelyn Persse and the suggestion of eroticism in those to Henrik Andersen reveal a late flowering of an emotional nature formerly kept under firm control. James's letters of encouragement to such literary friends and acquaintances as Kipling, Conrad, H. G. Wells, Edith Wharton, and Ford Madox Hueffer show a sensitivity to new talents in some cases radically different from his own.

In the letters and *The American Scene*, James describes his American experience with a novelist's art and an expatriate's sense of adventure in a foreign land. He visits Edith Wharton in Lenox and quips that her house was "a delicate chateau mirrored in a Massachusetts pond."[42] From Lenox, he writes that "everything today has a romantic freshness" and "is almost uncannily delightful and sympathetic."[43] Later in Philadelphia, he lectures on "The Lesson of Balzac" and is pleased with his performance. In Washington, he meets old friends and dines at the White House with "Theodore Rex," who proves to be a genial host. His stay at the Vanderbilts' Biltmore estate in North Carolina during a surge of winter cold drives him to Florida where he discovers a "blandness in nature of which I had no idea."[44] He lectures in Indianapolis, St. Louis, and Chicago, and declares much of the country he saw "rank with good intentions." Southern California, however, proves an enchanted landscape with days of "heavenly beauty" and flowers "which fairly rage, with radiance."[45] And the marvelous chapters on New York in *The American Scene* offer evidence of how quick he was to catch the note of the "modern" even as he gave vent to his nostalgia for the endangered and annihilated monuments of his youth.

Still, from the beginning of his sojourn, James writes to his English friends that he is homesick for England. After reporting on the handsome "checks" he received from his lectures, he confesses to Edmund Gosse that he "would rather live a beggar at Lamb House" than opulently in the United States.[46] Certainly, lecturing and the discomforts of constant travel taxed James's strength; he was oversensitive to the ugliness he encountered; and even the kindly assiduities of friends and wellwishers made him yearn for a quieter routine at "home." From Chicago, which impressed him as "black, smoky, old-looking," he exclaims that he prefers the "far end of Sussex" to Florida: "In the heart of golden-groves, I yearned for the shade of the old Lamb House mulberry tree."[47]

Upon his return to England, James applied himself to the task of revising and writing prefaces to the fiction he had chosen for the New York Edition. The publication of the Edition, *The American Scene* (1907), and two autobiographical works were among the highpoints of James's later years.

He was celebrated in essays by Conrad and the constant Howells, and in 1913, Ford Madox Hueffer saluted him as "the greatest of living writers." Recognition came to him in the form of honorary degrees from Harvard and Oxford universities, and, on his seventieth birthday, a large group of friends and admirers subscribed for a portrait of James to be painted by John Singer Sargent. In America, Elisabeth Luther Cary had already (1905) written a book-length study of James noteworthy for its discriminating praise.[48]

But although achievements and rewards were many and conspicuous, James had anything but an untroubled old age. He suffered from chronic depression and from old and new ailments; he was wounded by the rejection implied by the poor sales of the New York Edition; and he had to endure in a single year (1910) the deaths of his brothers Robertson and William, the latter of whom, as he told Wells, represented such "an inexhaustible authority" that without him "I feel abandoned and afraid, even as a lost child.[49] Of course, the ultimate blow came with the outbreak of the war and its threat to the three countries whose lands and cultures he had long loved. To Rhoda Broughton, he despaired in August 1914: "Black and hideous to me is the tragedy that gathers, and I'm sick beyond cure to have lived to see it."[50] As the months passed and the carnage became frightful, he deferred work on The Ivory Tower and could not finish The Sense of the Past, his attempt to escape the implacable present. He tells Hugh Walpole in November, 1914, that he has been helping to console the "Belgian wounded" and the "influx" of British soldiers at St. Bartholemews Hospital, and he cries out, in a letter to an old friend, that the death of Rupert Brooke was "too horrible and heart-breaking."[51] Almost overwhelmed by the unending slaughter, he had to suffer the personal humiliation of being lampooned by H. G. Wells, whose works he had inordinately praised, as a "leviathan retrieving pebbles . . . a magnificent but painful hippopotamus resolved at any cost . . . upon picking up a pea which has got into a corner of his den."[52]

His refusal to be considered an alien at this moment of England's peril inevitably dictated James's decision to lend his "imponderable support" to the "cause" by becoming a British citizen. In asking Prime Minister Asquith to act as one of his sponsors, he affirms his "wish to testify at this crisis to the force of my attachment and devotion to England."[53] Of course, he was castigated by chauvinistic American critics, but many others who resented American neutrality in the war hailed his act as chivalric and even heroic. At the beginning of the last year of his life, he received the Order of Merit from King George V. "And," in the words of Rebecca West, "on 28th February 1916, he died, leaving the white light of his genius to shine out for the eternal comfort of the mind of man."[54]

After the glowing obituaries, James's reputation suffered an eclipse that at times seemed almost total. Today, the "white light" is shining more brightly than ever.

A NOTE ON THE SELECTIONS

To give a sense of Henry James's fluctuating reputation among his contemporaries, I have included in this collection reviews of each of his major novels from leading journals and newspapers of his time. I have tried, moreover, to give almost equal importance to British and American reviews and to balance where possible favorable and unfavorable opinion. In selecting twentieth-century criticism, I have preferred relatively recent work to work that has been widely reprinted. Although limitations of space have prevented my doing justice to narratives that have been variously classified as long tales, novellas, and short novels, I thought it wise to include an essay on "The Jolly Corner," a work whose technical brilliance and close thematic relevance to the later novels entitle it to serve as a representative of the "long story." The highly individualistic essays by Conrad and Howells present reactions to James by a distinguished novelist from his adopted country and from his native land.

James W. Gargano

Notes

1. *Henry James Letters, 3, 1883–1895,* ed. Leon Edel (Cambridge, Mass.: Harvard University Press, 1980), 512. Hereafter referred to as *Letters, 3.*

2. Joseph Weisenfarth, *Henry James and the Dramatic Analogy* (New York: Fordham University Press, 1963); Walter Isle, *Experiments in Form: Henry James' Novels, 1896–1901* (Cambridge, Mass.: Harvard University Press, 1968); Michael Egan, *Henry James: The Ibsen Years* (New York: Barnes and Noble Books, Harper and Row, 1972), 26.

3. *The Notebooks of Henry James,* ed. F. O. Matthiessen and Kenneth B. Murdock (New York: Oxford University Press, 1961, reprint), 138–43.

4. *Independent* 48 (10 December 1896): 1693; *New York Tribune,* (27 September 1896), sec. 3, 2; *Literary World* 27 (26 December 1893):476–77; *Current Literature* 20 (December 1896):486–87.

5. *Nation* 64 (28 January 1897):71; *Academy* 50 (14 November 1896):385–86; *Dial* 22 (1 January 1897):22; *Chicago Tribune,* 10 November 1896, 3; *New York Times,* "Saturday Review of Books and Art," 31 October 1896, 4; *American* 26 (9 January 1897):29; *Critic* 26 (28 November 1896):335.

6. S. Gorley Putt, *Henry James: A Reader's Guide* (Ithaca, N.Y.: Cornell University Press, 1966), 311; Leon Edel, *Henry James: The Treacherous Years: 1895–1901* (New York: J. B. Lippincott, 1969), 167; Oscar Cargill, *The Novels of Henry James* (New York: Macmillan, 1961), 211: Walter F. Wright, *The Madness of Art: A Study of Henry James* (Lincoln: University of Nebraska Press, 1962), 109; Walter Isle, *Experiments in Form,* 39–76.

7. Matthiessen and Murdock, *Notebooks of Henry James,* 136.

8. *Critic* 27 (1 May 1897):301; *San Francisco Chronicle,* 14 March 1897, 4; *Independent* 49 (29 July 1897):49; *New York Times,* "Saturday Review," 20 February 1897, 1; *Athenaeum,* 6 March 1897, 308; *New York Sun,* 20 February 1897, 7; *Literary World* 28 (17 April 1897):126–127; *Academy* 51 (27 February 1897):256; *Current Literature* 21 (May 1897):388.

9. Laurence B. Holland, *The Expense of Vision* (Baltimore and London: The Johns Hopkins University Press, 1982), 112; Manfred Mackenzie, *Communities of Honor and Love In Henry James* (Cambridge, Mass., and London, England 1976: Harvard University Press), 89; Ronald Wallace, *Henry James and the Comic Form* (Ann Arbor: University of Michigan Press, 1975), 83, 85, 86; Weisenfarth, *James and the Dramatic Analogy*, 44–56.

10. *Literary World* 28 (11 December 1897):454–55; *New York Times*, "Saturday Review," 27 November 1897, 9; *Spectator* 79 (30 October 1897):603; *Pall Mall Gazette*, 11 October 1897, 10; *Nation* 66 (17 February 1898):135; *Book News* 16 (January 1898):289; *Independent* 49 (16 December 1897):1660.

11. *Critic* 29 (8 January 1898):21; *Academy* 52 (16 October 1897):89; *Bookman* (London) 13 (October 1897):22; *Literature* 1 (23 October 1897):19; *Athenaeum*, 6 November 1897, 629.

12. F. W. Dupee, *Henry James* (New York: William Sloane, 1951), 191, 193; Nicola Bradbury, *Henry James: The Later Novels* (Oxford: Clarendon Press, 1979), 19.

13. Harris W. Wilson, "What Did Maisie Know?" *College English* 17 (February 1956):279–81; Sallie Sears, *The Negative Imagination* (Ithaca, N.Y.: Cornell University Press, 1968), 24, 31, 32; Philip Weinstein, *Henry James and the Requirements of the Imagination* (Cambridge, Mass.: Harvard University Press, 1971), 72–96.

14. *The Novels and Tales of Henry James*, vol. 9 (New York: Charles Scribner's Sons, 1908), vi–vii.

15. *Spectator* 82 (6 May 1899):647; *Independent* 51 (8 June 1899):1565; *Dial* 27 (1 July 1899):21; *New York Sun*, 1 July 1899, 6–7; *Athenaeum* 113 (27 May 1899):651–52; *Pall Mall Gazette*, 8 May 1899, 4; *Bookman* (London) 16 (June 1899):81; *New York Tribune*, "Illustrated Supplement," 21 May 1899, 13; *Literature* 3 (6 May 1899):475–76; *Chicago Tribune*, 13 May 1899, 10; *New York World*, 24 June 1899, 6.

16. *Critic* 35 (August 1899):754–56; *Times* (London) 15 August 1899, 9; *Academy* 56 (13 May 1899):532–33; *Brooklyn Eagle*, 11 June 1899, 19; *Detroit Free Press*, 29 May 1899, 7.

17. Charles Thomas Samuels, *The Ambiguity of Henry James* (Urbana, Chicago, and London: University of Illinois Press, 1971), 162; Rebecca West, *Henry James* (New York: Henry Holt, 1916), 106–7; Edmund Wilson, "The Ambiguity of Henry James," *Hound and Horn* 8 (April/May 1934):403–4; Pelham Edgar, *Henry James: Man and Author* (New York and Boston: Houghton Mifflin, 1927), 134; F. R. Leavis, *The Great Tradition* (New York: New York University Press, 1964), 170; Isle, *Experiments In Form*, 203; Daniel Schneider, "James's *The Awkward Age*: A Reading and an Evaluation," *Henry James Review* 1 (Spring 1980):219, 227.

18. F. R. Leavis, *The Great Tradition*, 170; F. W. Dupee, *Henry James*, 197; Samuels, *Ambiguity of Henry James*, 161, 173; Edgar, *Henry James: Man and Author*, 141; Dupee, *Henry James*, 198; J. A. Ward, *The Imagination of Disaster: Evil and the Fiction of Henry James* (Lincoln: University of Nebraska Press, 1961), 97; Dupee, *Henry James*, 202.

19. *Henry James Letters*, vol. 4: 1895–1916, ed. Leon Edel (Cambridge, Mass.: Harvard University Press, 1984), 154–55. Hereafter referred to as *Letters, 4*.

20. *Letters, 4*, 198.

21. *Letters, 4*, 186.

22. *Bookman* (New York) 13 (July 1901):442; *Boston Evening Transcript*, 13 February 1901, sec. 2, 12; *Chicago Tribune*, 5 March 1901, 13; *Times* (London), 4 May 1901, 9; *Independent* 53 (14 March 1901):616–620; *Athenaeum*, 2 March 1901, 272; *San Francisco Chronicle*, 3 March 1901, 8; *Pall Mall Gazette*, 26 February 1901, 4; *Academy* 60 (23 February 1901):165–66; *Times* (London), 4 May 1901, 9; *New York Tribune*, 9 February 1901, 8; *Critic* 38 *(April 1901):368–70; *Current Literature* 30 (April 1901):493; *Literature* 8 (23 February 1901):144; *New York Times*, "Saturday Review," 16 February 1901, 112.

23. Rebecca West, *Henry James*, 107; *The Sacred Fount*, ed. Leon Edel (London: Rupert Hart-Davis, 1959), 5, 14, 15; Weinstein, *James and the Requirements of the Imagination*,

101; Isle, *Experiments in Form*, 222; Edmund Wilson, "The Ambiguity of Henry James," *Hound and Horn* 8 (April–May 1934):394; Wilson Follett, "The Simplicity of Henry James," *American Review* (May–June 1923), 315–25; Cargill, *Novels of Henry James*, 280–96; Jean Frantz Blackall, *Jamesian Ambiguity and The Sacred Fount* (Ithaca, N.Y.: Cornell University Press, 1965).

24. *Philadelphia North American*, 29 November 1903, sec. 7, 6; *San Francisco Chronicle*, 6 December 1903, 8; *New York Times*, 14 November 1903, sec. E, 818; *Pall Mall Gazette*, 13 October 1903, 4; *Lamp* 27 (December 1903):467–69; *Academy* 65 (October 1903):387; *Boston Evening Transcript*, 21 December 1904, 18; *Chicago Tribune*, 21 November 1903, 13.

25. *Athenaeum*, 28 November 1903, 714; *Spectator* 191 (12 December 1903):1030; *Literary World* 34 (December 1903):348.

26. Percy Lubbock, *The Craft of Fiction* (New York: Peter Smith, 1945), 158; E. M. Forster, *Aspects of the Novel* (New York: Harcourt, Brace, 1927), 229; F. R. Leavis, *The Great Tradition*, 161; F. O. Matthiessen, *The Major Phase* (New York: Oxford University Press, 1944), 39, 34.

27. Quentin Anderson, *The American Henry James* (New Brunswick, N.J.: Rutgers University Press, 1957), 208–31; William M. Gibson, "Metaphor in the Plot of *The Ambassadors*," in *Henry James: Modern Judgments*, ed. Tony Tanner (London: Macmillan, 1968), 304–15; Frederick C. Crews, *The Tragedy of Manners: Moral Drama in the Later Novels of Henry James* (Hamden, Conn: Archon Books, 1971), 30–56; John E. Tilford, Jr., "James the Old Intruder," *Modern Fiction Studies* 4 (Summer 1958):157–64; Christof Wegelin, *The Image of Europe in Henry James* (Dallas: Southern Methodist University Press, 1958), 359; Sister M. Corona Sharp, *The Confidante in Henry James: Evolution and Moral Value of a Fictive Character* (Notre Dame, Ind.: University of Notre Dame Press, 1963), 180; Sears, *Negative Imagination*, 129.

28. *Letters*, 4, 224.

29. *Contemporary Review* 82 (November 1902):756–57; *Independent* 54 (13 November 1902):2711–12; *Spectator* 89 (4 October 1902):498–99; *New York Sun*, 13 September 1902, 8; *Bookman* (London) 23 (October 1902):24–25; *San Francisco Chronicle*, 14 September 1902, Supplement, 4; *Bookman* (New York) 16 (November 1902):259–60; *Nation* 75 (23 October 1902):330–31; *New York Times*, "Saturday Review," 4 October 1902, 658; *Athenaeum*, 13 September 1902, 346.

30. *Academy and Literature* 63 (6 September 1902):235.

31. Matthiessen, *Major Phase*, 42–80; Anderson, *American Henry James* 237; Dorothea Krook, *The Ordeal of Consciousness in Henry James* (Cambridge: Cambridge University Press, 1962), 214; Samuels, *Ambiguity of Henry James*, 70; Edel, *Henry James: The Master: 1901–1916* (New York: J. B. Lippincott, 1972), 116; Daniel Mark Fogel, *Henry James and the Structure of the Romantic Imagination* (Baton Rouge and London: Louisiana State University Press, 1981), 84.

32. *Letters*, 4, 591.

33. *New York Sun*, 3 December 1904, 7; *Pall Mall Gazette*, 23 February 1905, 3; *Atlantic* 95 (May 1905):696; *New York Tribune*, 3 December 1904, 10.

34. *Critic* 43 (January 1905):20; *Athenaeum*, 18 March 1905, 332; *Lamp* 29 (January 1905):583–85; *Academy and Literature* 68 (11 February 1905):128–29; *Independent* 58 (19 January 1905):153–54; *Nation* 80 (26 January 1905):74; Robert L. Gale, *The Caught Image* (Chapel Hill: University of North Carolina Press, 1964), 251.

35. Krook, *Ordeal of Consciousness*, 240; Walter Wright, "Maggie Verver: Neither Saint nor Witch," in *Henry James: Modern Judgments*, ed. Tony Tanner (London: Macmillan, 1968), 316–26; Naomi Lebowitz, "Magic and Metamorphosis in *The Golden Bowl*," in *Henry James: Modern Judgments*, 328; Wallace, *James and the Comic Form*, 136–47; Daniel Schneider, *The Crystal Cage* (Lawrence: The Regents Press of Kansas, 1978), 189–93.

36. West, *Henry James*, 104–5; Edmund Wilson, "The Ambiguity of Henry James," *Hound and Horn* 8 (April–May 1934):404; Laurence B. Holland, *The Expense of Vision*, 331–407; Fogel, *James and Structure of the Romantic Imagination*, 85–137.

37. *Letters, 4,* 408.

38. *Letters, 4,* 422.

39. *Letters, 4,* 777–78.

40. *The Novels and Tales of Henry James,* vol. 25 (New York: Charles Scribner's Sons, 1917), v–vi.

41. *Novels and Tales of Henry James,* vol. 26.

42. *Letters, 4,* 325.

43. *Letters, 4,* 332.

44. *Letters, 4,* 351.

45. *Letters, 4,* 357.

46. *Letters, 4,* 352.

47. *Letters, 4,* 356.

48. Cary, Elisabeth Luther, *The Novels of Henry James: A Study* (New York: G. P. Putnam, 1905).

49. *Letters, 4,* 562.

50. *Letters, 4,* 713.

51. *Letters, 4,* 752.

52. H. G. Wells, *Boon* (New York: George H. Doran, 1915), 110.

53. *Letters, 4,* 764.

54. West, *Henry James,* 117.

Reviews and Contemporary Comments

[*The Other House:* A Fresh Power]   Anonymous*

The appearance of a new book by Mr. Henry James is always an event to the connoisseur of letters. It cannot be stated too explicitly or published too widely that *The Other House* is an event of the first order. In a small way it is a revolution. Mr. James has done something new. His name has been for long a synonym for cleverness and conscious skill, but on laying down this volume the reader is forced to confess that henceforward, if the writer so wills, it also is a synonym for power. The book has grip. Up to this time Mr. James's grip has apparently been nothing more than an exquisite sense of touch. The plot is compact of passion, terror, tragedy. Heretofore the author has avoided all but the decorous intellectual tragedies comprehended only by the elect, and has ignored the passions—perhaps because they are not well-bred—in favor of the perceptions. Here for the first time he permits himself a hand-to-hand bout with those elements of human nature and life which he has previously handled with gloves. The result is a book in which for once the crowning impression is not "What a clever writer!" but "What a powerful tale!" In literature, also, he who loses his life shall find it. Mr. James's reward for the perceptible amount of self-repression involved in the situation and handling of the story will be a wider, more diffused appreciation of its merits. . . .

In the way of subtle linking of motive with event and the interaction of character upon character, Mr. James has never done anything stronger or more artful. Granting the character of Rose Armiger—it is a good deal to grant, but we readily make the concession of her possibility for the sake of the result,—the argument of the whole thing is absolutely flawless. It is complicated, but its complexity is as coherent as that of some living organism. In all points of technique the book is really marvelous. Up to this time, the writer's most ardent admirers have never claimed for him a constructive ability of the first order as a novelist. When, some six or eight years ago, he abandoned the form of the novel and devoted himself to the study of the short story, it presently became apparent that he had the power of presenting a single situation, a detached phase of life, more completely and significantly than anyone else has ever done. It seemed that he

*Reprinted from the *Critic*, n.s. 26 (28 November 1896):335.

had found for the first time his *métier,* the work for which his rare talent was destined. The present volume overturns completely this theory of the ultimate use of Mr. James in literature, for in it he has applied his perfected method of the short story to the problem of the novel with an almost startling success. The entire action of the book takes place in two half days; a morning at Bounds, the house of Anthony Bream, and an afternoon at Eastmead, the home of Mrs. Beever. To so arrange the stage that in these two scant scenes the characters, motives and relations of the six personages who play leading parts, become obvious and their destinies clear, is a feat of dramatic construction beside which Sardou's most compact bits of craftsmanship seem clumsy and badly done. The accusation of artificiality, which might well have been brought against such a marvel of structure had the theme been one of Mr. James's customary intellectual motives, can hardly be sustained against a book so full of "pity and terror," so vibrant with the true tragic note, that the general reader is likely to overlook the construction altogether in favor of more absorbing qualities.

Better and more exciting than the discovery of a new force in letters is the revelation of a fresh power in an old friend. Mr. James has written for nearly thirty years to the delight of an audience fit though few. He now comes forward exhibiting qualities adapted to the subjugation of the many. Has he had them up his sleeve these three decades? Have life and art revealed themselves afresh to him in the "middle years"? Or is it only that he has resolved to conquer the populace? Readers of *Embarrassments* will remember the history of Ray Limbert, an exquisite literary artist whose productions did not sell, though he was continually making more tremendous efforts to be obvious and popular, more desperate bids for general acceptance. Each time he only succeeded in producing "a more shameless, merciless masterpiece." The temptation to compare Limbert and his creator is strong, but the latter will have the happier fate. If *The Other House* is in any sense a bid for popularity, it is preordained to be a successful one. The thrill of the story naturally is not for the readers of "shilling shockers," but it will appeal to many whom even the art of his short stories left cold. No one could have predicted that Mr. James would have undertaken the apotheosis of the police gazette, but this is practically what he has done, and he has made its footing firm upon Olympus. The book is a masterpiece, and we predict that the hour of the author's universality is at hand.

[*The Other House:* A Crude Melodrama]

William Morton Payne*

The Other House is the most readable book that Mr. James has produced for some years—a result following from the exigencies of its purpose rather than from any deliberate eschewing of his inconclusive aims and methods. The obvious thing about the book is its dramatic structure. It is a play in three acts; the speakers are always conscious of being on the stage, and the reader is always conscious that the connective tissue of the story—the passages of description and analysis—have for their sole purpose the production of those impressions that the playgoer gets through the medium of eyesight. In other words, what we see as stage-setting and play of feature has somehow to be described in the book, and is described so skillfully as to keep the scene in its detail ever before the mental vision. In this aspect, the thing is so well done that adverse criticism is hardly possible. But the action of the story is not altogether natural, and the tragic climax finds us inadequately prepared. We realize from an early moment that the heroine is an emotional creature, and we may guess at the depths of passion that lie beneath the surface of her nature, but for all that we are hardly prepared to find her guilty of so diabolical a thing as the deliberate murder of the child of the man whom she loves. This is the artistic flaw in the plot, transforming into crude melodrama what starts out to be a successful comedy of manners.

*Reprinted from the *Dial* 22 (1 January 1897):22.

[*The Spoils of Poynton:* Fine-Spun Work]
Anonymous

Mr. James, in these later years, is spinning finer than ever. It is not only that his material in this novel is scant. Trollope, Crawford, and a dozen others have wrought skillfully with as little matter. But in the treatment of his subject Mr. James absolutely neglects all the opportunities any other novelist would seize upon. In the present case we have a mother, a son, and two young women, all of the "upper middle class," and in all the book not more than half a dozen other sketches of character for relief. Speaking broadly, the mother wants the son to marry one of the young women, and he intends to marry the other, and does. There, with another deserving hero, or even without one, would be material enough and to spare for the sentimental novelist.

But Mr. James makes nothing at all of the situation that he might be expected to make. He has few turns in the generally straight course of his narrative, and not one of them is obvious. He allows nothing for the romantic taste that is in us all. The study of character is his single aim, but it is invariably study pursued with no idea of giving the shallow entertainment; with no dwelling upon eccentric traits humorously, with no tenderness for the weak, with no appeal either for laughter or for tears, and it must be

*Reprinted from the *New York Times*, "Saturday Review of Books and Art," 20 February 1897, 1.

confessed, with a result which, if pleasing to one's finer sense, is yet scarcely tangible.

The most appreciative reader of this volume of exquisite English, (always the only right word in the only proper place,) will lay it down with no definite idea in his mind of the identity of Mrs. Gereth, Owen, Fleda Vetch, or Mona Brigstock. Once in a while, in his earlier novels, Mr. James so presented a personage that one felt, for a time, one knew him or her; as, for example, the protagonist of *The American*, the girl in *The Tragic Muse*, and that horrid brother and sister in *The Princess Casamassima*. But who remembers their names now? In his later books his aim has surely been far from making us care much for the creatures of his imagination.

Mrs. Gereth is the type of good taste so highly developed that it has become almost a malady. So exquisite is her sensibility, so exacting her fastidiousness, that nearly every other woman she meets seems a "frump," and the popular literature and art, decorative, plastic, and graphic, of England at the close of the nineteenth century is to her unbearable. Yet when her son marries, she must give up Poynton, which is all perfect, without a false note, every room representing a lifetime of joyful labor in selection; and her son will marry Mona Brigstock, who will care for nothing there, and will desecrate the home with "bric-a-brac," things from Liberty's, and anti-macassars. As it turns out, Mona does "care" in a sort of animal way, without a touch of real appreciation; and that lends to the situation, as Mr. James treats it, an almost tragic tone.

The irony is appreciable, of course, but while Mr. James is bound to treat of Mrs. Gereth with a touch of irony, his sympathy with her, in all her trials, is sufficiently evident. It is sad to think that not one novel reader in ten thousand, probably, will be able to comprehend his and Mrs. Gereth's and Fleda Vetch's views of life, art, and conduct, leaving sympathy out of the question. But the appreciation of the one in ten thousand is worth working for, and the knowledge Mr. James must have that his delight in the book's subtlety and refinement, the grave, thoughtful piquancy which is the substitute for humor, will be keen while it lasts, is, perhaps, a sufficient reward. And counting all the tens of thousands of novel readers in the English speaking world, one from each of the tens of thousands will make up a company that is worth while. So that we need not grieve for Henry James.

[*The Spoils of Poynton:* The Triumph of the Inner Drama]   Anonymous*

If, however, [*The Other House*] seems to have been somewhat influenced by the theatre, nothing could be further removed from every sugges-

*Reprinted from the *Edinburgh Review* 197 (January 1903):75–76.

tion of things theatrical than *The Spoils of Poynton*, which appeared in the next year. Few, indeed, would have considered favourably, as the theme of a story, the fondness of a middle-aged lady for the furniture she and her late husband have collected. But it is one of Mr. James's peculiarities that he is extraordinarily independent of his themes, and one never can quite foresee to what uses he will put them. The old furniture at Poynton becomes the test of a girl's honour; of a girl who, when the story opens, knew the place not even by name, and of a point of honour which to many may seem an over-sensitive perversity. But it is a point of honour between a woman and a woman, a fine and rare thing, or perhaps, one should say, between a woman and her self-respect, a thing finer and rarer still. For the real issue of the work is the triumph over her desires of Fleda's jealous probity, and its final discomfiture by her passion. It is a study of wonderful subtlety, this slow capture of a heart. Breach follows breach in its wall, barrier after barrier falls in its highways, and all the while its owner is unconscious of defending it, and its assailant in ignorance of his success. Long after Fleda Vetch has surrendered, she is still fighting, and fighting not for terms but for ultimate victory. And the tragedy is that she obtains it. Obtains it, as it were, when her city is sacked and its defences broken, when she has lost all for which she fought. The distance between her counsel of honour to the man who was beseiging her, and her despairing capitulation, is increased for us by contrast between the overwhelming suddenness of her passion in victory, and the intriguing devices by which she had kept it so long at bay.

The book is illustrative, though not more so than many another, of the author's exquisite sense of beauty in the ministration of life, a sense which concerns itself chiefly with the ordering of human habitation, with houses and gardens and charming rooms, expressed by a style as mellow and as exquisite as the things which it describes.

> What he saw so intensely to-day, what he felt as a nail driven in, was that only now, at the very last, had he come into possession. His development had been abnormally slow, almost grotesquely gradual. He had been hindered and retarded by experience, and for long periods had only groped his way. It had taken too much of his life to produce too little of his art. The art had come, but it had come after everything else.

The words are from the reflections of Dencombe in *The Middle Years*, but they might be taken, in view of his wonderful development, for the author's own. He has in these stories of his later years at last come into possession. He had for long been driving in the wide rut of fiction where so many wheels go. He had done work of a quality which, however superior to that of his competitors, was still of their kind. It portrayed, to use a term which but imperfectly defines it, the outer drama of life, the expression in circumstances of character, the working out of temperament. But what he now depicted was the inner drama, the impression of circumstance on character, the working in of fate. He had at last "come into possession," and of a field completely his own. The intimacy of his new presentment, the delicate tracing of motive and impulse, and susceptibility to the involutions of the mind, make his old work seem almost superficial.

What Maisie Knew: High Water   Anonymous*

This latest novel from Mr. James's pen seems, beyond doubt, to touch his highest point. It is a work very difficult to criticise, very perplexing to appraise. But beyond and above all the one fact of its astounding cleverness stands forth. It is quite impossible to ignore that, if the word have any significance, and is ever to be used at all, we are here dealing with genius. This is a work of genius, as much as Mr. Meredith's best work, though on quite other human lines, as the readers of both need not be reminded. And the next point which may occur to a reader, as he lays down the book, is that the author has generously, wilfully, almost wantonly handicapped himself. He had selected a strange medley of sordid intrigue, in which some vivid and curious characters perform the antics of that human comedy on which Mr. James loves to dwell as much as his great contemporary. It was a *partie carrée,* a group hard enough in itself to conceive, set forth, and illumine in the subtle manner to which the author has accustomed us. But conceive that this medley, these intricacies of motive, this tangle and confusion of emotion, are all transmuted, reflected, determined through the mind of a little girl of eight years! The thing, one would say, was preposterous. What on earth, indeed, *did* Maisie know of all this terrible human imbroglio? She knew nothing—that is obviously the answer which Mr. James desires us to take from his story; and that very fact that she knew nothing, was really aware of nothing, stared on life through childish and innocent eyes, surveyed the dustheap and the dungheap with her incomplete and wondering vision—that fact composes the amazing difficulty of Mr. James's task. To render the action and the motives through Maisie's mind to the reader, and yet leave upon that virginal spirit the stain or shadow of no comprehension—such has been the author's work. His success is commensurate with the difficulty. Of all the figures that tread the mazes of the story—Farange, her father, Mrs. Beale, Sir Claude, even Ida herself—none is fixed so indelibly and marked with such personality as the child. Mr. James's plots do not bear the bald analysis of a review; they must be taken in the context. To any one who will drop his Hall Caines and Marie Corellis for a time and take the trouble to read through this book, every single act and feeling of the child will be pathetically convincing. The grime and squalor of the life of these characters make an impression upon the

*Reprinted from the *Pall Mall Gazette,* 11 October 1897, 10. The first paragraph of the review has been omitted.

reader. But they never touch Maisie. She is no heroine, of course; she is what her unnatural life made her—weak, yielding, a little deceitful, feebly affectionate, but above all ignorant, peace-loving, and possessed of that weary craving for rest and home and some one to cling to. To the last she is defeated, and even when Mrs. Wix carries her off in triumph, we are not quite certain if she has gained what was the desire of her heart.

What did Maisie know? There was little that she had not heard. Every vain, selfish, or cowardly character in the book pours confidences into her ears. She herself boasted to her father that she knew everything; she liked to know. The pathetic part of it, and yet the best part of it also, was that, as we have said, she knew nothing. We have remarked upon the surprising difficulties which Mr. James has thrown in his own way; and yet we should not be astonished to learn that Mr. James has conceived the book entirely for the sake of that central figure with its distressing problem. He is used to set himself hard tasks, and executes them whether any cares or not. This time we venture to think that he has achieved something which must strike even that mysterious and loose-headed person, the general reader. And yet, perhaps not; and, if not, at least he has enriched the heritage of our descendants.

[*What Maisie Knew:* Repellent to Taste and Feeling, to Law and Gospel]   Anonymous*

What Maisie Knew is of a quality incredible in a writer whose work has heretofore been, morally, beyond reproach. In what it says, still more in what it suggests, it ranks, except for a terrible underlying dullness, with the worst schools of French fiction. Maisie is a little child, not more than five or six years old, when her parents obtain a mutual divorce with an agreement that she shall divide her year equally between them. In the six months spent with her worthless father she hears her mother's name daily mentioned with oaths and foulest reproach. Going thence to an equally worthless mother, she learns, in language only less profane and foul, that her father is a profligate wretch. Neither spares one detail of coarse objurgation for pity at her helpless babyhood. Presently the pretty governess, hired by the mother, follows Maisie to the home of the father and becomes that father's mistress. A little later the mother makes a second marriage. Husband No. 2, a good-natured person, as weak and dissipated as, but less violent than, his predecessor, takes a fancy to the little girl, and she learns to adore him. She also adores the ex-governess, her father's mistress and

*Reprinted from the *Literary World* 28 (11 December 1897):454–55. The first paragraph of the review has been omitted.

later his wife. When, therefore, father No. 1, deserts wife No. 2, and goes to live with (and on) a third lady, and mother No. 1, having tried a variety of lovers (all with Maisie's knowledge and connivance), elopes with the latest, and father No. 2 and mother No. 2 form a connection, Maisie, by this time nine years old or so, sees no harm in the arrangement. She talks the situation over with her governess, and is prepared to accept it happily.

Such a plot seems inconceivable. Its author exhibits not one ray of pity or dismay at this spectacle of a child with the pure current of its life thus poisoned at its source. To him she is merely the *raison d'être* of a curiously complicated situation, which he can twist and untwist for purposes of fiction. One feels in the reading that every manly feeling, every possibility of generous sympathy, every comprehension of the higher standards, has become atrophied in Mr. James's nature from long disuse, and that all relation between him and his kind has perished except to serve him coldly by way of "material."

It goes without saying that the style of the book is jerkily incoherent. The characters, Maisie included, converse in vague inuendoes, and, as no answer is promised "in the next number," the readers of the story—may they be few—will probably never understand exactly what any one concerned said or did or meant. This is just as well, for what little one is able to understand is alike repellent to taste and feeling, to law and gospel.

[*What Maisie Knew:* An Ill-Focussed Photograph]   Anonymous*

What Maisie Knew is an attempt to print the figure of life as it falls upon the very acute vision of a little girl. Life as presented to her eyes is sufficiently unpleasant, as hers is spent alternately in the company of divorced parents who have each contracted fresh alliances. That, however, should rather have increased the interest of the story, and have produced a sharpness of outline and contrast which is the very quality it lacks. It is a bewildering blur of motive and action which has the same effect of irritation on the mind as an ill-focussed photograph upon the sight. If the promise of the title had been more closely adhered to, this might have been avoided, for throughout the book Maisie's knowledge is all too liberally supplemented by that of Mrs. Wix, her nurse, and Mrs. Wix is a bore of almost heroic proportions. She is the incarnation of the moral idea in an inferior mind, well enough in its way seen from a sufficient distance, but terrible when it sprawls microscopically distinct over the foreground of a picture. Mr. James had before shown a disposition to succumb to the attractions of unattractive women, and here he has permitted them com-

*Reprinted from the *Edinburgh Review* 197 (January 1903):76.

pletely to master him. Wise and foolish, moral and unmoral, all the women
in the story are almost entirely unentertaining.

The Evolution of Henry James   Cornelia Atwood Pratt*

It is perfectly understood that Mr. James is far and away the most finished writer of prose fiction our generation has produced. He who runs and
does not read knows as much as this, for the critics have been lavish in
their appreciation of his perfection of style and form. But while it would be
impossible to do too much justice to this particular aspect of his merit, it
has perhaps been dwelt upon to the exclusion of his more vital qualities.
These have suffered the misapprehension which is the share of the too-
perfectly-dressed human creature whom the world lightly estimates by his
garments, without taking stock of the reserves of character which alone can
dignify the best tailoring.

Should anyone whose attention has been concentrated upon the irre-
proachable vesture of Mr. James's work ask upon what its vital qualities depend, there are fifty answers. He has not sought the reward of the marketplace; he has rejected compromises; he has refused to sacrifice his especial
vision of excellence; he has served an exacting ideal of art with a patience
and a strength nothing short of super-human. How can work done in such
a spirit fail to be vital?

There are two things which the gods of art reward: patience and audacity. And the reward of patience is the greater of these. We learn this from
the maxims of our elders, and believe it not, but when we see the lesson
wrought out in life before our eyes it is more difficult to be sceptical. The
gradual evolution of Mr. James's work contains, if you like, an immense
moral lesson for the young artist, as well as a reproach to the worthy gentlemen who turn off a novel before breakfast every morning and correct the
proofs of the same that evening after dinner. It proves beyond a doubt,
indirectly, that playing to the gallery means loss of power, and, directly,
that the consistent service of "the God of Things as They Are" is fructifying
and profitable in the highest sense, the one safeguard against that disaster
of artistic dryness and importance with which middle life threatens the
worker in the things of the mind. From forty to fifty-five is the time which
tests the artist, as well as the prophet and the common man. Does he grow
a little commonplace, hard, clay-encrusted? Is the land of his youthful
dreams a country erased from his map of life? Is science more absorbing
than poetry and his bank account a little dearer than either? Then he has
taken the wrong turning, and is off the track of art. On the other hand, has
he kept his vision of good work? Has his insight deepened and his expres-

*Reprinted from the *Critic*, n.s. 31 (April 1899):338–42.

sion sweetened? Is he keener to catch "the note, the trick, the strange irregular rhythm of life"?

Along with his growing mastery of the tools of his trade, does there go
a broader comprehension of the material in which he works? Is his spell
more potent, his creative effort more effectual? Then is he justified, for
these are the natural sanctions that proclaim him called to his chosen labor.
The spectacle of a cumulative artistic life is as rare as it is convincing, and
this spectacle Mr. James furnishes for us in a very satisfying fullness.

He has been writing for a little more than thirty years. He has produced between thirty and forty volumes. Unlike the briefly triumphing
young talents with whom we have become so familiar of late, his first work
is far from his best. Yet certain things were clearly visible in his writings
from the beginning. His style was admirable even then. It was lucid, quiet,
elegant, but these qualities strike the reader as perhaps existing for their
own sake rather than because of their appropriateness to the matter in
hand. In *Watch and Ward*, his first novel, the style seems an end rather
than the readiest means. Thought and expression are not so entirely co-
ordinated as they later become. As for his subject-matter, he was evidently
resolved always to see life in its higher aspects; to consider its intellectual,
aesthetic, and its lighter social problems.

At the beginning of his career he considered these subjects with suav-
ity rather than with fervor. *Watch and Ward*, for instance, is an agreeable
story with a highly finished surface, which does full justice to the merits of
a good but uninteresting young man who adopted an orphan girl and
brought her up with a devotion that was ultimately rewarded. The best
thing in the book is the moral tenderness the writer shows for poor Roger,
who is bald, a trifle stout, immaculate, and precise,—just the kind of hero,
in fact, upon whom an author might be tempted to impose a life of renunciation. To say this is not to intimate that Mr. James exhibits any partiality
toward his creations such as existence would not be likely to show them.
He early took the resolve that in his pages life should speak for itself without other editorial comment from him than that implied in the choice of
subject. His work shows that he also held a definite theory of composition
whose first principle was that the whole should be greater than any of its
parts. His work is wonderfully even, and it is next to impossible to pick out
"strong passages" where the writer's force has been expended more lavishly
than elsewhere.

In one of his later stories, "The Figure in the Carpet," he recites the
strenuous endeavor of an ardent disciple to decipher the general idea, the
underlying design, which ran through all the work of an acknowledged
master of literature. If it is impossible to do this in his own case, one may
yet observe certain patterns which recur oftener than others. He has, for
instance, an especial fondness for considering the problems of the artistic
life, and has done some of his cleverest work about them, just as much of
his strongest writing has gone into stories whose fundamental proposition

is the elemental hgh-mindness of the young girl. The picturesque also has attracted him strongly, especially that phase of it produced by the contrast of character and circumstances as fixed in the Old World, with character and circumstance as evolved in the New. He recurs to this contrast again and again in his earlier works. *The American* and *The European* [sic] are the most highly finished examples of it, as *Daisy Miller* is the best known and *A Passionate Pilgrim* the most poignant and captivating. Of the six stories in this volume, four are absolute masterpieces, and the fifth is only saved from perfection by some vague lack of interest in the chief character. They have that final touch of fervor, of passionate creative interest, which testifies to the absorption of the artist in his work. Matter and manner are perfectly fused. The writer's talent glows at white heat, and the book indicates the high-water mark of his earlier period.

But the law of the artistic life is experiment, and some of Mr. James's subsequent experiments produced less happy results. It is avowedly his theory that "character is action, and action is plot." Conceding him this point of view, it must be admitted that some characters make better plots than others, just as some caterpillars spin handsomer cocoons than their fellows. There are many even of Mr. James's admirers who do not care for the plot which wove itself about Verena Tarrant, heroine of *The Bostonians;* and Christina Light after her transformation into the Princess Casamassima was almost equally disappointing as a centre of growth. These novels have more surface than depth, and the proper amount of emotion was not mixed with the minute observation that went to their construction. If this fact was apparent to their readers, we may readily assume that it did not escape the more exacting eye of their writer. Certainly they had no successors in kind.

The Tragic Muse, which was the first long novel following the *Princess Casamassima*, seems to mark an era in the author's production. Assuredly, for the last ten years the connotation of his work has been richer and its execution more brilliant than ever before. Up to the beginning of that time, there have always been moments when his perfections left the reader cold, but now he arouses enthusiasm rather than admiration. It is as if his search for perfection had grown into such a consuming passion that everything he turns out glows with the warmth of that central fire. Also he has become bolder in the handling of his tools. His hand is free at last after half a lifetime's apprenticeship, and the feats he performs, his bits of sheer craftsmanship, make us catch our breath. If he had written nothing else than the six volumes of short stories which followed *The Tragic Muse*, he would yet have an ample claim upon enduring fame. There is hardly a tale in "The Lesson of the Master," "The Real Thing," "The Wheel of Time," "The Private Life," "Terminations," and "Embarrassments," that is not a little miracle for execution, subtlety, and suggestiveness. In these volumes he begins to exercise his dexterity upon the problem of saying the unsayable, which has absorbed him still further since. That his success in so doing was marvellous will not be denied by any one who has read "The Private Life," or "The Altar of the Dead"—to name only two of the most remarkable of these tales. The latter story is a strange and deeply tender study wherein human constancy is given a fantastic outward form which satisfies us completely, in spite of its surface absurdity, because, while recognizing how untrue it is to the outer existence, we are aware in every fibre of its deep realism as toward the soul's life.

In one of his critical essays, Mr. James says that we measure the author by his execution. "The advantage, the luxury, as well as the torment and responsibility of the novelist is that there is no limit to what he may attempt as an executant, no limit to his possible experiments, efforts, discoveries, successes." If we are to estimate our author himself by this measure which he proposes, how are we to express ourselves as to his successes during the recent years? We may think what we please of the material used in *What Maisie Knew, The Spoils of Poynton, The Other House*, "In the Cage," "The Two Magics," and *The Awkward Age*, but as feats of execution, as plastic performances, there is simply nothing in our language with which to compare them. They are final. They stand alone. In his *Artist's Letters from Japan*, Mr. La Farge tells of a famous Chinese architect who lived more than two thousand years ago. When asked how he conceived his marvellous works, he replied that it was very simple; he put out of his mind everything but the thing he wished to do and his sense of relation to the divine mind. At the end of the first day he had forgotten the money he was to receive for his work; at the end of the second, he no longer remembered the applause which would be given to him, and very soon nothing was present to his consciousness save the Thing Itself which he desired to create. Then he was ready to go out into the forest and choose the timber of which his building should be wrought. Now and again, in art and in literature we come upon works of such extraordinary vividness, so completely seen, so detached and independent, that we know instinctively they have been shaped with the aid of this eternal formula. What Fortuny and Franz Hals did in painting, Mr. James has achieved in literature by his work of the last ten years. He has set forth the "Thing Itself" which he has sought to express. To do this, he has adopted whatever means will serve his purpose best. He alters his style at will, complicating it to serve complicated ends. The style of *Maisie*, "In the Cage," and *The Awkward Age*, shows hardly a trace of his wonted grace and transparency. But it has the deeper lucidity, for it succeeds in carrying to the reader's mind the exact impression the writer means to convey, as smoother sentences could not do. Resenting its difficulty at first, the reader finally comes to feel a triumph in reacting to the writer's purpose, a pleasure in assisting, with whatever intelligence is at his command, in the production of such a work of art as he divines Mr. James is driving at. It is something to play even a passive part in these audacious and brilliant performances. And to remain unconscious of them is to lose, if not the strongest, yet certainly the finest, satisfaction possible to the readers of our time.

Mr. Henry James Exasperates   Anonymous*

Perhaps the surest way to induce a novice to Mr. Henry James's work never to attempt another book of his would be to start the patient with *The Awkward Age*. As is always more or less true of Mr. James, the attraction of his style and substance (the two are almost inextricably one) fights a continuous battle with their irritation. And in this case, while attraction wins throughout to the extent of urging persistence in reading, irritation wins the rubber decisively as the book is closed. Both in substance and in verbal style he proves himself, as ever, a master of shades and suggestions. A delicate little touch here, a scarcely perceptible change in pressure there, a slight deflection of line not to be detected except under the microscope, and he has achieved the precise effect that he desired with extraordinary nicety. And the result is so complete that effort does not show in it, save that one is certain that no man could have reached such a degree of elaboration without effort. Mr. James's verbal style is a revelation to the normal slipshod person; for his awkward adverbial inversions of the type of "Do you like so very much little Aggie?" are not an exception, since they are due, not to carelessness, but to some perfectly unintelligible but consistent reason.

But the sense of irritation which inevitably accompanies such nonnatural elaboration of style, though there it is mastered by admiration, predominates in regard to the matter of this book. Almost entirely dialogue, it represents the speech and relations of a little set of people who are intensely clever talkers together, and have made a perfect science of their artificiality of talk. The tremendous plainness with which, in real fact, they call a spade a spade in speaking to each other, and canvass the motives and feelings of each other and their nearest, is supreme; but not for one moment would they ever call a spade verbally a spade. They would suggest it with every refinement of word-fencing. One of them is fined five pounds for "cheap paradox," and you feel that they would never let themselves, nor would Mr. James let them, be cheap at any price. But behind their subtlety of talk is the subtlety of mind of many of them, and behind that Mr. James's own subtlety; and what with one subtlety and another, it is really impossible to know where you are. Why did not Vanderbank marry Nanda? Because he did not wish to appear to be bribed by her threatened dowry, or because she wrote his name on that risky book which he lent her

*Reprinted from the *Pall Mall Gazette*, 8 May 1899, 4.

mother, or for some other equally vulgar reason? Mr. James is not going to make that too clear. You must work the suggestions and shades of allusions out for yourself. And, in honest truth, life is not long enough to warrant the conscientious working out of a novel. Most of these characters are not meant to be sympathetic; but the influence of the whole overwhelms them all. One cannot feel a permanently complete human interest in Nanda, or in that aggressively maiden person Aggie, or in "Mr. Mitchy," who ought to be very likable, or even in the comparatively simple old Rip Van Winkle from Beccles. These people undoubtedly perfectly understood each other as a rule, and Mr. Henry James understands them always; but the reader only by flashes. It has been said of Mr. Disraeli that at one time he became so affected that he positively affected affectation; and here Mr. James has refined refinement, subtilized subtlety, and suggested suggestions to bewilderment. That he continually gives the reader more ideas than can possibly be put in plain words, constitutes his degree of triumph as he proceeds; that he fails to give a complete idea of the whole proves that he has this time smothered himself with elaboration.

[*The Awkward Age:* A Thoroughly Disagreeable Study]
Anonymous*

Four hundred and fifty-seven pages of Henry James's analysis, intricacy, dry cleverness, and disheartening suggestiveness make a pretty big dose for one time. Such is *The Awkward Age*. To add further weight to the volume, its contents are divided into ten books and each book-dose must be swallowed conscientiously; and you will taste it all the way down. Somehow, we think that a simple, fairly tender chapter from the Bible would make the best "chaser."

In *The Awkward Age* we have a thoroughly disagreeable study of English society and manners; a study whose detail will occupy many, many hours of careful reading. The plot itself, a mere thread of a story, deals with a so-called love affair between a middle-aged man and the granddaughter of his early love. This elderly hero is really the only comfortable person in the book. The rest of the volume is given over to the worldliness, the selfishness, the scandals, and gossip of the numerous people who make up its world. It seems as though no word or look or act in their lives had escaped the author's attention. The critical exactness is marvelous. His observation and knowledge seem to grow keener with each new novel. But where will they end, that observation and knowledge? Will they swamp themselves finally in pessimism and unpleasantness and horrors?

Oh, Mr. Henry James, why do you write like that? You do not always

*Reprinted form the *Literary World* 30 (22 July 1899):227.

put sin into life, but you drain all the blood and warmth and goodness out of people, and leave them just with their sins, their wizened skin-and-bone sins. And dry sins are such awful things. Your people are dull or evilly clever, or common, or gross, or bad. But they are not big bad. They have no irresistible impetus of temperament. They have no fanatical or even childish enthusiasms. Their sins, their faults, their mistakes imply some ghastly mental element that suggests disease rather than passion. There are exceptions to this? Yes, surely. But the exceptions have not made your style or your reputation. Is this really the way you see life?

[*The Awkward Age:* The Ultimate Development of the Art of Vision]   Anonymous*

In 1899 appeared what is probably [James's] most distinctive effort, *The Awkward Age.* As a novel it lacks the delicate freshness of *The Spoils of Poynton* and the dramatic distinctness of *The Other House,* but as a study of life, which it almost professedly is, it surpasses, by its completeness, its sympathetic intrusion, its fine impartiality, anything that Mr. James has done. The life it deals with, the life of Mrs. Brookenham's circle, is as limited as, despite its limits, it is minutely complex. It lacks virility; it is, saving appearances, indifferent to virtue; it affects rather an easy accommodation than good manners; but its quick intelligence, its very detachment from the strenuous effort of life make it worth study. Mr. James has provided a touchstone for its vulgarities, its indifferences, its freedoms, in the shape of Mr. Longdon, the remnant of an older generation; but he views the contrast thus afforded with impartial eyes, for if he treat the younger without extenuation, he makes of Nanda, its representative, the most charming portrait in the book. And the book is confessedly a portrait gallery. Its ten parts are each labelled, like picture frames, with the name of a person, and Mr. James brings to the filling of each the ultimate development of the art of vision.

How completely such vision is an art, an art acquired from the observation of laborious years, one realises by studying its evolution. In his earlier work he draws directly from life. He is particular as to clothes, gait, the carriage of a head; he gives the profile, the relief; the exterior as exterior. Gradually as he progresses the outside ceases in itself to interest him; it would be almost impossible to "dress" his figures, there is scarcely a hint of period; he renders the outside only so far as it is significant; the exterior as interior. Finally he almost abandons direct portraiture; rendering by a few lines enough, but only just enough, to keep the figure in its place, and providing everything needful for its realisation from reflection only, that is

*Reprinted from the *Edinburgh Review* 197 (January 1903):77–79.

from its effect upon the other characters in his canvas. Even of Mrs. Brookenham, essential as she is to the scheme of *The Awkward Age,* we obtain no definite outline, only an appreciation of her prettiness, her flexibility, her flickering colour, her quavering tone, her lovely silly eyes, her effect of dimly tragic innocence. She gathers meaning and shape for us not from such vague touches, but with every word she speaks, and from every word that is spoken to her. We know enough of her beauty from the way her shadow falls upon her followers, we have a tribute sufficient to that "rather tortuous" mind in their replies. She takes on a personality, as it were, with every movement; she does nothing, she approaches no one, without acquiring substantiality. Nor is hers the only presence so to acquire it. The relief of every figure in her "little sort of set" is wrought in the same wonderful manner; by which everything is constructed, one might say, from some one's point of view. How far more subtle is it that the author should give us no conception of his characters but what is indirectly communicated, as it were, by themselves, a communication which also, as it is made, reveals the individuality of each. And his dialogue likewise is often of a supreme excellence. It renders the author's intention by the very difficulty with which his characters deliver it. You can feel in its perplexities, its indirectness, the vibration of their minds, those fluctuations of sense and of intelligence by which speech is shaped and coloured, and personality impressed, so that everything by the way of its saying tells at once the speaker's and the author's story. It is a tribute to its perfection that no extract could exhibit it; the point of each work spoken being so delicately dependent on its position in the narrative.

Houses of Cards

Anonymous*

For the full enjoyment of our Henry James, especially when he has but little story, in the conventional sense, to tell, and when his mood is subtly psychological, peace, perfect peace, and cushioned ease are indispensable requisites. The leisured tranquility of his manner, his keen, ingenious analysis of motive, his happy metaphors and figures—nay, even his startling little mannerisms, which suggest an influence rather than reveal a disciple—will else now and again escape notice. On these occasions Mr. James is no doubt caviare to the general. The mass of novel-readers cannot, then, appreciate, because they cannot understand him, and even those accustomed to his method must read him closely, must hark back ever and anon to note his drift, and *will* hark back more frequently of their own free will for the full enjoyment of those clear-cut and exquisitely set sentences.

Seldom, indeed, has Mr. James been so exacting in his demand on the

*Reprinted from the *Pall Mall Gazette,* 26 February 1901. A summary of the plot has been omitted.

reader's intelligence and attention as in *The Sacred Fount*. Never has his purpose been more obscure, never has his dialogue seemed so aimless, so that the author seems to be alluding to himself when he makes one of the characters exclaim, "Then why is it not simple to understand me? . . . I daresay the interpretation of my tropes and figures is not ever perfectly simple."

But the purpose becomes plain, and the seemingly aimless conversation acquires point to those who read carefully and possess their souls in patience, while there is the usual charm of style, and as usual the pages are strewn with good things which might be missed on a merely hasty perusal.

The story is told in the first person, and the narrator at once impresses us as a man of keen discernment . . . [But] while Mr. James with delightful ingenuity, baffles the reader's curiosity and leads him off constantly on false scents, he falls into the sin of over-elaboration and—alas! that it must be said—becomes fatiguing. For instance, the conversation between the narrator and Mrs. Brissenden, in which the latter, alluding to the number of flirtations Long has in hand, says, "Then he has nothing but *screens*. The need for so many does suggest a fire," is in Mr. James's best manner, and therefore excellent. But when the narrator details for whole pages the impressions he had formed at merciless length and with no other apparent aim in view than to bore, the reader is tempted to skip, and, if wise, will yield to the temptation. The closing conversation, too, admirable as it is for the greater part, should most certainly have been recorded in less than eighty pages. Still, these drawbacks to one's pleasure are neither many nor great.

The end of the story is both entertaining and annoying. It is annoying to find that the author has been making fun of us all through; it is entertaining to reflect how skillfully he has deluded us save in one instance. Long is not clever at all, but a supreme ass. Mr. James, however, has stooped to the sort of device the mere "mystery" novelist favours, and has represented him to us through the narrator as completely changed from a fool to a man of ability and originality, and only lets us discover at the end that the narrator has deceived himself. We are left doubtful, too, whether the changes in the other characters are far less than we have been given to understand. The narrator's pet theory may be mere extravagance, his impressions vain imaginings, and to him himself we are fain to say, as Mrs. Brissenden did, "My poor dear, you are crazy, and I bid you goodnight!"

Mrs. Brissenden and Lady John, in whose presence "imagination was but the wing of the insect that bumps against the glass," are finished examples of portraiture worthy of being on the line in the Henry James gallery. The narrator's "guid conceit" of himself is amusingly shown, and we are not at all sure that we ought not to have suspected him for the ass that he was long before the disclosure of the truth, while certainly the reader who is misled as to May Sever's (sic) real character has only his own obtuseness to blame.

The Sacred Fount is only for the few, but they, unless they resent the author's call for mental alertness in the reader will prize it highly, for, notwithstanding some shortcomings, it is, to give it its highest praise, worthy of its illustrious author.

[*The Sacred Fount:* Is It a Parody?]   Anonymous*

In an assembly of wise men a certain sage once propounded the question, "Whether a work of humour could ever be conceived and executed with such subtlety as should hinder the whole world from perceiving its aim?" After some disputation it was agreed that the possibility existed. Whereupon an Average Person who chanced to be of the company inquired what object such a work could have, and the sages answered that to the writer, on the one hand, this super-subtlety might afford entertainment, but, as regarded the readers, it was just as if they conned the writings of a dullard. Very respectfully we would venture to commend this apologue to the notice of Mr. Henry James. We have read *The Sacred Fount* . . . with care, as becomes those who value Mr. James's talent, and who have in the past—even in the quite recent past—derived pleasure and refreshment from his novels. The exact intention of the author having seemed to escape us upon a first reading, we read it again. Still finding outselves hazy about the meaning, a third perusal was adventured. And now, after so much hard, mental effort, after solitary wrestling, and after consultation with other readers, we are bound to admit that we have the dimmest of notions as to what *The Sacred Fount* is all about. The only explanation that seems possible is that Mr. James, annoyed by the folly of shallow admirers, who praise his books for their least praiseworthy qualities, has gone about to parody himself, and that he is now laughing in his sleeve at the sham enthusiasts who pretend to think this a great work. If there were really any danger of finding oneself among such people as fill the pages of *The Sacred Fount* with cryptic elliptical snatches of conversation, the only thing to do would be to join the Trappist Order and live under a vow of perpetual silence. Since no such people exist, it scarcely seems worth while to go to the trouble of inventing them.

*Reprinted from the *Times* (London), 4 May 1901, 15.

[*The Sacred Fount:* Analysis of Analysis]   Harry T. Peck*

Henry James is beyond all question in a bad way. He became morbid and somewhat decadent several years ago, when he wrote *What Maisie*

Knew and *In the Cage*, but even so, he was interesting, and one could read him through. When he wrote *The Awkward Age* we thought that it was only a temporary lapse; but now that he has produced *The Sacred Fount* he really seems to be sinking into a chronic state of periphrastic perversity. It is impossible to tell what the book is about without using almost as many words as Mr. James has wasted in the telling of it, and as when told it isn't worth one's while, we shall prudently refrain from the attempt. The manner of it all beggars description—the endless talk, the innumerable little inuendoes and hints and uncompleted sentences, the subtle speculations about nothing, the morbid analysis of thought and phrase and look and gesture, and then the analysis of the analysis. We have read everything that Mr. James has ever written, and many of his books we have read a dozen times, as we expect to read them a dozen times again, for they are a joy and a delight. No one can accuse us of approaching Mr. James's work in a Philistine spirit. None the less, we can not quite endure the sort of thing that he is writing nowadays. The casual person would say of the present Henry James that he is woozy; and though the term is not precisely academic we can not think of any other adjective that so completely fits the case. So let it go at that.

*Reprinted from the *Bookman* (New York) 13 (July 1901):442.

[*The Sacred Fount:* Subtlety Somewhat Overdone]   Anonymous*

The Sacred Fount, which appeared in 1901, offers an impediment to criticism by its very interest. Its theme, the transference of vitality by affection, is treated with scientific exactitude, and has so much to commend it for such treatment, that it is difficult to say how seriously the author considers it, or whether it or its consequence is to be considered subordinate, but if Mr. James intends his thesis seriously, he renders its elaboration much less convincing by compressing it into a week end. The entire action of the book only occupies the hours between the afternoon of Saturday and Sunday evening, a period long enough if utilised for observation only, but too short for the mental alterations which a change of circumstance works. Granting the condition to which May Server has been reduced by officiating as the Sacred Fount, one cannot imagine any benefit arising from so brief an intermission of her office as the time affords. Her malady is quite conceivable, but it is very much discounted by her recovery. But towards the finish of the book one is led occasionally to suspect that the author evades his own conclusions, and the final scene with Mrs. Brissenden closes in what reads like a hedging concession to the probable. It may be

*Reprinted from the *Edinburgh Review* 197 (January 1903):79–80.

that the ironic subtlety of Mr. James's amusement becomes so evasively fine in its conclusion as to pass for something else, but in that case the subtlety seems somewhat overdone.

[*The Wings of the Dove:* Society as Organized Cannibalism]

Anonymous*

. . . It would be unjust to give the impression that the reading of this extraordinary book is always like wading through glue, hunting phantoms in the fog, or endeavouring to see round several corners into the jungle of mixed motives by which the *dramatis personae* are actuated. The reader, if he has the persistence of an African explorer seeking to penetrate the gloom of the Aruwhimi forest, will eventually emerge into something like daylight. But before the quasi-illumination in the Ninth Book, after some four hundred and fifty pages of immensely tough reading, the author occasionally lapses into lucidity. It is in one of these lapses—on p. 148—that we get the *motif* or text of the entire story: "Kate did explain, for her listening friend: every one who had anything to give—it was true they were the fewest—made the sharpest possible bargain for it, got at least its value in return." Society, or that stratum of it which chiefly interests Mr. James, is a sort of organised cannibalism in which every one is more or less successfully employed in preying on his or her neighbour, much as the micro-organisms in the drop of ditch-water. Their methods vary, and the precise "value" they demand is not always to be estimated in cash. But the arch-vampire, the supreme harpy and anti-heroine of the plot, is Kate Croy, the pensioner of a wealthy widowed aunt, who employs as her chief instrument and tool in "working" everybody for all they are worth her amiable, impressionable lover, Merton Densher. We have called Kate a harpy because the desire of luxury and wealth is the ruling passion of her existence, and to secure her ends she does not hesitate to subject the man whom she loves, and is pledged to by the most solemn vows, to the humiliating ordeal of making up to, and, if need be, even marrying, a charming American girl, an heiress who is dying by inches of an incurable disease, and from whom Kate herself has received nothing but kindness. The plot fails owing to the interested intervention of another adventurer—a parasitic English Peer—and the story ends with the partial awakening of Densher to the true character of the women he loves.

Setting aside a good deal of wilful mystery-mongering, and exasperating mannerism, the talent displayed in the unravelling of this strange and unholy conspiracy is nothing short of amazing. Yet as we part from the

*Reprinted from the *Spectator* 89 (4 October 1902):498–99. The first half of the review, a complaint against James's "astonishing elusiveness," has been omitted.

"wonderful," "immense," and "prodigious" characters of Mr. James's novel, our sentiments towards them recall the story which is told of a *château* still standing in Switzerland. Once upon a time, so the legend runs, it was the home of a noble Knight who had four beautiful daughters. It chanced that he had to make a journey into a neighbouring valley, and returning suddenly by night before he was expected, he found the castle brilliantly illuminated. Wishing to ascertain what was the cause of this festivity without being observed, he got a ladder, climbed up it, and on looking through the window beheld his four beautiful daughters taking part in the most infamous orgies with four monks. His mind was at once made up: such people must not be allowed to live; so quietly summoning the neighbours, he barricaded the doors, piled faggots round the castle, set them on fire, and burned the guilty inmates to death. That is what we feel we should like to do with the characters in most of Mr. James's recent books,—shut them up and burn them at their dreary and morbid psychological orgies. We lament the concentration of such a distinguished talent on the portraiture of types which too often inspire horror without pity.

In Darkest James   F. M. Colby*

In Henry James's latest book, the two-volume novel, *The Wings of the Dove*, there are signs of a partial recovery. There are people who will see no difference between it and *The Sacred Fount* or *The Awkward Age*, but they are no friends of his. By what vice of introspection he got himself lashed to that fixed idea we cannot say, but it was clear that neither of those books was the work of a mind entirely free. In one aspect it was ridiculous; but if one laughed, it was with compunctions, for in another aspect it was exceedingly painful. This only from the point of view of his admirers. It is not forgotten that there is the larger class (for whom this world in the main was made) to whom he is merely ridiculous. They do not see why thoughts so unwilling to come out need be extracted.

In *The Wings of the Dove* there is the same absorption in the machinery of motive and in mental processes the most minute. Through page after page he surveys a mind as a sick man looks at his counterpane, busy with little ridges and grooves and undulations. There are chapters like wonderful games of solitaire, broken by no human sound save his own chuckle when he takes some mysterious trick or makes a move that he says is "beautiful." He has a way of saying "There you are" that is most exasperating, for it is always at the precise moment at which you know you have utterly lost yourself. There is no doubt that James's style is often too puffed up with its secrets. Despite its air of immense significance, the dark, un-

*Reprinted from the *Bookman* (New York) 16 (November 1902):259–60. The second half of the review, of a piece with the first half, has been omitted.

fathomed caves of his ocean contain sometimes only the same sort of gravel you could have picked up on the shore. We have that from thinkers who have been down him. But though this unsociable way of writing continues through *The Wings of the Dove,* it comes nearer than any other of his recent novels to the quality of his earlier work. It deals with conditions as well as with people. Instead of merely souls anywhere, we have men and women living in describable homes. . . .

[*The Wings of the Dove:* The Radical Fallacy of *L'Art pour L'Art*]

Anonymous*

. . . The truth seems to be that Mr. James has begun to show his age. There is a general impression that advancing age sees simple. Nothing of the kind; every year adds a facet to the human eye, and man in accumulating wisdom becomes ever more speculative, more disposed to talk about his experience rather than of it. So with Mr. James, the habit of contemplation, to which he was always addicted, has grown upon him with indulgence to such an extent that he not infrequently loses sight altogether of the object, which the reader is obliged in consequence to reconstruct for himself as best he can. It is this we find so afflicting; that it, whatever it may be, is all in the air, in Mr. James's mind or elsewhere, we have no way of knowing. His situations appear to be interesting, as far as we can make out from the indications he allows to escape him; at all events we are prepared to be interested, if he would only refrain from wrapping them away in what we must consider the mummy clothes of irrelevant reflection. In the seven hundred and fifty odd pages of the book before us, for instance, there are, to trust our impression, barely four score of dialog; while as for action, which one would expect to divide a novel, there is none worth mentioning. There is, indeed, little else but long, dull paragraphs of emotional tergiversation, wherein one loses all sense of direction for lack of one little clue, one simple straightforward word, which would, to be sure, if it were there, dispel the greater part of the story like a mirage.

To a plain man such doings will inevitably appear but the exercises of a mistaken ingenuity. But in reality they are not altogether so, they are rather more serious than that. In his essay on Flaubert he regrets that to this artist the spiritual should have offered little or no "surface." "He should at least," says Mr. James, "have listened at the chamber of the soul." And the stricture, while it may not be quite just to Flaubert, does

*Reprinted from the *Independent* 54 (13 November 1902):2711–12. The introductory paragraph has been omitted.

at least serve to suggest the meaning of Mr. James's own attitude. He is listening "at the chamber of the soul." And tho we might wish that his posture were a little less cramped and his message were a little more intelligible, still his intention is perfectly plain. Life is composed of two parallel currents, the stream of circumstance and the stream of consciousness. For obvious reasons, chiefly because such is the way of nature, it is the general practice of novelists to keep on the whole to the former, leaving the reader to take up for himself as much of the latter as he has inclination and capacity for. And if Mr. James reverses the natural order, suppressing incident and leaving the sequence of events to be pieced out by the reader's ingenuity, while he insists upon following the series of reactions which these hypothetical events are supposed to set up in the minds of his characters, he does so obviously in the hope of catching those subtle "psychic" states which he reproaches Flaubert with having neglected.

Now it would be fair to inquire of all this sort of thing whether "psychic" states are not fitter subjects for descriptive psychology than literature, whether, indeed, this conception of fiction does not show another of those strange confusions from which so many of our ideas appear to be suffering at present. At all events a writer who takes to such devices would seem guilty of throwing away his means of interest with a prodigality deserving, in case of bankruptcy, of no very great amount of sympathy; for it is just the advantage of the more usual and natural method that the reader has appetite only for a certain limited amount of subjective experience, precisely as much as he can get for himself, and no matter how much more is forced upon him is unable to digest it. But not to raise these moot questions, it is perhaps sufficient to point out that Mr. James's procedure, whether or no it is legitimate in theory, does at any rate in actual practice fail to accomplish its purpose and results simply in the bewilderment of the reader (or should we call him student?) and in the deformation of the novel to which it is applied. Art must always be in a very large measure representative, it must for the most part deal directly with the thing in itself, and if its substantial body be attenuated beyond a certain point it becomes a mere mist in the brain, a figment, a false illusion without reality or significance. The soul is all very well in its way, but to impoverish its body is certainly not to increase the efficiency of its manifestations. And further, in connection with the plot, to call it so, of this particular book, over which reigns a singular moral confusion wherein all natural feelings of pity and shame have been juggled away by some curious antic of the mind, it is worth while to notice the profound truth, that there is nothing so prone to depravity as unrelieved speculation, which, just because it has no issue and hence no corrective in conduct, tends of itself to become utterly dissolute and irresponsible. The fact is that Mr. James, together with some of his European neighbors, in forcing his "art," as he likes to call it, to such a point of refinement that its interest has come to be almost solely technical, has demonstrated incontestably the radical fallacy of *l'art pour l'art*, of art for art's sake, for art must exist for something besides itself or else be reduced finally to the composition of rhetorics.

The Ambassadors Anonymous*

[If clearness of expression be the first essential of a writer and the entertainment of its readers be the attraction of a novel, both Henry James and his latest work of fiction have fallen deplorably below the accepted standards. *The Ambassadors* is a large quarto volume of nearly 450 pages, which leaves its readers almost as much in the dark at the conclusion of its perusal as they are perplexed at its start by its author's involved sentences. It is a labor to drag oneself through the ponderous tome that is left unrewarded when the task is accomplished. Psychological analyses are so subtle and are carried to such a length as to become absolutely wearisome, while the characters are so intricate that doubt takes possession of the mind if they are understood even by their creator; certainly they remain puzzles to the public. It is not our intention to outline *The Ambassadors*. It would be an infliction on the reader. In brief, *The Ambassadors* is neither lucid nor interesting. It is a tangle which few persons will have the patience to attempt to unravel, even if that be possible. In putting down the book it is to range it with that incomprehensible style of literature which has lately been coming more and more into vogue, and with the regret that there has not yet arisen some American Boileau. In default of such critic and reformer it may be opportune to recall to the memory of Henry James and cite for the benefit of his less erudite emulators the maxim of the seventeenth writer, "Le sujet n'est jamais tot explique." [No accents used.]

*Reprinted from the *San Francisco Chronicle*, 6 December 1903, 8.

The Genius of Mr. James Anonymous*

The saying of William Blake, that the Venus of Milo was not carved but released from the block, is profoundly true of every work of art, and not least of imaginative literature. All the stories that ever shall be written are somewhere latent, and the business of the story-teller is less to create than to evoke. Evocation is peculiarly the method of Mr. Henry James; he does not tell a story, he divulges it, and nowhere is his method brought to a more perfect finish than in this his last and finest novel. Perhaps not the worst way to estimate the quality of an artist is to define what he is not,

*Reprinted from the *Pall Mall Gazette*, 13 October 1903, 4.

and the precise position of Mr. Henry James in contemporary literature becomes clearer by reference to other great living writers. In reading *The Ambassadors* you do not, as in reading a story of Mr. Thomas Hardy's, feel the breath of a woman on your cheek, nor are the situations stamped upon your brain, as by the ironic lightning of Mr. George Meredith. In *The Ambassadors* you are kept always a little aloof from the picture; you do not feel that the writer is in the least responsible for the creation of Mme. de Vionnet, or Strether, or Chadwick Newsome; he reveals them to you by the gradual stripping off of the veils which hitherto obscured them from your vision, or, rather, by his kindly though ironical correction of your own eyesight. It is with a shock of surprise that you remember to have been told by a distinguished man of letters of his own nationality that Mr. James belongs to the school of the Realists. Realistic in effect *The Ambassadors* undoubtedly is, but not at all in method; it is by the liberation of essential ideas, and not by the patient enumeration of facts, that the story is put before you. Consequently it impresses you as overwhelmingly like life, and the difference between this and realism is just the difference between truth and accuracy. Truth presupposes vision, but the accurate delineation of facts does not imply even observation. Now *The Ambassadors* affects you as the result of intense observation—a long time ago. The facts observed have been dissolved in the writer's consciousness, and are only now recrystallised out in a series of images coloured by just that tincture of the *menstruum* which makes the revelation in the truest sense personal and Mr. James's. Nor are the images as might be supposed, indefinite. A crystal is even more definite than a cut-glass lustre, only the history of its formation is entirely different, a crystal being the essential idea of the solution in which it secretly grows. As an example of the occult yet unwavering growth of Mr. James's characters into tangibility take Waymarsh. He looms through the earlier part of the book with his heavy speech and heavier silences, felt rather than seen, until he finally crystallizes out from the lips of Miss Barrace as "Sitting Bull." After that it is impossible to think of him in any other form. The other characters and their surroundings emerge in the same magical way, and very often precisely because they are not stated. They bcome apparent, say, as green becomes apparent to the eye fatigued with red; they are complementary to the thing described. In considering the thing spoken of you are conscious, in Mr. James's own words, of "the obsession of the other thing," and it is often enough the other thing which is essential to the story. Thus, you are never taken to Woollett, the American town from which Mr. James's "Ambassador," Strether, is sent to Paris to reclaim Chadwick Newsome, nor are you introduced to Chadwick's mother; yet in the recital of Strether's impressions of Paris, more particularly of the personality and surroundings of Mme. de Vionnet, who represents the disastrous entanglement Woollett supposes, you are made vividly to see the vulgarity of Woollett refinement and the essential inferiority of Mrs. Newsome. So vividly, indeed, that you go farther, perhaps, than the writer intends, and in recognising the crass "culture" which Chadwick so happily escapes, you are taken with curiosity to know the private emotion of, say, Boston over this book of Mr. James's, though, truly, there is the afterthought that just as Woollett, through the eyes of Mrs. Pocock and therefore implicitly of Mrs. Newsome, failed to see what Chad was become under the gracious influence of Mme. De Vionnet, so Boston would remain after all unmoved.

In considering Mr. James's revelation of his characters, we may, perhaps, be permitted to express what is likely enough a private grievance due to dulness. It needs the writer's explicit statement that Strether was fifty-five years of age to conquer our belief that he belonged on the right side of forty. It is not that Strether talks younger than his years, or acts as such; on the contrary, his words and actions come always as a surprise from one so young, and it would seem as if Mr. James himself were on guard against perplexity in the mind of the reader, since at least twice in the course of the story he reminds him that Strether was fifty-five years old.

For the business of evocation, for the development, as it were, of the latent images of his characters, Mr. James uses a style which, as the verse of Shelley is the very stuff of poetry, may be described as the delicate essentials of prose. He adds word to word warily, as a chemist would use a reagent to bring down a visible precipitate. He does not construct with words in the ordinary sense, because for him, as for every great artist, words are symbols rather than building materials. In relation to the ideas they betray they are as the visible peaks of submerged, deep-rooted mountains. The peaks are apparent, the mountains implied. Some of Mr. James's phrases positively make you jump. This, for example, of Waymarsh: "He met you as if you had knocked and he had bidden you enter." Yet for all the alertness of his style, it is not as if he performed before you, but rather as if you overheard a very old man murmuring to himself.

[*The Ambassadors:* A Perpetual and High Delight]

Anonymous*

Many will be frightened away from Mr. James's latest novel on account of its size. And it certainly is an appalling book to contemplate—432 extra large, extra solid, printed pages! Few but the confirmed admirers of Mr. James, and the adventurous, will attempt to read this, what appears to be, ponderous novel. To the admirers, the size will be but an added pleasure; to the adventurous, the very idea of "tackling" such a feat will prove stimulating, as an extremely high mountain lures the adventurous climber. Frankly I am an admirer, likewise I am adventurous so far as novel reading

*Reprinted from the *Literary World* 34 (December 1903):348. The plot summary has been omitted.

goes, therefore it was with the greatest pleasure that I took up *The Ambassadors* and sat down to read and enjoy it. After hours (this novel is not one to be read at one sitting, or even at two) of delightful enjoyment, I put the book down, saying to myself, "This is the real thing once more. Once more has Mr. James proved himself the master hand. While we have him and Edith Wharton and Joseph Conrad (Mr. Meredith no longer writes), we need not fear for English fiction, despite the historical novelists."

The scheme of the story is delightful . . . nothing "happens," and the entire time of the story is but three months. But the joy of the character work! The subtle charm that Mr. James spreads over the reader, as Paris absorbs the ambassadors,—all this is worth a hundred plots.

Never has Mr. James drawn two more real, more delightful, more finished, and perfect characters than Strether and Maria Gostrey. From the first moment of their meeting to their pathetic parting, they absorb the attention and delight the mind. She is the finished product of sophisticated life; he is the pliant material which you see formed before your eyes into the completed man. Circumstances had kept him narrow till he came to Paris, then he began to live. He says to Miss Gostrey: "It's a benefit that would make a poor show for many people; and I don't know who else but you and I, frankly, could begin to see in it what I feel. I don't get drunk; I don't pursue the ladies; I don't spend money; I don't even write sonnets. But nevertheless, I'm making up late for what I didn't have early. I cultivate my little benefit in my own little way. It amuses me more than anything that has happened to me in all my life. They may say what they like, it's my surrender, it's my tribute to youth." If this short quotation (the epitome of the whole book, in a way) does not appeal to you, do not try to read *The Ambassadors*. It will bore you.

This book could never be popular, even as Mr. James's other novels are popular, for its class of appreciative readers is so very limited. No really young people could understand it; no "simple people" would know what it was all about; no unsophisticated person could enjoy it; no "patriotic" American could stand it; few women would like it; no business men could find the time to read it; no one lacking a sense of humor could follow it. This leaves a very small class—the knowing—to appreciate the book. But for these it will be a marvel, a perpetual and high delight. For them there has been nothing like it in years.

A Master of Shades   Claude Bragdon*

A new book from the pen of Mr. Henry James is an event of importance, for since Meredith and Hardy have fallen silent, since Kipling has

---

*Reprinted from the *Critic* n.s. 43 (January 1905):20–22. About half of the review has been omitted.

become the unofficial censor of the British Empire, the self-crowned laure-
ate of torpedo boats and motorcars, and since Barrie finds his greater profit
in play-writing, Mr. James is the only Anglo-Saxon novelist of the first class
remaining. In craftsmanship and sureness of intention his work bears about
the same relation to the average current fiction that some fine and rare Oriental rug bears to a crazy-quilt. It cannot, however, be gainsaid that the
figure in his carpet grows more obscure and intricate with the passing
years; that it is woven with threads of sometimes too gossamer fineness.
His demands upon his readers are increasingly rigorous. Each successive
performance has come to resemble less and less a diverting trick with
cards, done with one eye on the audience, and more and more a game of
solitaire which—for the reader—sometimes fails to "come out," or it may
perhaps be figured better as a labyrinth with a dozen wrong turnings in
which it is possible to lose oneself, though to the attentive, leisurely, and
sympathetic reader (and Mr. James should have no other) the true path
through the maze never ceases to be in doubt.

The Golden Bowl is conceived and written in this later, this esoteric
manner of our author. It is addressed to the Cognoscenti, who are simply
all those having, in any degree approaching Mr. James's own, an insight
into those secret places of the human spirit which he essays to explore. Of
this dim limbo he is assuredly the Sherlock Holmes. . . .

There are so many things in [this remarkable novel]—the obscure
workings of hereditary traits, the seduction exercised by Europe on the
American imagination, the regenerative power of married love, the differences in the "moral paste" of individuals—that like her I feel that to help
myself too freely, to attempt to deal in other words, with all these aspects
in the space assigned to me, would "tend to jostle the ministering hand,
confound the array, and, more vulgarly speaking, make a mess," and so,
like Mrs. Assingham again, I pick out for the reader's consideration "a solitary plum."

If it be true, as Schopenhauer affirms, that a novel will be of a high
and noble order the more it represents of inner, and the less it represents
of outer, life, this latest novel of Henry James must be given a high place.
Throughout it is the inner life, the life of the passions, the emotions, the
affections of four people which is presented,—their souls' history, in other
words, with only just enough of time and place and circumstance to give it
verisimilitude, to make all vivid and real. The chronicle is accomplished
with an art beyond all praise: by formulating the questions which the soul
asks but which the lips fail to utter, by happy figures and comparisons
which fall thick and golden like ripe fruit, by making all the characters im-
possibly articulate and lucid—able "to discuss in novel phrases their complicated state of mind."

Those who lament the forsaking by Mr. James of his earlier themes,
and the abandonment of his more direct and objective manner, perhaps betray the limit of their own interests and perceptions. Like all men of origi-

nal genius arrived at maturity, the outward aspects of the world—manners, places, customs—no longer interest him exclusively. Little by little he has come to look for and to present the reality behind the seeming,—not circumstance, but the spiritual reaction of circumstance. Thus the Swedenborgianism of his father, like some pure, pale flower plucked from a cold Norwegian precipice, transplanted thence to a New England garden, blooms now in an English hothouse,—a thing to marvel at, a thing to be grateful for.

[*The Golden Bowl:* Thought as the Novelist's Sole Material]   Anonymous*

The theory of Impressionism has been summed up in the dictum of Monet, that light is the only subject of every picture. The theory of Mr. Henry James's art might also be put in a formula: "Human thoughts are the sole material of the novelist." Whoever fails to realize this elementary principle is sure to come to grief in his effort to follow a master never other than difficult. This principle alone accounts for the order in which events are narrated—or rather, they are not narrated at all. They are delineated only in so far and at such times as they are producing an effect on the inward life of one of his characters. Consequently they are never seen in a clear dry light, such as serves to display the events of Scott, or even Thackeray. We learn them always through the refracting medium of some person's mind—and that often is rather not his notion of the event in itself, but his suspicion of somebody else's notion of it. Now this is in reality the only way in which events, whether personal or historical, exist for any of us. "A fact when it is past becomes an idea," said Creighton. This truth, forgotten alike by most novelists and nearly all historians, is the justification of Mr. James's method. It gives us, of course, no ground for asserting his success. But one reason why some folks give him up is that they refuse to see that he is attempting what, to the best of our belief, has never been attempted before, even by the most "psychological" of novelists or poets, such as Browning. For even Browning's characters always display themselves to an audience. Not so with those of Mr. James. Here we are shown not the human heart under a microscope, as with the ordinary analytical novelist, but the soul developing itself from within, finding in other persons, circumstances, and happenings nothing but the matter of its thought. It is objected that Mr. James is super-subtle, and trails an idea through far too many windings, sets it in too many lights, refines and explains and exiguates, so to say, *ad nauseam*. This book will awaken this objection more

*Reprinted from the *Athenaeum*, 18 March 1905, 332. The last sentence of the review and a long final quotation have been omitted.

than ever. But let any one reflect on his thought upon any matter that concerns him personally; let him take only half-an-hour of it, and try to retrace all its involutions, and he will find himself ten times as full of distractions, of strange backward twists, of hesitations, of reasons and imaginings, as any of Mr. James's characters. The fact is brought out in this new book, for none of the *dramatis personae* is at all extraordinary. The impecunious but charming Italian prince who marries the daughter of a widowed American millionaire, his wife, his father-in-law, and his lover (the American girl of brilliant social qualities who marries the millionaire), are all commonplace persons enough. Indeed, the lack of greatness in his characters—their essential littleness—while it may enhance the realism of Mr. James's work, strikes us one of its serious defects as great art. The father continues so wrapped up in his daughter that the two former lovers are naturally brought together, and the plot turns on a peculiarly treacherous adultery. The gradual discovery of this by the princess, her desire to shield her father from the knowledge of it; his discovery of it, and desire to shield her; her success in finally severing her husband from his paramour and in securing his love, are the theme of the story. It is told—or, to be correct, it works itself out—with all the convincing realism of which Mr. James is a master. But it is very diffucult, for everybody is occupied in concealing from every one else what he or she knows; and even when they desire to convey the truth, it is commonly done by the statement of something else. The triumph of this method is shown in the scene between Maggie and her father, when, as a result of what she omits to say, the millionaire resolves to pack his traps and take his wife back for good and all to America. But for the "chorus work" of Bob Assingham and his wife the whole thing would be scarcely intelligible. As it is, the book is clear to those who think Mr. James worth a little trouble. The method, in spite of its "inwardness," is detached, cold, and, if the word is possible, a little cruel. But its mental agility, its likeliness, its atmosphere, are perfect. Why Mr. James should require so very disagreeable a situation to develope his study we cannot understand, but that he has elaborated it as no one else could, we are sure; indeed, we should have liked two more books in the novel, one giving the story as it affects the mind of Charlotte, the brilliant, hard, repulsive woman, and the other showing it in the mind of the millionaire, strange compound of shrewdness and simplicity, inexorable decision and inexhaustible kindliness. Mr. James can hardly achieve a greater success than that of making even one of his readers desire that the book were double its length. At the same time we trust that in the next book which he writes he will purge himself of certain mannerisms that are little more than affectations. He overworks the word "lucidity" even more than writers of an earlier age did that of "sensibility." He plays upon the phrase "There you are" as though the words were the strings of a violin. He puts the commonest and most obvious expressions in inverted commas, and we dislike his too frequently interrupting adverbs. Doubtless all are defensible as necessary on the hypothesis of the method. We grant the method, but deny the necessity. All the same, we admit that Mr. Henry James is at his best throughout this book. The final month at Fawns, especially the two scenes between Charlotte and Maggie, is a veritable triumph.

[*The Golden Bowl:* James as a Precious, Morbid Phenomenon]   Mary Moss*

As a rule it is the personal quality which makes for influence, but in Mr. James this quality has grown so exclusive as to be available only for Mr. James (and with him even one sometimes suspects auto-infection). *The Golden Bowl*, then, should be read, savored, reread. Indeed, this advice is superfluous. Once taken up, it pursues you. Mr. Verver with his horrible little convex waistcoat, the impeccable Maggie, her Prince, the Principino, poor peccant Charlotte—you think of nothing else for days. They even grow more alive after you flatter yourself you have done with them than while you are officially in their company. Bob and Fanny, the bric-a-brac dealers, the complaisant hostess of Matcham, forget them if you can! With all this, nevertheless, Mr. James is a marvelous hermit on a lonely isle; you must row out of the current to visit him. He is less cosmopolitan than utterly denationalized. More, even! He has deserted the earth and hovers in a wonderful, labyrinthine dimension of his own. He is a precious, morbid phenomenon, too exceptional for healthy discipleship.

*Reprinted from the *Atlantic Monthly* 95 (May 1905):696.

Mr. Henry James's Later Work   William Dean Howells*

. . . I have a theory that it is not well to penetrate every recess of an author's meaning. It robs him of the charm of mystery, and the somewhat labyrinthine construction of Mr. James's later sentences lends itself to the practice of the self-denial necessary to the preservation of this charm. What I feel sure of is that he has a meaning in it all, and that by and by, perhaps when I least expect it, I shall surprise his meaning. In the meanwhile I rest content with what I do know. In spite of all the Browning Clubs—even the club which has put up a monument to the poet's butler-ancestor—all of Browning is not clear, but enough of Browning is clear for any real lover of his poetry.

*Reprinted from the *North American Review* 176 (January 1903):125–37. This is the fourth section of a five-part essay. A few short references to previous sections have been omitted from this selection.

. . . Never, in my ignorance, have I had a vivider sense of London, in my knowledge a stronger sense of Venice, than in *The Wings of a Dove* [*sic*]. More miraculous still, as I have tried to express, was the sense he gave me of the anterior New York where the life flowered which breathed out the odor called Milly Theale—a heartbreaking fragrance as of funeral violets—and of the anterior New England sub-acidly fruiting in Mrs. Stringham. As for social conditions, predicaments, orders of things, where shall we find the like of the wonders wrought in *The Awkward Age?* I have been trying to get phrases which should convey the effect of that psychomancy from me to my reader, and I find none so apt as some phrase that should suggest the convincingly incredible. Here is something that the reason can as little refuse as it can accept. Into quite such particles as the various characters of this story would the disintegration of the old, rich, demoralized society of an ancient capital fall so probably that each of the kaleidoscopic fragments, dropping into irrelevant radiance around Mrs. Brookenham, would have its fatally appointed tone in the "scheme of color." Here is that inevitable, which Mr. Brander Matthews has noted as the right and infallible token of the real. It does not matter, after that, how the people talk,—or in what labyrinthine parentheses they let their unarriving language wander. They strongly and vividly exist, and they construct not a drama, perhaps, but a world, floating indeed in an obscure where it seems to have its solitary orbit, but to be as solidly palpable as any of the planets of the more familiar systems, and wrapt in the aura of its peculiar corruption. How bad the bad people on it may be, one does not know, and is not intended to know, perhaps; that would be like being told the gross facts of some scandal which, so long as it was untouched, supported itself not unamusingly in air; but of the goodness of the good people one is not left in doubt; and it is a goodness which consoles and sustains the virtue apt to droop in the presence of neighborly remissness.

I might easily attribute to the goodness a higher office than this; but if I did I might be trenching upon that ethical delicacy of the author which seems to claim so little for itself. Mr. James is, above any other, the master of the difficult art of never doing more than to "hint a fault, or hesitate dislike," and I am not going to try committing him to conclusions he would shrink from. There is nothing of the clumsiness of the "satirist" in his design, and if he notes the absolute commerciality of the modern London world, it is with a reserve clothing itself in frankness which is infinitely, as he would say, "detached." But somehow, he lets you know how horribly *business* fashionable English life is; he lets Lord Mark let Milly Theale know, at their first meeting, when he tells her she is with people who never do anything for nothing, and when, with all her money, and perhaps because of it, she is still so trammelled in the ideal that she cannot take his meaning. Money, and money bluntly; gate-money of all kinds; money the means, is the tune to which that old world turns in a way which we scarcely imagine in this crude new world where it is still so largely less the means than the end.

But the general is lost in the personal, as it should be in Mr. James's books, earlier as well as later, and the allegory is so faint that it cannot always be traced. He does not say that the limitless liberty allowed Nanda Brookenham by her mother in *The Awkward Age* is better than the silken bondage in which the Duchess keeps her niece Aggie, though Nanda is admirably lovable, and little Aggie is a little cat; that is no more his affair than to insist upon the loyalty of old Mr. Longdon to an early love, or the generosity of Mitchett, as contrasted with the rapacity of Mrs. Brookenham, who, after all, wants nothing more than the means of being what she has always been. What he does is simply to show you those people mainly on the outside, as you mainly see people in the world, and to let you divine them and their ends from what they do and say. They are presented with infinite pains; as far as their appearance (though they are very little described) goes, you are not suffered to make a mistake. But he does not analyze them for you; rather he synthetizes them, and carefully hands them over to you in a sort of integrity very uncommon in the characters of fiction. One might infer from this that his method was dramatic, something like Tourguénieff's, say; but I do not know that his method is dramatic. I do not recall from the book more than one passage of dramatic intensity, but that was for me of very great intensity; I mean the passage where old Mr. Longdon lets Vanderbank understand that he will provide for him if he will offer himself to Nanda, whom he knows to be in love with Vanderbank, and where Vanderbank will not promise. That is a great moment, where everything is most openly said, most brutally said, to American thinking; and yet said with a restraint of feeling that somehow redeems it all.

Nothing could well be more perfected than the method of the three books which I have been supposing myself to be talking about, however far any one may think it from perfect. They express mastery, finality, doing what one means, in a measure not easily to be matched. I will leave out of the question the question of obscurity; I will let those debate that whom it interests more than it interests me. For my own part I take it that a master of Mr. James's quality does not set out with a design whose significance is not clear to himself, and if others do not make it clear to themselves, I suspect them rather than him of the fault. All the same I allow that it is sometimes not easy to make out; I allow that sometimes *I* do not make it out, I, who delight to read him almost more than any other living author, but then I leave myself in his hands. I do not believe he is going finally to play me the shabby trick of abandoning me in the dark; and meanwhile he perpetually interests me. If anything, he interests me too much, and I come away fatigued, because I cannot bear to lose the least pulse of the play of character; whereas from most fiction I lapse into long delicious absences of mind, now and then comfortably recovering myself to find out what is going on, and then sinking below the surface again.

The Awkward Age is mostly expressed in dialogue; The Wings of a Dove is mostly in the narration and the synthesis of emotions. Not the synthesis of the motives, please; these in both books are left to the reader, almost as much as they are in The Sacred Fount. That troubled source, I will own, "is of a profundity," and in its depths darkles the solution which the author makes it no part of his business to pull to the top; if the reader wants it, let him dive. But why should not a novel be written so like to life, in which most of the events remain the meaningless, that we shall never quite know what the author meant? Why, in fact, should not people come and go, and love and hate, and hurt and help one another as they do in reality, without rendering the reader a reason for their behavior, or offering an explanation at the end with which he can light himself back over the way he has come, and see what they meant? Who knows what any one means here below, or what he means himself, that is, precisely stands for? Most people mean nothing, except from moment to moment, if they indeed mean anything so long as that, and life which is full of propensities is almost without motives. In the scribbles which we suppose to be imitations of life, we hold the unhappy author to a logical consistency which we find so rarely in the original; but ought not we rather to praise him where his work confesses itself, as life confesses itself, without a plan? Why should we demand more of the imitator than we get from the creator?

Of course, it can be answered that we are *in* creation like characters in fiction, while we are outside of the imitation and spectators instead of characters; but that does not wholly cover the point. Perhaps, however, I am asking more for Mr. James than he would have me. In that case I am willing to offer him the reparation of a little detraction. I wish he would leave his people more, not less, to me when I read him. I have tried following their speeches without taking in his comment, delightfully pictorial as that always is, and it seems to me that I make rather more of their meaning, that way. I reserve the pleasure and privilege of going back and reading his comment in the light of my conclusions. This is the method I have largely pursued with the people of The Sacred Fount, of which I do not hesitate to say that I have mastered the secret, though, for the present I am not going to divulge it. Those who cannot wait may try the key which I have given.

But do not, I should urge them, expect too much of it; I do not promise it will unlock everything. If you find yourself, at the end, with nothing in your hand but the postulate with which the supposed narrator fantastically started, namely, that people may involuntarily and unconsciously prey upon one another, and mentally and psychically enrich themselves at one another's expense, still you may console yourself, if you do not think this enough, with the fact that you have passed the time in the company of men and women freshly and truly seen, amusingly shown, and abidingly left with your imagination. For me, I am so little exacting, that this is enough. *The Sacred Fount* is a most interesting book, and you are teased through it to the end with delightfull skill, but I am not going to say that it is a great book like *The Awkward Age*, or *the Wings of a Dove*. These are really incomparable books, not so much because there is nothing in contemporary fiction to equal them as because there is nothing the least like them. They are of a kind that none but their author can do, and since he is alone master of their art, I am very well content to leave him to do that kind of book quite as he chooses. I will not so abandon my function as to say that I could not tell him how to do them better, but it sufficiently interests me to see how he gets on without my help. After all, the critic has to leave authors somewhat to themselves; he cannot always be writing their books for them; and when I find an author, like Mr. James, who makes me acquainted with people who instantly pique my curiosity by "something rich and strange," in an environment which is admirably imaginable, I gratefully make myself at home with them, and stay as long as he will let me.

Henry James: An Appreciation   Joseph Conrad*

The critical faculty hesitates before the magnitude of Mr. Henry James's work. His books stand on my shelves in a place whose accessibility proclaims the habit of frequent communion. But not all his books. There is no collected edition to date, such as some of "our masters" have been provided with; no neat row of volumes in buckram or half-calf putting forth a hasty claim to completeness, and conveying to my mind a hint of finality, of a surrender to fate of that field in which all these victories have been won. Nothing of the sort has been done for Mr. Henry James's victories in England.

In a world such as ours, so painful with all sorts of wonders, one would not exhaust oneself in barren marvelling over mere bindings, had not the fact, or rather the absence of the material fact, prominent in the case of other men whose writing counts (for good or evil)—had it not been, I say, expressive of a direct truth spiritual and intellectual; an accident of—I suppose—publishing business acquiring a symbolic meaning from its negative nature. Because, emphatically, in the body of Mr. Henry James's work there is no suggestion of finality, nowhere a hint of surrender, or even of mere probability of surrender, to his own victorious achievement in that field where he is master, Happily, he will never be able to claim complete-

*Reprinted from the *North American Review* 180 (January 1905):102–08.

ness; and, were he to confess to it in a moment of self-ignorance, he would not be believed by the very minds for whom such a confession naturally would be meant. It is impossible to think of Mr. Henry James becoming "complete" otherwise than by the brutality of our common fate whose finality is meaningless—in the sense of its logic being of a material order, the logic of a falling stone.

I do not know into what brand of ink Mr. Henry James dips his pen; indeed, I heard that of late he has been dictating; but I know that his mind is steeped in the waters flowing from the fountain of intellectual youth. The thing—a privilege—a miracle—what you will—is not quite hidden from the meanest of us who run as we read. To those who have the grace to stay their feet it is manifest. After some twenty years of attentive acquaintance with Mr. Henry James's work, it grows into absolute conviction, which, all personal feeling apart, brings a sense of happiness into one's artistic existence. If gratitude, as some one defined it, is a lively sense of favors to come, it becomes very easy to be grateful to the author of *The Ambassadors*—to name the latest of his works. The favors are sure to come; the spring of *that* benevolence will never dry up. The stream of inspiration runs brimful in a predetermined direction, unaffected by the periods of drought, untroubled in its clearness by the storms of the land of letters, without languor or violence in its force, never running back upon itself, opening new visions at every turn of its course through that richly inhabited country its fertility has created for our delectation, for our judgment, for our exploring. It is, in fact, a magic spring.

With this phrase the metaphor of the perennial spring, of the inextinguishable youth, of running water, as applied to Mr. Henry James's inspiration, may be dropped. In its volume and force the body of his work may be compared rather to a majestic river. All creative art is magic, is evocation of the unseen in forms persuasive, enlightening, familiar and surprising, for the edification of mankind, pinned down by the conditions of its existence to the earnest consideration of the most insignificant tides of reality.

Action in its essence, the creative art of a writer of fiction may be compared to rescue work carried out in darkness against cross gusts of wind swaying the action of a great multitude. It is rescue work, this snatching of vanishing phases of turbulence, disguised in fair words, out of the native obscurity into a light where the struggling forms may be seen, seized upon, endowed with the only possible form of permanence in this world of relative values—the permanence of memory. And the multitude feels it obscurely too; since the demand of the individual to the artist is, in effect, the cry, "Take me out of myself!" meaning, really, out of my perishable activity into the light of imperishable consciousness. But everything is relative, and the light of consciousness is only enduring, merely the most enduring of the things of this earth, imperishable only as against the short-lived work of our industrious hands.

When the last acqueduct shall have crumbled to pieces, the last airship fallen to the ground, the last blade of grass shall have died upon a dying earth, man, indomitable by his training in his resistance to misery and pain, shall set this undiminished light of his eyes against the feeble glow of the sun. The artistic faculty of which each of us has a minute grain, may find its voice in some individual of that last group, gifted with a power of expression, and courageous enough to interpret the ultimate experience of mankind in terms of his temperament, in terms of art. I do not mean to say that he would attempt to beguile the last moments of humanity by an ingenious tale. It would be too much to expect—from humanity. I doubt the heroism of the hearers. As to the heroism of the artist, no doubt is necessary. There would be on his part no heroism. The artist in his calling of interpreter creates (the clearest form of demonstration) because he must. He is so much of a voice that for him silence is like death; and the postulate was that there is a group alive, clustered on his threshold to watch the last flicker of light on a black sky, to hear the last word uttered in the stilled workshop of the earth. It is safe to affirm that, if anybody, it will be the imaginative man who would be moved to speak on the eve of that day without to-morrow—whether in austere exhortation or in a phrase of sardonic comment, who can guess?

For my own part, from a short and cursory acquaintance with my kind, I am inclined to think that the last utterance will formulate, strange as it may appear, some to us now utterly inconceivable hope. For mankind is delightful in its pride, its assurance, and its indomitable tenacity. It will sleep on the battle-field among its own dead, in the manner of an army having won a barren victory. It will not know when it is beaten. And, perhaps, it is right in that quality. The victories are not, perhaps, so barren as it may appear from a purely strategical, utilitarian point of view. Mr. Henry James seems to hold that belief. Nobody has rendered better, perhaps, the tenacity of temper, or known how to drape the robe of spiritual honor about the drooping form of a victor in a barren strife. And the honor is always well won; for the struggles Mr. Henry James chronicles with such subtle and direct insight are, though only personal contests, desperate in their silence, none the less heroic (in the modern sense) for the absence of shouted watchwords, clash of arms and sound of trumpets. Those are adventures in which only choice souls are ever involved. And Mr. Henry James records them with a fearless and insistent fidelity to the *péripéties* of the contest, and the feelings of the combatants.

The fiercest excitements of a romance *"de cape et d'epée,"* the romance of yard-arm and boarding-pike so dear to youth, whose knowledge of action (as of other things) is imperfect and limited, are matched, for the quickening of our maturer years, by the tasks set, by the difficulties presented, to Mr. Henry James's men's and women's sense of truth, of necessity—before all, of conduct. His mankind is delightful. It is delightful in its tenacity; it refuses to own itself beaten; it will sleep on the battle-field. These war-like images come by themselves under the pen; since, from the duality of man's nature and the competition of individuals, the life-history of the earth must in the last instance be a history of a really very relentless warfare. Neither his fellows, nor his gods, nor his passions will leave a man alone. In virtue of these allies and enemies, he holds his precarious dominion, he possesses his fleeting significance; and it is this relation, in all its manifestations, great and little, superficial or profound, and this relation alone, that is commented upon, interpreted, demonstrated by the art of the novelist in the only possible way in which the task can be performed; by the independent creation of circumstance and character, achieved against all the difficulties of expression, in an imaginative effort finding its inspiration from the reality of forms and sensations. That a sacrifice must be made, that something has to be given up, is the truth engraved in the innermost recesses of the fair temple built for our edification by the masters of fiction. There is no other secret behind the curtain. All adventure, all love, every success is resumed in the supreme energy of an act of renunciation. It is the uttermost limit of our power; it is the most potent and effective force at our disposal, on which rest the labors of a solitary man in his study, the rock on which have been built commonwealths whose might casts a dwarfing shadow upon two oceans. Like a natural force which is obscured as much as illustrated by the multiplicity of phenomena, the power of renunciation is obscured by the mass of weaknesses, vacillations, secondary motives and false steps and compromises which make up the sum of our activity. But no man or woman worthy of the name can pretend to anything more, to anything greater. And Mr. Henry James's men and women are worthy of the name, within the limits his art, so clear, so sure of itself, has drawn round their activities. He would be the last to claim for them Titanic proportions. The earth itself has grown smaller in the course of ages. But in every sphere of human perplexities and emotions there are more greatnesses than one—not counting here the greatness of the artist himself. Wherever he stands, at the beginning or the end of things, a man has to sacrifice his gods to his passions or his passions to his gods. That is the problem, great enough, in all truth, if approached in the spirit of sincerity and knowledge.

In one of his critical studies, published some fifteen years ago, Mr. Henry James claims for the novelist the standing of the historian as the only adequate one, as for himself and before his audience. I think that the claim cannot be contested, and that the position is unassailable. Fiction is history, human history, or it is nothing. But it is also more than that; it stands on firmer ground, being based on the reality of forms and the observation of social phenomena, whereas history is based on documents and the reading of print and handwriting—on second-hand impression. Thus fiction is nearer truth. But let that pass. A historian may be an artist too, and a novelist is a historian, the preserver, the keeper, the expounder, of human experience. As is meet for a man of his descent and tradition, Mr. Henry James is the historian of fine consciences.

Of course, this is a general statement; but I don't think its truth will be or can be questioned. Its fault is that it leaves so much out; and, besides, Mr. Henry James is much too considerable to be put into the nutshell of a phrase. The fact remains that he has made his choice, and that his choice is justified up to the hilt by the success of his art. He has taken for himself the greater part. The range of a fine conscience covers more good and evil than the range of a conscience which may be called, roughly, not fine; a conscience less troubled by the nice discrimination of shades of conduct. A fine conscience is more concerned with essentials; its triumphs are more perfect, if less profitable in a worldly sense. There is, in short, more truth in its working for a historian to detect and to show. It is a thing of infinite complication and suggestion. None of these escape the art of Mr. Henry James. He has mastered the country, his domain, not wild indeed, but full of romantic glimpses, of deep shadows and sunny places. There are no secrets left within his range. He has disclosed them as they should be disclosed—that is, beautifully. And, indeed, ugliness has but little place in this world of his creation. Yet it is always felt in the truthfulness of his art; it is there, it surrounds the scene, it presses close upon it. It is made visible, tangible, in the struggles, in the contacts of the fine consciences, in their perplexities, in the sophism of their mistakes. For a fine conscience is naturally a virtuous one. What is natural about it is just its fineness, an abiding sense of the intangible, everpresent, right. It is most visible in their ultimate triumph, in their emergence from miracle, through an energetic act of renunciation. Energetic, not violent: the distinction is wide, enormous, like that between substance and shadow.

Through it all Mr. Henry James keeps a firm hold of the substance, of what is worth having, of what is worth holding. The contrary opinion has been, if not absolutely affirmed, then at least implied, with some frequency. To most of us, living willingly in a sort of intellectual moonlight, in the faintly reflected light of truth, the shadows so firmly renounced by Mr. Henry James's men and women stand out endowed with extraordinary value, with a value so extraordinary that their rejection offends, by its uncalled-for scrupulousness, those business-like instincts which a careful Providence has implanted in our breasts. And, apart from that just cause of discontent, it is obvious that a solution by rejection must always present a certain apparent lack of finality, especially startling when contrasted with the usual methods of solution by rewards and punishments, by crowned love, by fortune, by a broken leg or a sudden death. Why the reading public which, as a body, has never laid upon a story-teller the command to be an artist, should demand from him this sham of Divine Omnipotence is utterly incomprehensible. But so it is; and these solutions are legitimate, inasmuch as they satisfy the desire for finality, for which our hearts yearn with a longing greater than the longing for the loaves and fishes of this earth. Perhaps the only true desire of mankind, coming thus to light in its hours of leisure, is to be set at rest. One is never set at rest by Mr. Henry

James's novels. His books end as an episode in life ends. You remain with the sense of the life still going on; and even the subtle presence of the dead is felt in that silence that comes upon the artist-creation when the last word has been read. It is eminently satisfying, but it is not final. Mr. Henry James, the great artist and faithful historian, never attempts the impossible.

Recent Criticism

The "Jourdain" Relationship of Henry to William James in *The Spoils of Poynton*

Richard A. Hocks*

In turning [from "The Real Thing"] to *The Spoils of Poynton* (1897), we turn from a virtually flawless tale which can engender opposing interpretations to a novel whose problematic nature has elicited disagreement only less notable than that of *The Turn of the Screw*.[1] Neither our alpha nor omega critical reader of "The Real Thing," *The Portrait of a Lady*, or *The Ambassadors* would ever consider that James was there "uncertain of his intention." But these were R. P. Blackmur's words about *The Spoils of Poynton*,[2] and many readers would agree, I suspect, if only because it is clearly established that the novel marks an important transition in James's career: it is his attempt to salvage the debacle of the playwriting period by appropriating the scenic art into his longer fiction. According to Leon Edel the novel was literally "a turning point in the fiction of Henry James."[3]

At the same time, this book has been the recipient of at least one small tributary line of consistent argument, though it is well overshadowed by its general problems of interpretation. It has been regularly cited—if not really examined—as the demonstrable source for Henry's ethical repudiation of William's pragmatism. The repudiation lies, according to this argument, in the contrast between the moral sensibility of the heroine Fleda Vetch and that of Mrs. Gereth, the widow and mistress of Poynton Park, whose antique home and unsurpassing collection of art objects and furnishings are subject by English law to possession by her son Owen upon his marrying. Mrs. Gereth, the argument continues, is someone with whom we initially sympathize in her plight and (like Fleda herself) we admire for her aesthetic capacities embodied in Poynton, but who ultimately shows up morally expedient, materialistic, utilitarian—"pragmatic"; Fleda, on the other hand, is ultimately shown to be the spokesman for Henry's own opposing ethic—absolute, idealistic, categorically imperative.[4] The repudiation of William's pragmatism as such is said to occur late in the story when the two ladies have their celebrated quarrel and each gives her respective view of

*Reprinted with the permission of the University of North Carolina Press and the author from *Henry James and Pragmatistic Thought: A Study in the Relationship Between the Philosophy of William James and the Literary Art of Henry James* (Chapel Hill: University of North Carolina Press, 1974), 134–51.

life. When entertaining this argument, we must remember, obviously, that it rests in turn on an entirely sympathetic (or completely "reliable") reading of the heroine and "register," Fleda Vetch, and not on the possibility that she is a classic study in hysteria or neurotic behavior, tending toward that of the famous governess. That is what the larger critical argument centers on.

If my examination of William's thought in relation to Henry in this study has pointed to anything, it points to the fact that this last possibility, that Fleda is an unreliable neurotic, is too easy and inappropriate a line to take in responding to the ethical issue just mentioned. The governess, after all, is left at the end of the tale with her arms around a child she may have frightened to death, whereas Fleda's only tangible harm, assuming she is neurotic, is to herself in the form of renunciation of all her best chances—something endemic to Jamesian protagonists even when we do not think them neurotic. Besides, this is the same lady James was to praise as a "free spirit" and the embodiment of "appreciation" in his later "Preface" to the novel.[5] More to the point generally might be Henry's own unawareness that he "unconsciously antipragmatised," but even there we could perhaps say that he was several years away from knowing what he was to believe about William's thought. And meanwhile we do have William by 1897 becoming increasingly critical of Henry's later manner—except that he certainly failed to see any repudiation of his own ethic in *The Spoils of Poynton,* which is a piece he happened to single out for high praise.[6]

The real issue, on William's side at least, is of course whether his thought really is mere expediency and materialism; and if I have not answered that already in these pages, I do not see how I possibly can. That he is a utilitarian is another matter, and one that perhaps can use some further amplification. The issue grows more engaging in its complexity when we turn back to Henry's side of it. For it is perfectly possible to assume, as Yvor Winters does, for example, that Fleda Vetch represents James's own "absolute" moral viewpoint,[7] while not necessarily having William's pragmatism in mind as the opposite and repudiated ethic of the novel. In my ensuing remarks I should like to address this last point along with the entire question of a repudiation of pragmatism. If I seem therefore to slight some of the other thematic content—the novel's implicit Ruskin- or Arnold-like critique of Victorian society, for example—it is the result of this particular ethical focus.[8]

Mrs. Gereth, we must remember, is designated by James in his "Preface" as one of the "fools" or "figures" along with the more obvious cases of Mona and Mrs. Brigstock and Owen. They are all of them "fixed constituents," he says, and *on that basis* different from Fleda Vetch, the "free spirit."[9] It is most significant that James would proffer such a distinction—and most appropriate, given the "Jourdain" relationship. A "fixed constituent" means a character who cannot change, cannot grow, a static instead of a dynamic character, as we would say. But this very distinction is for James's art fundamentally grounded in turn on his engagement with reality in its flux and process. A "fixed constituency" can no more comprise James's sense of human freedom than it can his view of fictional rules, like those of Walter Besant; and it likewise cannot comprise William's view of reality or human choice, both of which must allow for the genuine "novelty" in human affairs and which thus disallows "moral holidays" implied by fixed systems, ethically as well as epistemologically. And so to call Mrs. Gereth a "fixed constituent" is practically to have prima-facie evidence that, whatever she represents, it is most unlikely to be William's thought.

In the story itself she is not motivated in her conduct or in her views just by her passion for the lovely objects themselves at Poynton: she is "fixed" by her all-consuming idea in respect to them and in connection with which she has spent most of her life in assembling and, like a monarch, surveying them. The objects are the particulars she finds meaning in, in the same sense that William's intellectualist opponents make particulars serve their notion of the real:

> It was not the crude love of possession; it was the need to be faithful to a trust and loyal to an idea. The idea was surely noble; it was that of the beauty Mrs. Gereth had so patiently and consummately wrought. Pale but radiant, her back to the wall, she planted herself there as a heroine guarding a treasure. To give up the ship was to flinch from her duty; there was something in her eyes that declared she would die at her post. . . . Her fanaticism gave her a new distinction. . . . She trod the place like a reigning queen or a proud usurper; full as it was of splendid pieces it could show in these days no ornament so effective as its menaced mistress.[10]

These observations come to us via our Jamesian "register" Fleda Vetch, and we may, of course, choose to distrust them. But there is certainly nothing in their import that is out of joint with the conduct and stance of Mrs. Gereth throughout the novel. Perhaps the more discriminating point is that Fleda here chooses a viewpoint and expression which also reveal her own idealism and absolutism. Then again, the passage as a product of James's narrative consciousness seems to participate in irony, even while presenting the sentiments which have caused Fleda to side initially with Mrs. Gereth in the dispute. Already, then, we find ourselves, in evaluating such passages, having to keep quite a number of matters distinguished: James's view of Mrs. Gereth, his attitude toward Fleda, the modifying context of this relatively early point in the story, and even his viewpoint on the issue of beauty. In order to clarify my own general position about so many intersecting matters, I am first going to engage in a "Jacobite" evaluation and reading of the passage above. I believe it would read something like this: James, as he so often does, is employing here a "double consciousness"; we are early in the story; Fleda has yet to discover that her fine moral sensitivity cannot be superseded even by her equally fine artistic one; nevertheless, James has managed here to convey masterfully not only the erroneous view which she holds, at this point, of Mrs. Gereth's position in the dispute, but also her own warmth and generosity: qualities which may take her for a while into a wrong turning, but will, in the long run, take her far beyond the merely "artistic" norm she imputes to Mrs. Gereth and on to the truly artistic one where, with her author, moral values and "patiently wrought beauty" are one; James accomplishes all this, and at the same time stands "behind" his heroine and, with comic discipline and rhetoric ("heroine guarding a treasure," "menaced mistress"), points delicately and satirically at the limitations of Mrs. Gereth, all of which is the more remarkable for his not detracting from Fleda's own superior qualities.

I cannot conceive of a Jamesian enthusiast disapproving of that reading, unless he happens to believe that Fleda Vetch is the Master's brilliant portrait of a neurotic and not his ethical spokesman. I myself do not disapprove of it—or I would not have made it as elaborate as I have. I subscribe to it almost wholeheartedly, if perhaps a little less rhapsodically, one octave lower on the keyboard (as also, doubtless, my hypothetical enthusiast). Nevertheless, it is that octave lower which makes me ask: what does it mean to say that Fleda's view of Mrs. Gereth is at this point erroneous? Is she not rather perfectly correct about Mrs. Gereth, her error lying in her very accuracy rather than the expression of a temporary mistake "despite" her good parts? In other words, is the issue fundamentally a *conjunctive* or a *disjunctive* one? Her error resides in her accuracy at assuming, as she does here with Mrs. Gereth, that someone's behavior ("practice") can be justified primarily by recourse to a noble idea alone—even the idea of beauty. For as she becomes more and more involved in this dispute, and more and more "unfixed" in her own loyalties, she will discover that this present lovely idea itself has consequences which get her enmeshed with people and people's feelings, including her own. Then comes the difficult question of how one best "uses" all concerned. The attempt to *use* people well is not shoddy because it is utilitarian: it is in fact the heart of any ethical question, even though one sometimes hesitates before employing the word "use" in this way, so little currency does it seem to have now.

At the same time, Fleda's notion, insofar as it pertains to Mrs. Gereth, is quite correct. Mrs. Gereth has the classic intellectualist mentality: like William's opponents, concepts for her are not things to "re-direct" and come back into experience with; they stand stately and removed from "mere" occurrences and consequential process. Let us see:

> The great wrong Owen had done her was not his "taking up" with
> Mona—that was disgusting, but it was a detail, an accidental form; it was
> his failure from the first to understand what it was to have a mother at
> all, to appreciate the beauty and the sanctity of the character. . . . One's
> mother, gracious goodness, if one were the kind of fine young man one

ought to be, the only kind Mrs. Gereth cared for, was a subject for poetry, for idolatry.

[49]

This passage is not, like the previous one, complicated by the "registering" viewpoint of Fleda. It belongs entirely to Mrs. Gereth, even
though not a direct quotation, and can remind us that James has as many "in-
between" areas in his panoramic-scenic method as in his view of reality itself. In any case, this passage is supposed to represent William's thought?
If it has to represent anything along these lines, I would rather call it a
caricature of William's opposition. But of course it represents nothing along
these lines, and is Henry's very solid characterization of Mrs. Gereth. It is
just that, James's mind being what it is, such a flawed viewpoint probably
will appear intellectualist in William's sense. Mrs. Gereth's captivation by
an idea is correlative to her prescriptiveness and "infallibility." The absolutist, not especially bothered by particulars, is secure in his knowledge of
what is central and what is peripheral. Thus Fleda to Mrs. Gereth: " 'I gave
(Owen) my opinion that you're very logical, very obstinate and very
proud.' " And Mrs. Gereth replies: " 'Quite right, my dear: I'm a rank
bigot—about that sort of thing!' Mrs. Gereth jerked her head at the contents of the house. 'I've never denied it. I'd kidnap—to save them, to convert them—the children of heretics. When I know I'm right I go to the
stake. Oh he may burn me alive!' she cried with a happy face"(114).

We shall want to remember this extravagant remark about a possible
"burning" and the context in which it is uttered, when we later come to
address the novel's conclusion. Meanwhile we see once again the quality of
Mrs. Gereth's presumption, which remains intact throughout the greater
part of the novel. She is one of James's many Walter Besants, those who
think a priori, who know in advance what is what, and are therefore not
embued with "the possible other case."[11] Mrs. Gereth has presumed, practically from the start, that Fleda, unlike Mona Brigstock, would be just the
person for Owen—i.e., just the sort of daughter-in-law who would continue
to cherish and properly administer the lovely Poynton objects. And it is
precisely because James's own mentality differs from hers that this presumption is quite accurate—Fleda really *is* just the person for Owen. She
has fallen in love with him, and because she really does love him honor-
ably, she therefore cannot *be* "just the person" for Owen in Mrs. Gereth's
scheme. The same is true of the elder lady's presumption that Fleda, like
herself, has the true artistic empathy for the spoils. Again, she could not
be more wrong for being right. Fleda's difficulty here is that, not unlike
the poor pragmatist, she cannot take any moral holidays: her empathy for
the objects is "true," all right; so true that she is eventually compelled to
respond to them *contextually*, in all their relations and ramifications ("consequences"), which is what gets her embroiled with them as the occasion
for people's conduct. If I may be forgiven such a "utilitarian" perspective—

it is exactly her having the artistic sensibility ascribed to her by Mrs. Gereth that impels her to deal with the spoils in terms of what they are "proceeding-to-do," how they are "known-as," and hence she cannot play the game according to Mrs. Gereth's prescribed injunctions. But Henry James *can*, because he knows artistically that the value of such injunctions, like those of Walter Besant, lies wholly in the meaning one attaches to them. That is the mentality of his operative irony because it is thoroughly conjunctive in its dramatic manifestation.

In the blurb of the Penguin edition of this novel we find the following quite typical sort of comment and paraphrase: "(Fleda) is in love with Owen Gereth and genuinely appreciates the contents of Poynton for themselves. But she scrupulously stands aside when he gets engaged to the coarse and insensitive Mona. . . ."[12] The whole import of my previous remarks is that, except for the very beginning—and then again at the very end, as we shall presently see—Fleda cannot and does not appreciate the objects "for themselves"; her refusal to find inherent properties or essences in them throughout the conflict is only less than James's own throughout the entire novel from cover to cover. As for such expressions as "but she scrupulously stands aside"—we must try to remember that James's art is not primarily a "but" art; it is a "because" and a "for-that-very-reason" art. It is the art of William James's formulation of reality as pluralistic novelty—"the same returns not, save to bring the different."[13]

Mrs. Gereth's many presumptions culminate in what is one of the more satisfying structural "re-directions" in James's fiction. Fleda, having confronted Owen's own eventual declaration of love and proposal to her at her sister Maggie's house, has after considerable excruciation refused him unless the affianced Mona herself releases him from his pledge. She sends Owen back in the hope that he will be released, since Mona has become so adamant and furious over not getting the objects (Mrs. Gereth having carted them off to the dower house at Ricks), that she appears ready to break things off. Fleda then returns several days later to London in answer to a summons from Mrs. Gereth, only to learn that the elder lady has, in her latest—and last—melodramatic move, packed up and sent every last "spoil" back to Poynton itself:

> Mrs. Gereth stood there in all the glory of a great stroke. "I've settled you." She filled the room, to Fleda's scared vision, with the glare of her magnificence. "I've sent everything back."
> "Everything?" Fleda wailed.
> "To the smallest snuff-box. The last load went yesterday. The same people did it. Poor little Ricks is empty." Then as if, for a crowning splendour, to check all deprecation, "They're yours, you goose!" the wonderful woman concluded, holding up her handsome head and rubbing her white hands. But there were tears none the less in her deep eyes.

(211)

Thus we see the tenacity of Mrs. Gereth's "fixed" idea, the logical extension of her fanaticism. She has properly fixed Fleda's wagon by virtue of that presumption of hers. Not duped for a moment, when she heard that her son had gone searching for her young protégée, she saw (naturally) the embodiment of her own plan. Her great act is her "sign," her "token" of knowledge. The only trouble with such knowing what you are about intellectualist-fashion is that the consequences may not always allow the curtain to drop amid the applause. She has done the one thing that now can lose Owen back to Mona, as Fleda, in sending him away, has done the one thing Mrs. Gereth could never entertain in her anticipation. It is at this point—and not before—that we turn the page and have the well-known quarrel between the two ladies wherein Henry is supposed to have repudiated William's "pragmatism." But let us look back at Fleda's character and ethic more closely.

I would be the last to say that Fleda Vetch is not idealistic. William's ethical pragmatism, if we can grasp it without supplying present-day connotations of the word, is itself most idealistic. The point is here that we must see Fleda's particular quality of idealism, not just call her idealistic and then quasi-mechanically equate that with absolutism. That she speaks ethically for Henry James (whatever her "ism") is not cut and dried, for his later fiction remains a "more-and-less" affair in this as in other matters.[14] That she is his chosen "viewpoint" is not definitive, for so are the narrators of "The Liar," *The Aspern Papers, The Sacred Fount*, and *The Turn of the Screw;* as well as John Marcher and Herbert Dodd in *The Beast in the Jungle* and *The Bench of Desolation*—to name several narrative "deputies" not, to my mind, at least, his ethical spokesmen. Nor should we overlook the possibility that a central James character with whom he is on the whole sympathetic may proceed from one ethical orientation to another, and then back again—though always remaining, to a greater extent than with almost any other writer, "in character." Nevertheless, I do think that James's comments about Fleda Vetch in his later "Preface," stressing her "appreciation," her "character," and her "free spirit" are genuine and adhere correctly to the reading experience of the novel. I would even say that her "appreciative" qualities as James defines them—her capacity, as James later said, to "both see and feel" as well as her not being "able," like the stronger-willed Mrs. Gereth and "triumphantly" willed Mona—do constitute ethical qualities James admires;[15] furthermore, they are the very ones implicated in William's claim, earlier discussed, that anyone who thinks his law lax ought to try keeping it one day.

I have several times pointed out in the course of this study that in William's pragmatistic thought the ethical view just cannot be divorced from the epistemological view. The character of Fleda Vetch is a particularly apt illustration and parallel. When she accidentally meets up with Owen Gereth on a shopping trip, and he seems to want to lengthen their meeting, Fleda reflects as follows: "He unduly prolonged their business together, giving Fleda a sense of his putting off something particular that he had to face. If she had ever dreamed of Owen Gereth as finely fluttered she would have seen him with some such manner as this" (63).

This is most "Jamesian," a quality not, we see, necessarily dependent upon sentences a page long, although to accomplish what he just has above usually demands longer sentences. The quality lies in Fleda's previous impressions of Owen as terminating and tumbling into the present one. She does not think of her present perception as something to be explained or modified through attachment to some preconceived reality. She thinks in just the reverse fashion: i.e., Owen seems to be putting something off; I have not before seen him act like this; and with respect to my previous knowledge of him, were I now to imagine that person as nervous, his behavior would resemble the phenomenon I presently perceive. Of course it would be easier for James to have Fleda thinking: "Good heavens, he's acting differently: he must really be fluttered." And such a statement would be far easier for a conceptualist or "saltatory" reader (or critic) to accommodate.[16] But it would also take us out of James's world, implying as it does a disjunction between the present, nervous Owen and the former un-nervous Owen. And, viewed in this light, the *former* Owen would be the *real* Owen; the present nervousness only a new "attribute" intruding on the scene. Instead, Fleda's thinking makes Owen's most recent behavior in effect the continual and ongoing basis for "Owenness." It captures the very heart of William's whole point about consequential pluralistic "novelty."

But the real issue now is the ethical correlative to such epistemological considerations. Fleda's "use" of others morally is the cognate to the sort of thinking above. What the epistemology insists upon is the undermining of the subject-object separation. Fleda's "appreciation" is her constantly imputing to others her own best and most recent motives—always making them morally "present." Let us go to her celebrated scene with Owen, when she sends him back to Mona, the scene that has irritated quite a number of critical readers as much as it will upset Mrs. Gereth herself when, after sending the spoils back to Poynton, she later learns from Fleda that this scene had taken place:

> "Then in God's name [Owen pleads] what must I do?"
> "You must settle that with Mona. You mustn't break faith. Anything's better than that. You must at any rate be utterly sure. She must love you—how can she help it? *I* wouldn't give you up! . . . The great thing is to keep faith. Where's a man if he doesn't? If he doesn't he may be so cruel. So cruel, so cruel, so cruel!" Fleda repeated. "I couldn't have a hand in that, you know: that's my position—that's mine. You offered her marriage. It's a tremendous thing for her." Then looking at him another moment, "*I* wouldn't give you up!" she said again.
>
> (196–97)

This entire scene has perplexed many a reader, and I do not wish to diminish some of its problems—for example, Fleda's characteristically retreating "upstairs" (like a Victorian heroine) for fear of breaking down before Owen's passion. My concern is that of the ethical content of Fleda's character. For the Jacobite critic she is either James's surrogate moral absolutist or else the Master's brilliantly done neurotic, and for the anti-Jacobite she is the second without the Master's knowledge. It seems to me that, even if we are to find her excessive, the quality of her ethic remains utilitarian; and if it seems awfully "fine" for being utilitarian, then so much the worse for our understanding of utilitarian. It is utilitarian because she refuses to prescribe ("You must settle that with Mona"); utilitarian because she does not base her position on anything transcendent, but rather on the human contracts and pledges made by fallible people. The "faith" she speaks of is that everybody, including even the Monas of the world, must get the fairest shake possible, because we do not have the final word that their position is less ordained than ours. It is utilitarian because its eye is to consequences: no matter how deserving we are convinced that we are, our actions can cause cruelty. Utilitarian, finally, because the matter remains provisional: *if* Mona will agree to call off the engagement, *then* Fleda and Owen can marry.

Her ethic here is furthermore pragmatistically oriented—that is, parallel to William's own broadening or "radical" aspects of utilitarianism—in that Fleda characteristically *creates* a possible other case about Mona, projects a version of the other girl as someone for whom Owen's earlier proposal is "a tremendous thing," someone who "must" love him because Fleda herself does. The saltatory mind can immediately say that Fleda is merely creating Mona in her own image; and that is so to the extent that she does project, in Henry's language, the "possible other case" for what "*might*, blessedly be," and makes Mona's feelings coalesce with her own. To the same saltatory mind that sounds simply like making others into yourself. In fact it is just the reverse: it is conceiving of each person as so distinctively individual that you are willing continually to subsume your own views into them rather than classify them as Other, which would then take the spark of human life and dignity out of them—one which you know is there because you have it yourself. That is the sort of "use" Fleda makes of Mona, and it is extraordinarily characteristic of her throughout the novel.[17] The fact that neither Mona nor Owen deserves such good usage cannot alter Fleda's fundamental response in this regard. It is an extreme position and an extreme ethic, and one which is rather easy to confuse with its conceptualist opposite—making others conform in an extreme way to your own idea. The reason the two are easily confused is that they *are* both extreme and opposite and therefore seem to resemble one another; and the reason Fleda's is likely to be thought the other is that we rarely see *her* ethic in people, but we do see the other one. James himself is most capable and adept at presenting the other one: John Marcher, the narrator of *The Aspern Papers*, and the governess are good examples of it in his fiction. Fleda is instead an extreme case of William's ethic.

Late in the novel, in the aftermath of Owen's marriage to Mona, Mrs. Gereth expresses her bewilderment to Fleda, this time about Owen himself; that is, if Fleda had been "idiotic" in pursuing her "scruples" beyond all reason, there was still Owen's discovery in the whole dispute of the ugliness of Mona's character—and yet he now seemed content. Fleda, however, observes: " '[Mona's] a person who's upset by failure and who blooms and expands with success. There was something she had set her heart upon, set her teeth about—the house exactly as she had seen it.' " And Mrs. Gereth cries: " 'She never saw it at all, she never looked at it!' " But Fleda counters:

> "She doesn't look with her eyes; she looks with her ears. In her own way she had taken it in; she knew, she felt when it has been touched. That probably made her take an attitude that was extremely disagreeable. But the attitude lasted only while the reason for it lasted. . . . When the pressure was removed she came up again. . . . her natural charm reasserted itself."
> "Her natural charm!"—Mrs. Gereth could barely articulate.
> "It's very great; everybody thinks so; there must be something in it."
>
> (254–55)

The novel never allows us to test this evaluation of the couple by Fleda. But one thing, I hope, is clear: this evaluation could never come from someone who is supposed to embody Henry's repudiation of William's thought. And note that it continues Fleda's characteristic "use" of others. Moreover, it is one time we could hardly confuse such usage as its opposite of making Mona into Fleda's idea and self, for Fleda is certainly not someone who blooms and expands with success.

And so: in the celebrated quarrel scene between Fleda and Mrs. Gereth (occurring, we must remember, only after the elder lady's comic "apotheosis" in sending the objects back to Poynton as well as Fleda's sending Owen back to Mona) the two women do not so much reveal their opposing ethics, or ideologies, as they reinforce and enrich the full meaning of the dramatic context—much like those supposed "thematic" statements earlier discussed in "The Real Thing," aesthetic statements best "re-directed" right back into the psychological moments that gave birth to them. Shortly after Mrs. Gereth condemns Fleda's "wonderful exactions" and "sweet little scruples," and wonders why her son had not "snapped his fingers at your refinements" (219, 220), Fleda cries out her defense that many readers consider—along with the statements to Owen about keeping faith—the very touchstone of her ethical consciousness and that of Henry James:

> "You simplify far too much. You always did and you always will. The tangle of life is much more intricate than you've ever, I think, felt it to be.

You slash into it," cried Fleda finely, "with a great pair of shears; you nip at it as if you were one of the Fates!"

(224)

If this is a touchstone of Jamesian morality, we should at least include the finishing line to it: " 'If Owen's at Waterbath he's there to wind everything up.' " Not only does this take away some of the bloom of profundity, it shows that Fleda could not be more wrong for being right: Owen, we later learn, is indeed winding things up, but not as Fleda bravely imagines.[18] What James is once again doing is making his ideological pronouncements arise out of a context only to be "re-directed" right back into it, and thus making the very relationship itself totally "empirical" in William's sense. Fleda, in short, has become increasingly apprehensive that Mrs. Gereth's unforeseen act may have lost her Owen, and that her own earlier insistence to Owen that he keep his pledge may have the dire consequences she was willing to risk. The quality of James's art lies just in such unstiffening and mediating. It is really beginning to come home to Fleda that she *is* going to lose Owen, just as earlier she so nobly said that she might. Such is James's actual "tangle of life" and "intricacy" of the human comedy. Like William's unseverable stream of reality it cannot be cut with a shears, because it is thoroughly conjoined.

Mrs. Gereth, for one, perceives what is involved in Fleda's fine rhetoric about "the tangle of life": " 'You don't believe a word you're saying,' " she responds: " 'I've frightened you, as you've frightened me: you're whistling in the dark to keep up our courage' " (224–25). But the recognition here is not gratuitous either. It does involve Mrs. Gereth's inability to comprehend Fleda. In fact Fleda's present fright, which the elder lady perceives, drives it home to *her* that all expectations are lost. She immediately continues: " 'I do simplify, doubtless, if to simplify is to fail to comprehend the inanity of a passion that bewilders a young blockhead with bugaboo barriers, with hideous and monstrous sacrifices. I can only repeat that you're beyond me. Your perversity's a thing to howl over' " (225).

Mrs. Gereth begins this speech with a "slow austere" shake of the head, and becomes increasingly furious until she is almost ready to howl. And, once again, she too could not be more wrong for being right: her simplifying *is* her incomprehension; and she creates for herself a Fleda in the image of her incomprehension—blockheaded and perverse; her imputation to Fleda of monstrous sacrifices comes from the same source: Mrs. Gereth *will* have a sacrifice, after her own "crowning splendour" of having sent back the spoils! But what is almost of equal importance is that Mrs. Gereth's anger, culminating in these remarks above, also expends itself with them. Not only does she calm down, and the two ladies exhaust themselves with their argument, but their relationship reestablishes itself for the remainder of the novel, if anything on the closest and most legitimate footing since they first met. Thus, not only does a reading of Fleda's repudiation of Mrs. Gereth's "pragmatism" do violence to the context leading up to the quarrel but even to what follows afterward. It also, as we have seen, thoroughly misconstrues the ethical bases for both Mrs. Gereth and for Fleda. Henry James's "tangle of life" proceeds and, like William's definition of truth, is in the making.

The difficult and controversial dénouement, the burning down of Poynton Park, is for the most part outside of the ethical focus I have been addressing. But I would like to comment on its possible place or appropriateness, if only to stress what are often the implications for James's art of the "Jourdain" relationship. The critical problem with the potentially melodramatic conflagration that closes the novel has been one, first, of deciding whether James knew his full intention in the story and, second, assuming he did, what the fire was then meant to symbolize. More recently Leon Edel has said that it stands for James's own theatre period and vocation going up in smoke,[19] and that seems plausible; but it neither supports nor rejects the critical question of its symbolic content or artistic appropriateness for the novel as a whole. The general tendency has been to see it as some kind of symbolic underscoring of Fleda's necessary renunciation of earthly or material gain—poetic justice which deprives her of tainting her pristine fineness and absolute morality; or else the parallel aesthetic point of tainting her hard-won recognition that true art exists beyond its mere physical embodiment, an idea reminiscent of, say, Hawthorne's "The Artist of the Beautiful."[20]

If we were instead to shift our basic orientation away from such symbolic realms proper and "re-direct" our focus back into the context in which it occurs, I believe we can see another quite different rationale for it, and one at least as satisfying as those proposed above. It should be remembered that Fleda only begins to think of the lovely objects once again as "too proud, unlike base animals and humans, to be reducible" to anyone's mere ownership—Mona's or her own—after the conflict has been resolved against her and she faces the prospect of a future alone with only lost alternatives (235). In other words, just as we have seen that she initially joined up with Mrs. Gereth on the basis of a lovely "idea," then had to discover through the conflict that such ideas cannot be divorced from their consequences or implications, she now as a lonely and rejected girl becomes vulnerable to responding—or responding—to the same lovely "idea" of the spoils detached from time, place, or human conflict.

The advantage of our keeping this perspective is that it adheres so well to the text during those chapters following the quarrel with Mrs. Gereth and culminating in Fleda's trip to Poynton and discovering the fire. First there is the pathetic search for Owen, the telegram, the full reconciliation with Mrs. Gereth, the response to Ricks and the modest furnishings of the "maiden-aunt," and the growing acquisition of her "serene" and "lucid" stoicism. Owen's surprising letter, requesting that she go to Poynton and take the "gem of the collection," is a Jamesian tour de force of mystery and ambiguity, but its effect on Fleda, coming when it does in her situation, triggers a response from her that is unmistakable and unambiguous. We can literally watch her becoming increasingly enamored of an "idea." Starting with natural bafflement, she proceeds "little by little" to endow it with significance and idealism. She "would go down to Poynton as a pilgrim might go to a shrine"; she "would act with secret rapture"; she would have a gift more splendid and joyful "than the greatest she had believed to be left her"; the time was "to dream of and watch for; to be patient was to draw out the sweetness"; it was "an hour of triumph, the triumph of everything in her recent life that had not held up its head." And still her response builds and expands:

> She moved there in thought—in the great rooms she knew; she should be able to say to herself that, for once at least, her possession was as complete as that of either of the others whom it had filled only with bitterness. And a thousand times yes—her choice should know no scruple: the thing she should go down to take would be up to the height of her privilege. The whole place was in her eyes, and she spent for weeks her private hours in a luxury of comparison and debate. . . . (S)he would on the spot so handle and ponder that there shouldn't be the shade of a mistake.
>
> (259–61)

In one conjunctive, seamless, sequence (a single two-page paragraph in the text) Henry James has modulated his heroine's response from one of initial bafflement at Owen's request to the heady imaginings seen here. This very progression equates perfectly with the description by William James, given in an earlier chapter, of how the human mind can mistakenly arrive at a "sublime" saltatory explanation or Idea.[21] But we need not revisit William's epistemology to see that Fleda's initial perplexity has turned into "triumph," her sense of the possible other case which characterized her conduct has evaporated into "completeness," her commitment to human fallibility become now no "shade of a mistake." Henry's own doctrine for all of this is his well-known distinction between the real and the romantic, contained in his "Preface" to *The American*. Fleda has cut the "rope" which keeps the "balloon of experience" tied to the earth.[22] And that means, vis-a-vis William, that she is out in the great conceptualist Beyond.

The Poynton fire, then, is what brings her back. For what all "symbolic" readings of the fire inadvertently distort is that the fire qua fire is never given in the text; that is, the final scene takes place at the train station, and is rendered through high comedy—Fleda's impassioned remarks to a most bewildered porter followed by her conversation with the stationmaster, who tells her what has happened. This does not mean, however, that the scene exists and is written satirically at Fleda's expense. There is great sympathy for her when, after finally grasping that Poynton is gone, she feels herself "give everything up" and, standing in the smoke from the fire a mile away, covers her face and speaks the final lines of the novel: " 'I'll go back' " (266).

It is the appropriately written scene, then, for what has happened to Fleda since she lost Owen. Her "go(ing) back" symbolizes, if you will, her reattachment to actuality, and even conveys that circular quality we have seen again and again in this study in connection with James's letter to Henry Adams—one seems to be back again at the beginning, except that being "back" means more than it did.[23] Similarly, Fleda's built up reveries and imaginings have been "redirected" back into their ongoing consequences, and the result is a rude awakening. Thus, in contradiction to the many "symbolic" readings of the Poynton fire, I am suggesting the purpose and effect of the dénouement is almost one of setting up and then rejecting such symbolic realms—or at least the transcendent correspondences such readings imply. Judged this way, the scene would function basically like the concluding stanzas of the Robert Frost poem earlier examined in this book.[24]

It cannot be too greatly stressed, however, that the deflation of Fleda's "idea" in no way undermines what is basically James's compassionate and sympathetic view of her. For that very reason the scene is a delicate "compromise" between its comic and tragic elements. And if we do not respond to them both simultaneously, we are again rejecting that positive, middle, "in-between" territory demanded by a pragmatistic mediating view of the real. If I may appropriate the ethical language and criteria of my discussion of Fleda herself, James is here "using" his character well. Had he not subjected her to this rude awakening, he would not have fully respected her as a created "center"—in effect a real person, a someone who, like Isabel Archer, is not a "fixed constituent." And not to have allowed her to fall prey to her lovely "idea" at the particular *time* and *context* she did, would have disallowed her fallibility as a human being, also making her a "fixed constituent." The pragmatistic mind cannot give favors in those ways.

At the same time, my reading of the novel's ending does come round to making the point that commentators have always sensed about the conclusion, that it somehow recapitulates the central conflict. It does indeed, as Fleda once again engenders her aesthetic ideal disembodied from time and place and people, and then must give it up. James has seen his character through in the "Jourdain" way; his consistency in this respect is fully intact.

If, then, *The Spoils of Poynton* remains, as I suspect it will, an important "problem" novel in James's canon, perhaps the reason must be sought elsewhere than in the character of Fleda per se: if the problem is not at the level of ambulation, perhaps it is at the level of imagination; if not at the "Jourdain" level as such, perhaps it is at the level of imagination; if not at the "Jourdain" level as such, perhaps at the deepest structural level of polarity—a level anterior even to its "Jamesian-ness." Walter Isle observes that the free spirit is necessarily "fixed" by the conditions of life in which it finds itself, and that the novel reveals the "gap between perception and act," the "irreconcilable split between the self and life."[25] Such seem the effects of Fleda's successive defeats and Mona's triumphs. At the same time, Laurence Holland maintains that the novel "turns on the paradox that the renunciation and the hope, the sacrifice and the vision, virtually create each other; the act of renunciation and the vision of possession are the source and image of each other."[26] To the extent that readers sense these various contraries to be reconciled through the work, to that extent the novel becomes less of a problem. These relationships—between freedom and conditions, perception and act, self and life, renunciation and possession—*are* cases of genuine polarity. That they are made to relate imaginatively *as* polar—relate, that is, in the positive way Holland speaks of—would be altogether clear were the novel under discussion *The Portrait of a Lady*, in which these very same cases and deep structural network of polarity sustain it throughout. To the extent, however, that a reader senses what Isle calls a "gap" or "irreconcilable split" between them (not as a thematic issue, but in the full matrix of the work itself), to that extent one can speak of James's "uncertainty" in intention—or ambiguity. The issue, as always, is between dichotomy and polarity, between juxtaposition and interpenetration.[27] In my judgment *The Spoils of Poynton* is ultimately unified organically through polarity, but not nearly so clearly and obviously as in much of James's comparable best fiction. Indeed, its prevailing tenor of indeterminacy does not only make it compatible with still another of William's philosophic doctrines; it also give this book its affecting power—as if its very tentativeness, like Henry's famous metaphor of the silken web of consciousness, draws reader after reader to it.

Notes

1. From *Henry James & Pragmatistic Thought: A Study in the Relationship between the Philosophy of William James & the Literary Art of Henry James* (Chapel Hill: University of North Carolina Press, 1974), pp. 134–151. Edited by the author. The " 'Jourdain' Relationship" refers to the best known of Henry James's repeated claims of identity of his work with the thought of William: "Then I was lost in the wonder of the extent to which all my life I have (like M. Jourdain) unconsciously pragmatised. You are immensely & universally *right.*" In Moliere's *Le Bourgeois Gentilhomme*, "M. Jourdain" discovers from the Philosophy Master that for forty years he has without knowing it been speaking "prose." James is saying that William's thought identifies his own idiom—his prose. William, like the Philosophy Master, in no way causes or determines that idiom, but he does name it. William's *Pragmatism* (1907), the book which elicited this response by Henry, is subtitled *A New Name for some Old Ways of Thinking*. The study exhibits the various ways that William's thought in effect keeps naming Henry's "way of thinking" in the novelist's writing.

2. R. P. Blackmur, "Introduction," *The Aspern Papers* and *The Spoils of Poynton* (New York: Dell Publishing Co., Inc., 1959), p. 12. A good summary of critical argument over *The Spoils* and in particular the character of Fleda Vetch may be found in Oscar Cargill, *The Novels of Henry James* (New York: Macmillan Co., 1961), pp. 218–43, supplemented by James W. Gargano, "*The Spoils of Poynton*: Action and Responsibility," *Sewanee Review* 69 (1961):650–60, and Robert C. McLean, "The Subjective Adventure of Fleda Vetch," *American Literature* 36 (1964): 12–30.

3. Leon Edel, *Henry James: The Treacherous Years: 1895–1901* (Philadelphia and New York: J. B. Lippincott Co., 1969), p. 161.

4. This was the argument proposed in the first of Eliseo Vivas's two notes in "Henry and William (Two Notes)," *Kenyon Review* 5 (1943): 580–94. In *The James Family* (New York: Alfred A. Knopf, 1947), p. 683, F. O. Matthiessen concedes that some readers might believe that Henry was "warning" William in *The Spoils of Poynton;* nevertheless, "Fleda (Vetch)," Matthiessen feels, "though WJ [*sic*] may not have so recognized her, was essentially one of his underdogs," whereas William himself could "have indicated the psychological weaknesses in HJ's free spirits, in so far, at least, as they were represented by the extreme case of Fleda, who was fastidious to the point of being neurotic." Vivas's argument—the moral opposition— is most fully restated by William H. Gass, "The High Brutality of Good Intentions," *Accent* 18 (1958): 62–71, in which both *The Portrait of a Lady* and *The Spoils of Poynton* are brought to bear on the issue. For Gass "[t]he impatience which James generates in the reader and expresses through Mrs. Gereth is the impatience, precisely, of his brother: for Fleda to act, to break from the net of scruple and seize the chance . . . but Fleda Vetch understands, as few people in Henry James ever do, the high brutality of such good intentions. She cannot accept happiness on the condition of moral compromise." Finally, Walter Isle in *Experiments in Form: Henry James's Novels, 1896–1901* (Cambridge, Mass.: Harvard University Press, 1968), pp. 86, 110–11, cites Vivas's argument as "central to the moral scheme of the novel" and equates Mrs. Gereth with "pragmatism" and "a pragmatic conception of value"; his point, however, is that James shows the limitations both of Fleda Vetch's "altruistic idealism" and Mrs. Gereth's "pragmatism."

5. Henry James, *The Art of the Novel*, ed. R. P. Blackmur (New York: Charles Scribner's Sons, 1934), p. 129.

6. Matthiessen, *The James Family*, p. 337. William on occasion could respond positively to Henry's later manner, especially in shorter works. Thus he speaks of the "hard enamel finish" of the collection *The Better Sort* (1903).

7. Yvor Winters, *In Defense of Reason* (Denver: Alan Swallow, 1947), p. 338. Winters nevertheless views the effect of Fleda's morality on the reader as "essentially neurotic," p. 320.

8. The most satisfying discussions to date of this difficult book are by Walter Isle, *Experiments in Form*, pp. 77–119, Lawrence Holland, *The Expense of Vision: Essays on the Craft of Henry James* (Princeton: Princeton University Press, 1964), pp. 57–113, and James Gargano's "*The Spoils of Poynton:* Action & Responsibility."

9. Henry James, *The Art of the Novel*, pp. 129, 131.

10. Henry James, *The Spoils of Poynton*, in *The Novels and Tales of Henry James* (New York: Charles Scribner's Sons, 1908), 10:46–47. Subsequent references will be to this volume of the New York Edition and will appear in brackets just after the quoted material.

11. Projecting "the possible other case" is the heart of James's definition of "operative irony" in *The Art of the Novel*, p. 222. James's entire scheme of individuals who are wrong for the right reasons, and vice versa, is built on this conception.

12. Henry James, *The Spoils of Poynton* (London: Penguin Books, 1963).

13. William James, *Some Problems of Philosophy: A Beginning of an Introduction to Philosophy* (New York: Longmans, Green & Co., 1911) p. 147.

14. The use of "more-and-less" throughout the essay, as well as "re-direction" and certain other highlighted phrases or terms, i.e. "mediated," "conjunctive," etc., refers to key ideas in William James's pragmatistic thought—especially his epistemology of human consciousness—elaborated elsewhere in the study.

15. Henry James, *The Art of the Novel*, pp. 129, 131.

16. "Saltatory" refers to William James's epistemological opponents in his book *The Meaning of Truth* (1909), a book Henry James highly praised and with which he again identified his own work. William opposes "saltatory" relations, i.e. jumping from one end term to

another, to his own view of "ambulatory" relations, or "made out of intervening parts of experience through which we ambulate in succession." The issue has to do with the nature and drama of cognition. Henry, like William, is, in William's words "ambulatory through & through," inasmuch as knowing occurs through "a bridge of intermediaries, actual or possible"—the later prose idiom of the novelist.

17. A good example of this same quality is Fleda's enormously warm response to and "creation" of the character of the deceased maiden-aunt of the dower house at Ricks. See especially her conversation with Mrs. Gereth in chap. 21, where she lauds Mrs. Gereth's artistic arrangement of the maiden-aunt's modest furnishings and then invokes intimately the very moral character of the deceased lady—all of which Mrs. Gereth finds both amusing and yet fascinating, as though "finding herself seated at the feet of her pupil" (249). It is also true, however, that the maiden-aunt probably inspires Fleda by having lived a life of renunciation and dignity. The sheer extent of this quality in James's heroine can be seen too in her reaction at one point to Owen's dress, when, after responding favorably to his attire, she thinks: "this in turn gave him—for she never could think of him, or indeed of some other things, without the aid of his vocabulary—a tremendous pull" (150).

18. Walter Isle has also noted this "wrong conclusion" from Fleda's declaration, *Experiments in Form*, p. 112.

19. Edel, *The Treacherous Years: 1895–1901*, pp. 163, 164.

20. See, for example, Blackmur, "Introduction," p. 14, and Isle, *Experiments in Form*, pp. 114–17; on the other hand, McLean's reading of the ending, "The Subjective Adventure of Fleda Vetch," pp. 28–29, as the "burning away" of Fleda's "illusion" may seem at first similar to mine, but it is actually as far—even farther—from my reading than the "symbolic" ones I criticize. His entire argument for her "subjective adventure" is a matter of reversing things into "unreliability." His casual reference to Fleda's "ethical relativism," p. 19, has no relationship whatever to my discussion of her ethic, and is instead his singly turning-the-screw on previous commentary on her "superior" morality.

21. See William James, *The Meaning of Truth* (New York: Longmans, Green and Co., 1909), pp. 142–44. This is again part of William's argument on behalf of "ambulation."

22. Henry James, *The Art of the Novel*, pp. 33–34.

23. James's "ambulatory" mode in the late prose can be shown as constantly circular, while yet each "return" accrues additional meaning. A letter to Henry Adams was used in the study to illustrate and elaborate this pragmatistic principle. James spoke of his best work as possessing "superior roundness."

24. The poem is "Neither Out Far Nor In Deep"; the explication brings out the same "circular" principle above.

25. Isle, *Experiments in Form*, pp. 92–93, 108, 117.

26. Holland, *The Expense of Vision*, p. 109.

27. The principle of Coleridgean polarity is invoked throughout this study as the ultimate source for James's artist unity and the expression of his creative process. It is also proposed as the undergirding principle for operative irony, especially those instances where characters are wrong for the right reasons (i.e. John Marcher) or vice versa (i.e. Lambert Strether). In this respect James's polarity exhibits a level of unity deeper than any accounted for in William's doctrines, in which unity is always said to reside in experience itself as "conjoined," "concatenated," "confluent" (note how closely these conceptions correspond to "ambulatory relations" made by "intervening parts of experience"). As a devoted pluralist, William perhaps "slighted" the unifying principle, but that issue does not alter nor is it pertinent to the "Jourdain" relation of Henry to William's thought. Polarity in Henry James is the power or agency he shares with *other* great imaginative writers, whereas William's doctrines, including that of experience-as-"confluence," are what enunciate Henry's *distinctive*, or "Jamesian," elements. On this general issue of James's polarity while yet incorporating all William's doctrines, see especially pp. 115–120 in this study.

Moral Geography in
What Maisie Knew

Jean Frantz Blackall*

The difficulties for the reader of *What Maisie Knew* are inherent in the remarkably complex technical problem James set himself, that of rendering the intellectual and moral evolution of a child. Because Maisie is represented as passing from very early childhood to the verge of adolescence, she does not have the more nearly fixed perspective of an adult protagonist. Only at the end is she old enough to be confronted with a major decision without the sacrifice of verisimilitude. Confronting her with such a trial, however, was the means by which James could achieve depth as well as ironic effect. Hence he begins with a heroine whose perceptions are oriented to the material world and ends with one who is more concerned with abstractions. Because Maisie is still very young at the end, there is also a discrepancy between the conclusion of the plot and the symbolic conclusion. She can now think independently, but on the morning that she tries it, Mrs. Wix helps with the back hooks. In other words, Maisie's independence of spirit cannot be corroborated by an independent action on her part, such as Isabel's returning to Gilbert Osmond or Milly Theale's leaving her fortune to Densher. Instead, Maisie goes off to England with Mrs. Wix, to the consternation of most readers. And because Maisie remains a child, limited in knowledge and in the terms with which to frame concepts, the maturing of her conviction depends to an uncommon degree on schematic symbolization. Normally James can rely more heavily on conversation to bring out point of view and on more subtle imagery than is at Maisie's command. Maisie's rapidly changing perspective, the final discrepancy between action and symbolism, and the perhaps excessive dependence on symbolism in the Boulogne scenes all make particular demands upon the reader.

The thematic statement of the novel, and particularly the interpretation of its ending, becomes clearer, however, when one scrutinizes James's techniques for projecting Maisie's mental development. For despite the limitations of her knowledge Maisie's insights consistently modify and increase, and her power to evaluate adult behaviour exists from early in the novel. By examining the nature of the methods and terms she adopts to reason out her perplexities one can discern the development of her mind and insights. By tracing the augmentation of her knowledge one can see the basis and context for each of her choices. In what follows I should like to illustrate this process in the early chapters and then to focus upon the subtle symbolic plotting of the Boulogne scenes, which has consistently been neglected despite the amount of thoughtful criticism addressed to this work. My purpose is to orient the reader to Maisie's level of understanding

*Reprinted from the *University of Toronto Quarterly* 48 (Winter 1978/79):130–48. Reprinted by permission of the author and University of Toronto Press.

apart from his adult consciousness of the ironies attendant upon her naive perceptions of the adult world and of her own relationships to it. By this mode of approach it can be shown that *What Maisie Knew* is consistent with the James canon both in its affirmation of an ideal stance (whatever the cost to the suffering protagonist) and in its characteristic fusion of aesthetic and moral values.[1]

I

F. W. Dupee observes that "Maisie first sees [the universe of her elders] as a jumble of material particulars: loud laughs, quarreling voices, violent hugs and equally violent pushes, beards, teeth, eyes and eyeglasses, jewels, cigars." "To know the actualities of things" Maisie must piece these together.[2] In undertaking this task her principal difficulty is one described by James in his preface: "Small children have many more perceptions than they have terms to translate them; their vision is at any moment much richer, their apprehension even constantly stronger, than their prompt, their at all producible, vocabulary."[3] None the less, Maisie progressively adopts terms of comparison and description from the only sources of information at her disposal: games or playthings, stories, and outings about London. By examining subjects, relationships, and experiences she understands, she seeks to characterize the people and to impose order on the unrelated particulars of the adult world she does not understand.

Such a task is initially perplexing and the adult world out of focus, diverting but not informative: "She was taken into the confidence of passions on which she fixed just the stare she might have had for images bounding across the wall in the slide of a magic lantern. Her little world was phantasmagoric—strange shadows dancing on a sheet" (23). Furthermore, Maisie's nurse discourages seeking knowledge:

> By the time she had grown sharper . . . she found in her mind a collection of images and echoes to which meanings were attachable—images and echoes kept for her in the childish dusk, the dim closet, the high drawers, like games she wasn't yet big enough to play. The great strain meanwhile was that of carrying by the right end the things her father said about her mother—things mostly indeed that Moddle, on a glimpse of them, as if they had been complicated toys or difficult books, took out of her hands and put away in the closet.
>
> (25)

Maisie, for that matter, is herself most concerned with holding things by the right end: "He said I was to tell you, from him, . . . that you're a nasty horrid pig!" (26). Thus far James underscores the fact that there is no evaluative faculty operative in Maisie's mind. Presently, however, she is old enough to re-examine the confiscated toys: "It was literately a moral revolution. . . . The stiff dolls on the dusty shelves began to move their arms and legs; old forms and phases began to have a sense that frightened her" (28). The consequence is that she makes her first independent decision, that she will no longer serve as a "messenger of insult" (28).

Next Maisie tackles the problem of her father's relationship to her governess, Miss Overmore, whom she had had to leave behind when she returned to her mother's house. Maisie asks direct questions, to be met with bursts of laughter and *doubles entendres* from her father and judgments on his "horrid" humour from Miss Overmore. Maisie recognizes that she has committed an error, and decides to reason out the matter with her French doll rather than to press her inquiries among the house-maids: "Little by little . . . she understood more, for it befell that she was enlightened by Lisette's questions" (41). Though Lisette cannot always supply answers, she is helpful in gauging the change in Miss Overmore after her marriage to Beale: "Even Lisette, even Mrs. Wix had never, [Maisie] felt, in spite of hugs and tears, been so intimate with her as so many persons at present were with Mrs. Beale and as so many others of old had been with Mrs. Farange" (58). And she supplies Maisie with a much needed measure for registering the degree of her delight with her new stepfather: "he was by far the most shining presence that had ever made her gape. . . . No, nothing else that was most beautiful ever belonging to her could kindle that particular joy—not Mrs. Beale at that very moment, not papa when he was gay, nor mamma when she was dressed, nor Lisette when she was new" (59). The initiation of this relationship finishes Lisette; hereafter Sir Claude will be Maisie's most reassuring companion. This is one of the first of those substitutions of interest by which her maturing can be gauged. She now happily sets out for her mother's house with Sir Claude.

School has never been an oppressive matter under the preoccupied Miss Overmore (Mrs. Beale) or the ignorant Mrs. Wix, but Mrs. Wix has introduced Maisie into her own limited intellectual world: "She took refuge on the firm ground of fiction . . . Her conversation was practically an endless narrative, a great garden of romance" (37). From this garden Maisie plucks all the characterizations she needs for the present: Sir Claude, when he laughed at Mrs. Beale "looked quite as Mrs. Wix in the long stories she told her pupil, always described the lovers of her distressed beauties—'the perfect gentleman and strikingly handsome' " (62). Maisie returned with him to Mrs. Wix as a "rescued castaway" (66) and "set her teeth like an Indian captive" (67) in obedience to his request that she not tell her mother any particulars about his visit to Mrs. Beale. Finally, when she sees her mother for the first time in a year, she applies her reading to account for

> her ladyship's remarkable appearance, her violent splendour, the wonderful colour of her lips and even the hard stare, the stare of some gorgeous idol described in a story-book, that had come into her eyes in consequence of a curious thickening of their already rich circumference. Her professions and explanations were mixed with eager challenges and sudden drops, in the midst of which Maisie recognized as a memory of

other years the rattle of her trinkets and the scratch of her endearments, the odour of her clothes and the jumps of her conversation.

(68)

These characterizations all happen to be accurate, despite their fictional origins. But Maisie's comprison of her mother's eyes with those of an idol most immediately indicates that her perspective is changing. Until now Ida has been one of those obscure muddles of intensive particulars that Maisie could not assemble, "all kisses, ribbons, eyes, arms, strange sounds and sweet smells" (26), but now such a conglomeration is "a memory of other years." Maisie has hit on an image that focuses her sense of her mother's presence, and the "gorgeous idol," which accounts not only for Ida's artificial, theatrical eyes but also for her great height and metallic splendor (119–23, 168), will be implicit in every subsequent view she has of Ida. She here indicates her progress in imposing order on the concrete elements of her world.

Once a source of confusion and now parts which can be organized into a large visual pattern, observed particulars will eventually become for Maisie the index to obscure adult facts and relationships. She will note, for example, that the American Countess's "brightness" lies in her possessions; her drawing-room is that "of a lady . . . whose things were as much prettier than mamma's as it had always to be confessed mamma's were prettier than Mrs. Beale's" (145). She will discern that Sir Claude's resources are not unlimited (despite the fact that he has been an easy distributor of shillings); her father can "offer her the privilege of six rows of chocolate bonbons, cutting out thereby Sir Claude, who had never gone beyond four rows" (148). And the Countess's smile, which is "interested" like that of the Captain, suggests a logical equation: "Papa's Captain—yes—was the Countess" (158).

Meanwhile, one sees that Maisie's judgment is undergoing modification as well as her ability to interpret material particulars. When she characterized Sir Claude as a perfect story-book hero, she was trying to catch the effect of his "brightness" upon her; and seeing herself as an Indian captive was make-believe. To the reader the possible limitations of such a hero in non-fictional situations are more apparent, as well as the ironies implicit in Maisie's self-characterization. Most important, however, these images (62, 67) emphasize by contrast the greater degree of her discrimination after a short interval (79–80). Maisie is about to make her first judgment of Sir Claude. She had agreed willingly not to mention how much Mrs. Beale appeared to like him because her own earliest conviction had been of the value of not carrying tales. But when Sir Claude ever so lightly invites her sanction of a plan for Mrs. Beale to pay her a visit, "And if you should suggest . . . that we might somehow or other, hide her peeping in from Mrs. Wix—" (79), Maisie makes her second moral discrimination, between withholding a comment and committing a deceitful act: "There came to her from this glance at what they might hide the first small glimpse of something in him that she wouldn't have expected. There had been times when she had had to make the best of the impression that she herself was deceitful; yet she had never concealed anything bigger than a thought" (79–80).

Thus we see that Maisie's perspective is constantly maturing. She has exchanged an undiscriminating point of view for an analytic and judicial one, a transition marked by her putting aside simpler for more complex toys. She has exchanged the companionship of her doll for that of Sir Claude. By drawing on story-books she has been able to characterize her feelings about her mother and Sir Claude. The methods that I have so far illustrated are consistent in the novel. Since Maisie constantly draws on her immediate experience to interpret situations, her substitution of more "adult" references for childish ones progressively marks her greater knowledge, and the relevance of her comparisons indicates the degree of her understanding. After the Folkestone chapters, however, there is a deepening of effect. Although this change is ostensibly occasioned by Maisie's growing older, it is also consequent upon a modification in James's technique for projecting her mental experiences.

II

Until now the narrator has been overtly guiding the reader, helping him to grasp Maisie's perspective and insights by explicitly stating the comparisons and points of resemblance that she makes. He has been describing Maisie's point of view or state of mind. Or alternatively he has been prompting the reader's responses by invoking a metaphorical language appropriate to Maisie in substance but beyond her in implication. The "games" figures ironically describe her condition and her perceptions of the world. For the most part, however, Maisie has been preoccupied with interpreting material particulars and with defining her sense of persons. The added complexity in the Boulogne chapters is that she is more consistently delving into the world of ideas. In order for her to figure in the judgment scene at the end of the novel, James must sustain the effect of her mind at work on an abstract problem. He must represent the pulls and pressures she experiences in trying to reach a decision that relates to moral concepts without expressing these concepts.

To achieve these ends James sustains Maisie's point of view by objectifying rather than conceptualizing her alternatives. "I so despair of courting her noiseless mental footsteps here that I must crudely give you my word for its being from this time forward a picture literally present to her" (221). Maisie moves from one setting to another in Boulogne. Each of these gradually accrues symbolic overtones as a consequence of who is present there, of what that person and Maisie see and talk about, and of subtle verbal promptings that associate one such occasion with another. As the reader watches Maisie go from one to another setting or recalls something that happened in one or another, he is in fact perceiving her mind at work in an externalized, correlative pattern. Though James's technique is far more subtle, it resembles that of the morality play, in which an Everyman moves physically among symbolized alternatives. Maisie for her part moves in a symbolic landscape. In what follows my objectives are to identify those settings that function symbolically, to propose how their symbolic meanings accrue and what they may be, and then to show how, on the final day, the day of decision-making, Maisie's actual peregrinations about the city of Boulogne with Sir Claude objectively correlate the internal process of decision-making, how her moral choice is enacted in "a picture literally present to her," and to us as readers.

At Boulogne the action has temporarily halted. Sir Claude has fled with Maisie, and deserted by Ida at Folkestone, he calls himself "free." But he has limited funds and does not know what Mrs. Beale's next move will be, so he makes no further plan. On the second day Mrs. Wix arrives to be Maisie's companion. When Sir Claude hears from Mrs. Beale, therefore, that she has been deserted by her husband, he sets out for London despite Mrs. Wix's protests. Mrs. Wix is horrified at Sir Claude's move, and she takes advantage of his absence to indoctrinate Maisie in her own version of what it means to have a moral sense.

Mrs. Wix is also susceptible to Sir Claude's bounty, however, so that she and Maisie avail themselves of the equipage reserved for them in his absence and spend much of their time in outings: "Best of all was to continue the creep up the long Grand" Rue to the gate of the *haute ville* and, passing beneath it, mount to the quaint and crooked rampart, with "its rows of trees, its quiet corners and friendly benches where brown old women in such white-frilled caps and such long gold earrings sat and knitted or snoozed. . . . They sat together on the old grey bastion; they looked down on the little new town . . . and across at the great dome and the high gilt Virgin of the church" (211). This rampart of the *haute ville* is the most prominent of the Boulogne settings both because of the number of sustained references to it and because it is dominated by the view of the golden Virgin. Edwin T. Bowden has pointed out the "psychological realism" of Maisie's "find[ing] herself idly interested in the madonnas of the National Gallery or the great golden madonna of Boulogne. . . . To a little girl hated by one mother and cynically made use of by another, the madonna image would naturally evoke an instinctive fascination." Ward S. Worden observes that the Madonna "serves to emphasize the unworldly quality of Maisie's purity and knowledge, and the sacrifice that she, unlike all the adults, finds the strength to make."[4] Though one grants both these interpretations, the implications of the Madonna are still more various. As a commanding figure this one symbolizes a new point of reference in Maisie's sensibility and thought.

Formerly her mother's looming figure has dominated the horizon of Maisie's childhood in a physical sense and, in the metaphor of the idol, in a symbolic sense as well. But at Folkestone Maisie rejected Ida, faced up to her, was angered rather than frightened by her for the first time. Thus the statue of the Madonna, because it is a traditional symbol of devoted motherhood and because it appears just after Maisie and her own mother have parted company, replaces the figure of the idol with all its connotations of artificiality and remoteness and hardness and paganism. In rejecting Ida Maisie also casts off symbolically all those qualities in Ida that are alien to herself. She thereby initiates a process of divesting herself of adult influences that will persist throughout the scenes in Boulogne. "They went back to the rampart on the second morning—the spot on which they appeared to have come furthest in the journey that was to separate them from everything objectionable in the past" (212). Now under the tutelage of Mrs. Wix but not solely dependent on her, Maisie seeks a new point of reference. She is not to find it in Sir Claude or Mrs. Beale, the substitutes for her real parents, but in a form of conviction that is partially symbolized in the figure atop Boulogne Cathedral. On Maisie's intellectual horizon the Madonna supplants the idol and thereby suggests a change in her moral orientation.

This implication is supported from a different quarter. In *What Maisie Knew* light and dark do not have traditional symbolic connotations of good and evil but clearly represent Maisie's superficial reactions and preferences. Thus Mrs. Beale has always been bright or radiant, likewise Sir Claude, Beale Farange with his blond beard, and Ida in her bejewelled splendour. The American Countess's drawing-room, whatever sinister connotations may attach to it for the reader, was to Maisie the most brilliant place she had ever seen. Mrs. Wix, on the other hand, has always been dingy because, viewed externally, as Maisie originally viewed everyone, Mrs. Wix is old and ugly.[5] The Countess, for all her bright possessions and her kindness to Maisie, which Maisie acknowledges (216), is grotesque, "almost black" (142). Most notably, the paintings of the Madonnas in the National Gallery had no charm for her when she was younger—and when she was primarily under the influence of Sir Claude—because she saw them externally and not for qualities they might symbolize. These were "gaunt" (100), "ugly Madonnas" with "uglier babies" (99). Now for the first time a pleasing brightness attaches to something that has also the connotations of "elevated" or "fine": this is "the high gilt Virgin" (211), "the great golden Madonna" (214), "their gilded Virgin" (224). and when one of the old women on the rampart delights Maisie and Mrs. Wix by speaking to them, the brightness of the figure blends into a much broader prospect, thereby promoting another symbolic connotation.

> She watched beside Mrs. Wix the great golden Madonna, and one of the earringed old women who had been sitting at the end of their bench got up and pottered away.
>   "Adieu, mesdames!" said the old woman in a little cracked, civil voice—a demonstration by which our friends were so affected that they bobbed up and almost curtseyed to her. They subsided again, and it was

shortly after, in . . . a phase of almost somnolent reverie, that Maisie
most had the vision of what it was to shut out from such a perspective so
appealing a participant [as Sir Claude]. It had not yet appeared so vast
as at that moment, this prospect of statues shining in the blue and of
courtesy in romantic forms.

(214)

The Madonna not only has supplanted the past and all in that past which
is alien to Maisie's own nature, but also suggests the beauty to Maisie of
certain other qualities as yet imperfectly definable but which imply gracious and kindly attitudes in human relationships as these find expression
in "forms." In these moments Maisie is moving beyond the childish enjoyment of bright surfaces (the Countess's drawing-room, Mrs. Beale's bright
form, the Madonna as an object) toward an intuitive understanding of
brightness as an abstraction inherent in certain modes of conduct.

This is something of the process through which Maisie wordlessly
passes while she sits on the bench on the rampart. That she is exploring
imaginatively beyond Mrs. Wix's depth is pointed out as far as her historical sense is concerned (211), but that she is exploring beyond Mrs. Wix's
depth morally as well may also occur to the reader. In more explicit and
conscious terms Maisie ponders the magnitude of the sacrifice Mrs. Wix
has proposed: that she give up "her stepmother and her relative" (213),
who is also, because of these very relationships to Maisie, Sir Claude's
"greatest intimate" (213). Maisie senses that Mrs. Wix is right: "her perception of reasons kept pace with her sense of trouble" (213). Yet her natural
disposition as well as her lifelong habit is to keep the peace, so that she is
not ready to break with Mrs. Beale. She recalls that her parents called each
other "low sneak" for good reason (213), and neither is she ready to see Sir
Claude liable to such an epithet from Mrs. Beale. Finally, she reasons that
her father's defection has after all left her step-parents solely responsible
for her (217). For the moment, therefore, Maisie tries to avoid a crisis by
proposing a domestic foursome, and thereby brings down Mrs. Wix's fury
upon her. They end their morning weeping in mutual antagonism, but by
early afternoon "the idea of a moral sense mainly coloured their intercourse" (220). From this exchange with Mrs. Wix the rampart takes on two
further identifications in addition to those it derives from the proximity of
the Madonna. Here Maisie initiates the period of moral debate which is to
terminte in her rejecting each in turn of her adult companions in favor of
an independent position shared with none of them. And because Mrs. Wix
is her companion here and the instigator of these struggles, the rampart
also suggests her as a character and her influence.

The second symbolic setting is the *plage* and its environs, the part of
Boulogne which stirs Maisie's imagination and wonder from her first hours
in the city: "Her vocation was to see the world and to thrill with enjoyment
of the picture; she had grown older in five minutes and had by the time
they reached the hotel recognised in the institutions and manners of

France a multitude of affinities and messages" (185). That first morning the *plage* crystallized for her all the colourful, the enjoyable, and the adventurous elements in foreign travel: "The place and the people were all a picture together, a picture that, when they went down to the wide sands, shimmered, in a thousand tints, with the pretty organisation of the *plage*, with the gaiety of spectators and bathers, with that of the language and the weather, and above all with that of our young lady's unprecedented situation" (186). Here is that same imaginative response to the bright and the beautiful, coupled with the same instinct for order that leads Maisie to associate shining statues with romantic forms. The *plage* to Maisie is both a source of delightful impressions and a pleasing "organisation" of them.

Maisie's affinity for order is the side of her character that makes her susceptible to Mrs. Wix's moral instruction, since the observance of forms in human relationships may be the expression of convictions. The imaginative side of Maisie, on the other hand, is what Mrs. Wix cannot comprehend. While they sit together on the rampart she pries into it suspiciously and unsympathetically (212). The possibility of Mrs. Wix's being insensitive rather than Maisie morally obtuse is underscored when they take a walk along the beach: "The bathers, so late, were absent, and the tide was low; the seapools twinkled in the sunset and there were dry places as well, where they could sit again and admire and expatiate: a circumstance that, while they listened to the lap of the waves, gave Mrs. Wix a fresh fulcrum for her challenge. 'Have you absolutely [no moral sense] at all' " (220). A second insight prompted by this setting, then is that it measures Maisie's imaginative response to variety and beauty against Mrs. Wix's lack of this kind of susceptibility. The *plage* symbolizes the qualities that Maisie shares with Sir Claude just as the rampart stands for those she shares with Mrs. Wix.

There is another side to Sir Claude, however. When he and Maisie walked here on their first day in Boulogne (220), suddenly she lost his attention: "he stood there and with a kind of absent gaze—absent that is, from *her* affairs—followed the fine stride and shining limbs of a young fishwife who had just waded out of the sea with her basketful of shrimps" (188). This detail is weighted for Maisie as well as for the reader because she has begun to note the consistency with which he is distracted by attractive women (170–1, 182). His consistent distraction likewise finds a correlative in a setting in which diversion from any more urgent preoccupations is the order of the day. The *plage*, while Maisie moves under the moral aegis of Mrs. Wix, becomes a place of fleshly diversion and of irresponsibility: "they wandered again up the hill to the rampart [on the second day] instead of plunging into distraction with the crowd on the sands or into the sea with the semi-nude bathers. They gazed once more at their gilded Virgin: they sank once more upon their battered bench; they felt once more their distance from the Regent's Park [Mrs. Beale's house fronts the park]" (224).

The most sinister of the three principal Boulogne settings, however, is the salon that forms part of Sir Claude's suite at the hotel. This little room stands for the temptations that visit Mrs. Wix and Sir Claude and to which each succumbs. At first it would seem to be another of Mrs. Wix's moral strongholds, for here on her first evening in Boulogne she tearfully pleads with Sir Claude not to return to London and Mrs. Beale. Here the next evening, not without compunction (222), she instructs Maisie in the basis for judging Sir Claude and Mrs. Beale (chapter 26). That she is effective in the latter interview is apparent from the fact that Maisie in their subsequent conversation withholds all the reasons for not "sacrificing" Mrs. Beale to which she had cleaved in their exchange on the rampart that morning. At worst the salon in relation to Mrs. Wix would seem to remind us of her humourless, oppressive morality, which sends Maisie fleeing to the adjacent balcony to refresh herself with a renewed draught of the customs and manners of France (223).

In fact, however, the salon is Mrs. Wix's weakness. Maisie perceives on their way upstairs the very first night that their comfortable quarters have already begun to work upon Mrs. Wix's susceptibilities. She notes the grandiosity with which her governess refers to "their own apartments," "as if she had spent her life in salons" (200). And then, ironically, Mrs. Wix proceeds to chastise Sir Claude in a "little white and gold salon which Maisie thought the loveliest place she had ever seen except perhaps the apartment of the Countess" (190). Now the American Countess's apartment more than anything else was the realization of what money could buy. Everything of hers was the product and emblem of gold, from her "gilded nooks" (145) and "yellow silk sofa" (148, 157) to Beale Farange with "his wonderful lustrous beard" (146) and his "laced yellow uppers" (156). "You've an eye, love! Yes, there's money. No end of money" (156). So too the present confrontation is implicitly founded upon the question of what money can buy. Can Sir Claude purchase Mrs. Wix as the Countess acquired Beale Farange, with gold? Poor Mrs. Wix has never had enough money. To her even a modest amount symbolizes security. Maisie notes Mrs. Wix's imaginative grasp on "their own apartments" this evening simply because she had observed even in the old schoolroom days at Ida's that the desire for a roof over her head is a primary motive with Mrs. Wix. It was, for example, more directly accountable for Mrs. Wix's pressing Sir Claude to establish a home for Maisie than solicitude for Maisie's own plight:

> [Maisie] recognized the hour that in troubled glimpses she had long foreseen, the hour when . . . she shouldn't know "wherever" to go. Such apprehension as she felt on this score was not diminished by the fact that Mrs. Wix herself was suddenly white with terror: a circumstance leading Maisie to the further knowledge that this lady was still more scared on her own behalf than on that of her pupil. A governess who had only one

frock was not likely to have either two fathers or two mothers: accordingly, if even with these resources Maisie was to be in the streets, where
in the name of all that was dreadful was poor Mrs. Wix to be?

(90)

Secondly, because Mrs. Wix is poor, she has never enjoyed a status in life,
so that she is equally susceptible to money, or even to a kind word, as a
token of the acknowledgement of her existence. At Ida's "what dazzled
most was [Sir Claude's] kindness . . . not only the five-pound note and the
'not forgetting' her, but the perfect consideration" (70). "Even to the hard
heart of childhood there was something tragic in such elation at such hu-
manities: it brought home to Maisie the way her humble companion had
sidled and ducked through life" (70). Whenever Mrs. Wix has money or a
new dress, she glows (190), becomes assertive (194), because these give her
a new status. In Boulogne "it was perhaps half an effect of her present ren-
ovations, as if her clothes had been somebody else's: she had at any rate
never produced such an impression of high colour, of a redness associated
in Maisie's mind at *that* pitch either with measles or with 'habits' " (190).
These are the reasons, of course, why, with a whole new wardrobe from
Sir Claude (189) and a courteous send-off and a ten-pound note from Ida
(192), Mrs. Wix might pass in Boulogne "almost for sublime" (221). But her
sublimity, as again Maisie will perceive, consists in the extent to which she
resists temptation, not in her overcoming it.

When Sir Claude leaves them in Boulogne on the third day, Maisie
watches Mrs. Wix's temptation proceed in material terms. Certainly she
does not neglect Sir Claude's bounty in order to avenge herself on him for
having fled to Mrs. Beale: "They had ordered coffee after luncheon, in the
spirit of Sir Claude's provision, and it was served to them while they
awaited their equipage in the white and gold salon. It was flanked, moreover, with a couple of liquers, and Maisie felt that Sir Claude could scarce
have been taken more at his word" (219). Maisie understands, however,
that one in Mrs. Wix's position can be bribed with security, which to some
extent Sir Claude can offer her:

> Her appetite was a sign to her companion of a great many things and
> testified no less on the whole to her general than to her particular condi-
> tion. She had arrears of dinner to make up, and it was touching that in a
> dinnerless state her moral passion should have burned so clear. She par-
> took largely as a refuge from depression, and yet the opportunity to par-
> take was just a mark of the sinister symptoms that depressed her. The
> affair was in short a combat, in which the baser elements triumphed, be-
> tween her refusal to be bought off and her consent to be clothed and fed.

(210)

When two days later Mrs. Wix shows an equal susceptibility to being
bribed with consideration—which Mrs. Beale, newly arrived in Boulogne,
now offers her in order to get her way with Sir Claude—Maisie becomes
more coolly critical. She becomes "quite as interested in Mrs. Wix's moral

sense as Mrs. Wix could possibly be in hers; it had risen before her so pressingly that this was something new for Mrs. Wix to resist" (235). She and her governess have been united, hand in hand, on the ground of their mutual adoration of Sir Claude (226). Will Mrs. Wix now reverse herself for the sake of Mrs. Beale's consideration and the guarantee of support that Mrs. Beale's assurance seems to imply? Presently convinced that Mrs. Wix is not holding out, Maisie challenges her:

> "You don't answer my question," Maisie persisted. "I want to know if you accept her."
> Mrs. Wix continued to hedge. "I want to know if *you* do! . . ."
> "Him alone or nobody."
> "Not even *me?*" cried Mrs. Wix.
> ". . . Oh, you're nobody!"
>
> (241)

Satisfied that Mrs. Wix has been shaken, Maisie in a word rejects her along with Mrs. Beale. It is a delightful irony that Mrs. Wix, who has driven Maisie to the point of feeling the obligation to judge people morally, should become Maisie's first victim when she herself shows moral inconsistency.[6]

The respect in which the salon represents Sir Claude's temptation and defeat is obvious. Mrs. Beale simply usurps it, the room in which of all "their apartments" Mrs. Wix and Maisie have most gloried and by which they have measured their well-being: "They mounted to their apartments . . . and it was Maisie who . . . threw open the white and gold door. . . . [Their] situation had put on in a flash the bright form of Mrs. Beale" (227). Hereafter the salon is principally identified with Mrs. Beale, her presence in it frequently remarked (231, 238). And when Maisie awakes next morning to learn that Sir Claude has returned, Mrs. Wix underscores the point: " 'The salon isn't ours now. . . . It's theirs' " (247). She and Maisie and the pull they represent on Sir Claude's affections and sense of obligation have lost out to the greater attraction of Mrs. Beale.

III

The likeness of James's method to that of a morality play is most apparent on the last day. Now, the symbolizations having been set by the long preamble in Boulogne, Maisie is actually to choose. Now she moves, sometimes literally, sometimes in thought, among settings which symbolize her alternatives, trying to resolve a moral issue. Her companions are Sir Claude, the only adult whom she has not yet rejected, and an occasional personification she invokes to help her see things more clearly.

She awakes, after oversleeping, to Mrs. Wix's ominous announcements that Sir Claude has returned and that the salon is no longer theirs. She tries to "wake" also the "faculty of gladness" but is unsuccessful (242). While Maisie dresses, facts that will be involved in her imminent choice are underscored in a conversation with Mrs. Wix; the facts, for example, of Sir Claude's weakness and of Mrs. Beale's tenacity. At last, aware how "tremendously grave" the situation is, "Maisie spoke as if she were now dressed quite up to the occasion; as if indeed . . . she had put on the judgement-cap, 'I must see him immediately' " (247).

She goes to the salon, but Sir Claude is not there. He is on the balcony. This is Maisie's own setting, which symbolically reconciles the height and perspective of the rampart with the pleasure which the *plage* symbolizes in a less refined form. Over its rail "Maisie had hung a long time [on the evening Mrs. Wix catechized her] in the enjoyment of the chatter, the lights, the life of the quay made brilliant by the season and the hour" (223). Here Maisie, hearing a song about "amour," had wondered if it reached Mrs. Wix inside. "Maisie knew what 'amour' meant too, and wondered if Mrs. Wix did; Mrs. Wix remained within, as still as a mouse and perhaps not reached by the performance" (223–4). What the balcony has suggested to Maisie came out more explicitly next day when she wondered "how Mrs. Wix, with a devotion not after all inferior to her own, could put into such an allusion [to Sir Claude's fear of Mrs. Beale] such a grimness of derision" (225). In short, Maisie and Sir Claude are natures attuned, and because they are alike she loves him even though she comes to see his weakness. Her love is not corroded by judgments of him as Mrs. Wix's is—and the balcony is the setting in which this distinction between loving and judging first began to occur to Maisie. This last day begins, then, with Sir Claude and Maisie together: he emerges from the balcony which has been Maisie's, to which neither Mrs. Wix nor Mrs. Beale has ventured, for neither of them has experienced the kind of attachment Maisie and Sir Claude feel for each other.

Sir Claude is dressed for a holiday, "in light fresh clothes . . . [which] gave him a certain radiance" (248). But Maisie is no longer satisfied with bright externals. When, embarrassed, he hesitates to hold out his arms to her, "his pause made her pause and enabled her to reflect that he must have been up some time, for there were no traces of breakfast; and that though it was so late he had rather markedly not caused her to be called to him. Had Mrs. Wix been right about their forfeiture of the salon?" (248). By the time that they arrive at a café for breakfast, she is convinced that Mrs. Wix was right: "he had brought her out . . . to imitate indeed a relation that had wholly changed, a relation that she had . . . seen in the act of change when, the day before in the salon, Mrs. Beale rose suddenly before her" (253). Meanwhile Maisie delights in the café. Its "shaded, sprinkled coolness, [was] the scene, as she vaguely felt, of a sort of ordered mirrored licence, the haunt of those—the irregular, like herself—who went to bed or who rose too late" (252). An "ordered licence" has always been the combination that has appealed to Maisie. Now in a "jesting postponing perverting voice," which she recognizes is Sir Claude's fear speaking (253), not Sir Claude, he proposes that she desert Mrs. Wix and come to live with Mrs. Beale, near him, on the continent: "I put it to you. *Can* you choose freely?" (260). "Well," Maisie concludes for the moment, "it seemed wonderfully regular, the way he put it; yet none the less, while she looked at it as judiciously as she could, the picture it made persisted somehow in being a combination quite distinct—an old woman and a little girl seated in deep silence on a battered old bench by the rampart of the *haute ville*. It was just at that hour yesterday; they were hand in hand; they had melted together" (261). Here Maisie is reluctant to find the same fault in Sir Claude for which she had rejected Mrs. Wix. She and her governess had "melted together" for adoration of him, and then subsequently Mrs. Wix indicated that she seemed capable of betraying him for the security which an alliance with Mrs. Beale might represent. Is Sir Claude equally capable of betraying Mrs. Wix for what he wants? This is a new perplexity. Till now Maisie has been wearing the judgment cap, proceeding according to the "Mrs. Wix" side of her nature. Now she would like a respite: "Have we got to go back to the hotel? . . . I think I should like to see Mrs. Wix first" (263). Hereby Maisie successfully postpones decision-making. She cannot decide without a final estimate of Mrs. Wix, but Mrs. Wix is at the hotel, and they will not return to the hotel: "If they were afraid of themselves it was themselves they would find at the inn. She was certain now that what awaited them there would be to lunch with Mrs. Beale. All her instinct was to avoid that, to draw out their walk, to find pretexts, to take him down upon the beach, to take him to the end of the pier" (264–5). Afraid like Sir Claude, and for the moment evasive like Sir Claude, Maisie seeks the locale which suggests diversion, irresponsibility. And the "truants" (265) in fact spend all the interim between Sir Claude's question at breakfast and Maisie's answer late that afternoon in the lower city. There is no question of visiting such heights as Maisie has reached with Mrs. Wix. They go to the opposite extreme of irresponsibility, to "the far end of the *plage*" (265).

Eventually they go to the railway station for the Paris afternoon papers, and here Maisie's impulse to flee is excruciating. If they were to take the Paris train, she would in effect have decided to throw over Mrs. Wix. During these moments, however, she notices that the proprietor of the book stall in the station is "one of her favourite old women, in one of her favourite old caps" (265). The old women have appeared nowhere but on the rampart. One of them bidding her good-day had brought to Maisie's mind the possibility of a beauty in forms. Symbolically, then, her thoughts have left the station, the lower city in general, for the rampart, just as Maisie and Mrs. Wix had done literally yesterday. And Maisie's decision, when she gives it in a moment, represents a fusion of the two impulses in her that have been symbolized in the *plage* and the rampart. Her choice has been anticipated symbolically in her liking for the balcony "Yes, I've chosen. . . . I'll let her [Mrs. Wix] go . . . if you'll give up Mrs. Beale" (267). Maisie will prefer pleasure (Sir Claude) to forms (Mrs. Wix) if Sir Claude will prefer forms (his obligation to Maisie) to license (Mrs. Beale). The precedent that exists for Maisie is that her father preferred the Countess, with her "gilded nooks," to his parental relationship to her. Will Sir Claude, her surrogate father, prefer the bright presence of Mrs. Beale to her? But she is no longer acquiescent to adult demands out of the desire to please. She rejects pleasure divorced from forms: Sir Claude's proposal in the café had merely "seemed wonderfully regular." In reconciling the disparate elements in her own character Maisie hereby achieves an independence which is instantaneously signaled by her being no longer afraid (267). She has been afraid of herself in that she might allow her fear of Mrs. Beale or her love for Sir Claude to overrule her capacity to choose freely.

Now she has confronted him with exactly the same choice that has tormented her. Since he is a frailer agent, she supports him under the burden of his decision-making: "When at last they lounged off it was as if his fear, his fear of his weakness, leaned upon her heavily as they followed the harbour" (268). Back at the hotel, she encourages him to choose as she has, to come from the *plage* to the rampart rather than to the salon, to prefer pleasure modified by principle to pleasure divorced from principle:

> "If I give up Mrs. Beale—? . . ."
> "I won't even bid Mrs. Wix good-bye, Maisie continued . . . I'll go up to the old rampart."
> "The old rampart?"
> "I'll sit on that old bench where you see the gold Virgin."
> "The gold Virgin?" he vaguely echoed. But it brought his eyes back to her as if after an instant he could see the place and the thing she named—could see her sitting there alone.
>
> (269)

But Sir Claude makes the opposite choice, and that is why he sees Maisie sitting alone on the rampart, and why he will no longer be on the balcony when Maisie looks back at the end (280).

The subsequent battle in the salon is the dramatized restatement of all this process through which Maisie has passed spiritually, that of being tempted and tested by opposing forces. Now the theatre of Maisie's consciousness yields to the actual theatre of her final cataclysmic encounter with the competing adults. The appropriateness of her returning here is that the salon has been the testing-ground, the temptation, of both Mrs. Wix and Sir Claude. Here the one has succumbed to the bright lure of money and the other to that of sex. Now Maisie in her turn must irrevocably choose, and their previous weakness is the measure of her present strength. She rejects Mrs. Beale, parts reluctantly with Sir Claude, and subscribes to the custody of Mrs. Wix. She does not subscribe to Mrs. Wix as an individual, for Mrs. Wix, when she failed Maisie, became "nobody." James does weight Mrs. Wix's position. He identifies the periods of her influence with the rampart setting dominated by the symbol of the Virgin; she is both motherly, a figure of nurture, and a moral catalyst for Maisie. Secondly, he specifies that she is unafraid of herself and consequently of other persons. Sir Claude is afraid of himself and therefore never free of the manipulation of others; his weakness is the source of their power. Maisie, when in the railroad station she resists the temptation to flee decision-making, immediately has the same source of power as Mrs. Wix: "her fear . . . had been dashed down and broken" (267). But that she has forged for herself an independent personal conviction is manifest. Utterly rejecting the baseness and self-interest of Mrs. Beale, Mrs. Wix's lack of imagination and susceptibility to bribery, and Sir Claude's irresponsibility, she has accepted the moral imperative of Mrs. Wix modified by the appreciative faculty, by the sensibility of Sir Claude. She thereby becomes the childish prototype of all those F. W. Dupee has described as James's "greater figures," in whom "conscience is a form of sensibility, a style of life, a state of mind to which judgment is alien and goodness for goodness's sake immaterial. Intelligent without being intellectual, moral but not ethical, they reflect very little on conduct itself; and mainly they do what they have to do in order to be themselves."[8] That Maisie has rejected all her adult companions in a sense is what she herself knows when she says at the end, "I feel as if I had lost everything" (273). The price of her knowledge is that she has spiritually accepted the burden of responsibility for her own fate. Her reward is implied in the deeper sense of Sir Claude's remark, the answer to the question he himself had put her in the café: " 'she's free' " (277)—free to choose, yes but also capable of choosing freely.

Notes

1. Interpretations of this novel have tended to find expression in polar formulations. Is Maisie irrevocably corrupted by her experiences or does she escape untainted? The present reading affirms the latter view, which is also the majority view. (See Joseph A. Hynes, "The Middle Way of Miss Farange: A Study of James's *Maisie*," *ELH*, 32 [December 1965], 528–53, for a substantial bibliographical note indicating the positions held by previous interpreters.) If one grants that Maisie in some sense rises above her experience, however, there remains the question of the nature of her own peculiar insights and judgment at the end. Is she merely a pragmatic player in the game of renunciations that is forced upon her, and therefore a bruised survivor, as Hynes concludes? Alternatively, has she achieved moral insight sufficient to sustain her in a fallen world or is Maisie's own peculiar vision aesthetically informed? These contrasting emphases are represented by James W. Gargano in *"What Maisie Knew: The Evolution of a 'Moral Sense',"* *Nineteenth-Century Fiction*, 16 (June 1961), 33–46, and Tony Tanner in *The Reign of Wonder* (Cambridge: Cambridge University Press 1965), pp. 278–98, whose fine studies I have in mind in proposing, none the less, that Maisie's ultimate stance represents a fusion of moral and aesthetic impulses. There remains, finally, the question of the tone of the novel, initially formulated by F. R. Leavis and Marius Bewley in their debate over whether James's "comedy" here is essentially Dickensian or Jacobean, informed by laughter or horror (*The Complex Fate* [London: Chatto and Windus 1952]). The Jacobean argument has been elaborated by Martha Banta in "The Quality of Experience in *What Maisie Knew*," *New England Quarterly*, 42 (December 1969), 483–510, and Sallie Sears's reading asserts the logical extreme of the view that the reader is being entertained rather than deeply moved (*The Negative Imagination* [Ithaca, N.Y.: Cornell University Press 1968], pp. 28–31). The assessment of tone largely depends on how the individual reader responds to the ironies evoked by the contrast between Maisie's immediate perceptions of the adult world and the

grim realities of her condition. The extreme possible attitudes towards Maisie are illustrated, say, in the contrasting responses that James invites in *The Awkward Age* by his initial presentation of Little Aggie and Nanda, the one a caricature of innocence, and therefore amusing; the other a sentient victim, and therefore pathetic. My own reading of *Maisie* with regard to its symbolic plotting affirms a middle view. Because Maisie's perspective matures, the nature of the reader's response shifts gradually from a qualified laughter, dependent on her naivety, towards compassion and respect, consequent upon her growing spiritual autonomy.

2. F. W. Dupee, *Henry James*, rev. and enlarged ed. (Garden City, N.Y.: Doubleday 1956), p. 167.

3. *What Maisie Knew* (Garden City, N.Y.: Doubleday 1954), p. 10. Parenthetic page references hereafter refer to this text, which reproduces that of the New York Edition.

4. Edwin T. Bowden, *The Themes of Henry James*, Yale Studies in English, vol. 132 (New Haven: Yale University Press 1956), pp. 84–5; Ward S. Worden, "A Cut Version of *What Maisie Knew*," *American Literature*, 24 (January 1953), 504. For contrasting, and in my view untenable, interpretations, see Oscar Cargill, *The Novels of Henry James* (New York: Macmillan 1961), pp. 257–8; and Juliet Mitchell, "*What Maisie Knew*: Portrait of the Artist as a Young Girl," in *The Air of Reality*, ed. John Goode (London: Methuen 1972), pp. 185–6.

5. James perhaps indulges in a little *jeu d'esprit* by characterizing her as a burned-out candle: "[Her hair] played a large part in the sad and strange appearance, the appearance as of a kind of greasy greyness, which Mrs. Wix had presented on the child's arrival. It had originally been yellow, but time had turned that elegance to ashes, to a turbid sallow unvenerable white" (35). ("That elegance" is "its glow" in the first edition.) From time to time, either under the duress of moral indignation or of after-dinner liquers, the candle gets lit (190–1). She will momentarily flare up, not without sputtering, in the end (194), but she will also be susceptible to Mrs. Beale's manipulations. Her name suggests wick and wax: fire and pliability.

6. That Maisie judged accurately is twice confirmed. From Mrs. Wix's revelation to Maisie next morning that she feels Sir Claude walked out on Ida rather than vice versa (245), one can see that she had earlier switched allegiance from Ida, her employer, to Sir Claude not because Ida had established a liaison with Mr. Perriam as she then implied (86), but because Sir Claude represented bread and butter: " 'Supplies be hanged, my dear woman!' said their delightful friend. 'Leave supplies to me—I'll take care of supplies' " (92). That afternoon, when Maisie returns to the salon with Sir Claude, she learns from Mrs. Beale that Mrs. Wix has agreed to a domestic foursome (270), the exact reversal of her position on the rampart. Hence Mrs. Wix's behaviour is absolutely consistent gauged not according to her moral sense but according to her spirit of compromise.

7. Such matters as failure to keep one's word and desertion are accessible to Maisie as the bases for moral judgments without her having knowledge of adult sexual behaviour. Her ability to judge Sir Claude immoral for Mrs. Wix's reasons is not the test of Maisie's own integrity (innocence), as Sallie Sears seems to imply, nor is the reader without reference points for determining "any final attitude to take toward Maisie" if he ponders such mentalpictures as she contemplates in this interview. (*The Negative Imagintion*, pp. 24–5, 32.)

8. *Henry James*, pp. 106–7.

The Awkward Age

Marcia Jacobson*

In a New York Edition preface nearly as inadequate as the preface to *The Tragic Muse*, James presents *The Awkward Age* as a novel that started from a humble impetus and emerged as a significant technical success. He began, he tells us, with an interest in "minor 'social phenomena' " (IX, vi), the crises produced in English households when a daughter can no longer be relegated to the schoolroom but is considered too immature because of her unmarried state to be admitted to the adult conversation downstairs. As a theme, "It was not," he continues belittlingly, "a fine purple peach, but it might pass for a round ripe plum" (IX, vi). The *roman dialogué* practiced in the eighties and nineties by the popular French writer "Gyp" (Sibylle Gabrielle Marie Antoinette de Riquette de Mirabeau, Countess de Martel de Janville) and her follower Henri Lavedan struck him as the ideal form for such a light work—but with the text type set to look like a conventional novel, which James deemed more attractive to the English reader than the French playbook form. The resulting novel, however, greatly exceeded James's expectations. It grew to an extraordinary length according to some principle of which he professed absolute incomprehension, and it outgrew its initial association with "Gyp" to become more dense and complex than her work and at the same much tighter in construction. Looking back at the novel, James concluded, "The thing carries itself to my maturer and gratified sense as with every symptom of soundness, an insolence of health and joy" (IX, xxiii)—and he felt this in spite of the fact that the reception of the book had provoked his publisher to remark, "I've never in all my experience seen one [a book] treated with more general and complete disrespect" (IX, xv).

We have no reason to doubt James's satisfaction with the novel. But his account of the novel's origins is suspect. Examination of the book in its literary context reveals James's indebtedness to two enthusiasms of the nineties: the English dialogue novel and the New Woman novel. This background in turn accounts for the amplitude of James's book: both the dialogue novel and the New Woman novel were associated with issues larger than the "minor 'social phenomena' " that James began with; when added to his germ, they transfigured it. This is another of the many cases in which James's friends worked in the genres that he too tried, and did so with considerably more popular success than he had. We can assume that as in other cases, his sense of dignity governed his silence on the popular context of his work. But such silence has had the unfortunate effect of diminishing James's novel. Although modern critics have occasionally observed that *The Awkward Age* presents a richer picture of contemporary British life than

*This work appeared originally in the *Philological Quarterly*, 54 (Summer 1975):633–46; it was later incorporated in *Henry James and the Mass Market* (University: University of Alabama Press), 121–38. It is reprinted with permission from the *Philological Quarterly* and the University of Alabama Press.

James's preface suggests, his silence has permitted many to read this book, like *Maisie,* simply as a technical experiment—in this case overstressing James's indebtedness to the drama with its scenes and dialogue—or as an event in James's psychological history.[1]

The dialogue novel in English probably owes its initial impetus to "Gyp," although her novels were not available in translation until the mid-nineties and the form had appeared earlier in England. *Punch* ran occasional dialogues through the eighties and published a regular series called "Voces Populi" starting in 1888, while *Black and White* began a series called "The World We Live In" in 1892.[2] These series dialogues were short, unrelated or loosely related dramatizations of amusing social difficulties, prose cartoons in effect. The form was soon picked up by other newspapers and weeklies in both America and England, and the notion that witty dialogue was somehow appropriate to popular journalism may account for the willingness with which *Harper's Weekly* agreed to run *The Awkward Age.*[3] Once a popular taste for the form was evident, books in dialogue also began appearing—sometimes set up like playbooks, sometimes looking like conventional novels, and sometimes combining both forms. The public was eager for the genre no matter what it looked like.[4]

We know James read one English dialogue novel and can reasonably assume he saw others. In 1893, his friend E. F. Benson published *Dodo; A Detail of the Day,* a novel that attracted wide attention because it was generally understood to be a roman à clef fictionalizing Margot Tennant's witty and articulate social circle, the "Souls." Although James was not a member of the group, he could claim acquaintance with its members, and this circumstance alone probably would have prompted his interest in the book.[5] But we need not speculate, for James did read an early version of this book and reacted by commenting "delicately" on it: in one of his autobiographies, Benson notes James's response as being a "wisely expressed opinion, that opinion, in fact, being no opinion at all"[6] and quotes part of a letter in which James speaks rather generally of the value of style. In addition, James probably saw the work of other friends. F. Anstey (Thomas Anstey Guthrie) was the anonymous author of *Punch's* "Voces Populi" as well as other dialogue pieces and serials for *Punch.* He published a number of collections of these dialogues in the nineties along with *Lyre and Lancet: A Story in Scenes* (1895), a novel-length work. Violet Hunt published parts of her first dialogue novel, *The Maiden's Progress: A Novel in Dialogue* (1894), in a variety of journals, including *Black and White* and the *Pall Mall Gazette.* Since James published in the former and read the latter, he probably saw some of the sketches if not the novel as a whole. Hunt was soon recognized as an accomplished writer of the genre, and her next novel, *A Hard Woman: A Story in Scenes* (1895), was extensively reviewed and advertised. There were best sellers in the genre too. *The Dolly Dialogues,* by Anthony Hope (Anthony Hope Hawkins), first published as sketches in the

Westminster Gazette, appeared in book form in 1894 and was nearly as popular as his other book of the same year, *The Prisoner of Zenda*,[7] while Ellen Thornycroft Fowler's *Concerning Isabel Carnaby* was a best seller in the year that James wrote and began serializing *The Awkward Age*. It is against this background, in part, that James's novel should be judged.

Two observations must be made about these popular novels. First, the dialogue form serves no real function. Its use in *Dodo* is understandable, for the book depicts a circle famous for its witty and free talk. But Benson brings no critical intelligence to bear on this fact: his fictional characters simply talk a great deal because their life models did. Benson does not ask what their conversations tell us about the society he is depicting. In other novels, there is even less justification for the dialogue form. The characters are educated, articulate upper-class Englishmen and women, but none of the books depicts a group as tightly knit and as self-consciously intellectual as the "Souls." Instead, what we have in Anstey's, Hope's, and Hunt's books is talk for its own sake, emphasized by an extremely high percentage of dialogue in each book, chapters that are anecdotal in nature, and the use of the word "dialogue" or "scene" in the titles, calling the prospective reader's attention to the form. Fowler's novel is more conventional: the percentage of dialogue is high but the sections of dialogue are introduced by substantial prose passages. Yet here too the talk is not functional: situations often seem to exist so that characters can have an opportunity to talk, and they talk on far longer than need be.

James, as we might expect, used the dialogue form very self-consciously. His letter to Henrietta Reubell about *The Awkward Age* implies that, like Benson, he too had the "Souls" or a similar group in mind when writing: "I had in view a certain special social (highly 'modern' and actual) London group and type and tone . . . clever people at least would know who, in general, and what, one meant."[8] The novel itself, however, has never been identified as a roman à clef; instead, the talkative circle represents contemporary English upper-class society in general. James opens his novel with a conversation between Mr. Longdon, a man of fifty-five who has not been in London for the past thirty years, and Vanderbank, a man of thirty-four who is a member of the circle in question. Their discussion defines modern London life, identifying "talk" (IX, 11) as the factor which distinguishes it from the life Longdon had known there in his youth. And as James brings out the uninhibited quality of the talk, he hints—even this early in the book—that social life established on such grounds necessarily entails a loss. Van speaks for the moderns: "it strikes you that right and left, probably, we keep giving each other away. Well, I dare say we do. Yes, 'come to think of it,' as they say in America, we do. But what shall I tell you? Practically we all know it and allow for it and it's as broad as it's long. What's London life after all? It's tit for tat!" Longdon "earnestly and pleadingly" asks, "Ah but what becomes of friendship?" (IX, 19–20). In the remainder of *The Awkward Age*, James answers Longdon's question by allowing London life to reveal itself through its particular kind of talk. The dialogue form thus becomes a means of examining a society critically.[9]

The second point to be made about the dialogue novel is that with some variations the story of a flirtation involving a heroine who is in the much-used word of the period, "clever," is a favored plot.[10] Benson's Dodo is the most tough-minded of the heroines. She marries for status and money, not love, and continues to flirt with the man she cares for. When the death of her husband frees her, she becomes engaged to the man she loves but makes a second socially advantageous marriage. Although the way she uses men is distasteful, she captivates those around her with her beauty, her spontaniety, and above all her audacity. With her insincerities, her concern with social status, and her sharp tongue, she prefigures Hunt's much less attractive Hard Woman. Dolly Foster, in Hope's book is a sweeter example of the type. She too has rejected one suitor for a man of higher social status, but in her case, she seems to have acted wisely: her rejected suitor rather enjoys the role of disappointed lover. From his safe vantage point, he flirts with Dolly through the numerous dialogues in which she appears and talks of love in those in which she does not. While Dodo is brash, Dolly is more subtle, always pretending to an innocence she does not have. But her pretence is not malicious and she brings genuine delight to her friends. Isabel Carnaby is a third variation. She is not as pretty as Dolly and Dodo, but she is more intelligent and often witty. She is torn between her worldly impulses and her better self, and her struggle occupies most of Fowler's book. Ultimately her better instincts win and she marries a man who is both good and intelligent, though poor. In choosing him, she rejects a suitor whom she does not truly love but who could offer her a fine social position. She thus avoids repeating Dodo's mistake and so gratifies popular fondness for sentimentality and moral platitude.

Hunt's first heroine is particularly interesting in relation to her literary peers and to *The Awkward Age*. She is Mary Elizabeth Maskelyne, nicknamed Moderna, and as her name indicates, cast in a somewhat different mold from Dolly and Dodo. The book begins with her coming-out at eighteen and ends with her engagement at twenty-seven. In the nine intervening years, Moderna develops as something of a New Woman. She enjoys making herself attractive to men, but after a brief engagement to a straitlaced and over-protective suitor, she decides that she will remain a "bachelor girl." She never develops any sort of feminist ideology but instead expresses her modernity by self-indulgently doing what she wants. What she wants is never really risqué—at its worst, it is a timorous association with a Bohemian crowd—but her behavior is enough to make her mother feel quite displaced by her modern child.[11] Mrs. Maskelyne, expressing a common maternal sentiment in the nineties, laments that her daughter "wants to know, she wants to gain her own experience, she doesn't care to make use of her mother's before her. A mother is only a kind of helpless Survival of the Unfittest. . . ."[12] But at the end of the novel, Moderna behaves in the most traditional manner and decides to marry a wealthy, strong-willed, conservative English Lord. It is impossible to tell whether Hunt means to disparage Moderna's values, which she had treated rather sympathetically at first, or whether she is unthinkingly using a traditional romance ending.

In *The Awkward Age,* James varied the convention of the clever heroine in a significant way: she is no longer a young woman like her predecessors; instead, she is the *mother* of a young woman. Like her fictional predecessors, Mrs. Brookenham has a quick wit, ready sympathy, and a self-confidence that keep her at the center of her social circle. Her usual manner is neither as brash as Dodo's nor as sweet as Dolly's, yet she often plays at incomprehension or conciliation to avert a quarrel in her drawing room, and at the end of the novel, she acts as audaciously as Dodo. She is also similar to Moderna—but not to Moderna's mother. "[T]he modern has always been my own note" (IX, 166), Mrs. Brook tells her friends. And "the modern," as she interprets it, means acting as if she were younger than her forty-one years. This is most apparent in her relationship with her daughter, Nanda, who has just been allowed to leave the schoolroom and sit with the adults "downstairs." Nanda is sixteen or eighteen—perhaps nineteen; Mrs. Brook lies about her age. Further, Mrs. Brook tends to deny parental responsibility for her child: "Why *should* I ask any [questions]—when I want her life to be as much as possible like my own . . . From the moment she *is* down [stairs] the only thing for us is to live as friends. I think it's so vulgar . . . not to have the same good manners with one's children as one has with other people. She asks *me* nothing" (XI, 177). While Mrs. Maskelyne feels abandoned by her daughter, Mrs. Brook has virtually abandoned hers by treating her as a friend with whom one does not interfere. In casting his heroine as an older woman, James has inverted the traditional relationship between mother and daughter—and the inversion has major consequences for his novel.

As a result of her mother's denial of responsibility, Nanda herself takes on the abdicated maternal role. With a premature gravity, she feels that at eighteen her character has taken its final shape: "what I am I must remain. I haven't what's called a principle of growth" (IX, 214). This sense of maturity is reflected in Nanda's treatment of those around her. She offers her unhappily married and somewhat slow-witted friend Tishy Grendon the solace and direction a mother might a child. To Mr. Longdon, who loved her grandmother in vain, she offers both the affection that her grandmother withheld and the instruction in the ways of the present that a parent should offer. At one point, when she and Longdon are solemnly reflecting on the differences between past and present, "she put out to him the tender hand she might have offered to a sick child" (IX, 231). It is a telling gesture that beautifully characterizes their relationship. And even more important, she provides her mother with the guidance Mrs. Brook will not grant her. Nanda cannot help but recognize that her presence in her mother's drawing room necessarily causes guests to watch what they say out of deference to her unmarried state. According to her mother, she thoughtfully absents herself: "She won't have a difference in my freedom. It's as if the dear thing *knew*, don't you see? what we must keep back. She wants us not to have to think. It's quite maternal!" (IX, 166). It is appropriate that Nanda resembles not her modern young mother, but rather her old-fashioned grandmother.

Like many of her fictional predecessors, Mrs. Brook's main interest is her extramarital flirtation. But James complicates her situation through his inversion of the mother-daughter relationship. Mrs. Brook has picked the nouveau riche Mr. Michett as the member of her circle whom she would like for Nanda's husband. But Nanda is attracted to her mother's admirer, the aristocratic and impoverished Vanderbank. When Mrs. Brook learns this—and it says something for her own state of infatuation that she must be told and cannot perceive for herself—her first reaction is, "he'll never come to the scratch" (IX, 91). This is probably an accurate appraisal of Van. Although men of the 1890s frequently waited until their mid-thirties to marry, Van seems to be one of the numerous constitutionally cold men in James's work. His attention to his clothes and his comfortably furnished home despite his relatively tight finances suggest a finicky man whose own needs come first. His relationship with Mrs. Brook is, in spite of the jokes of their mutual friends, an innocent flirtation and not an affair. When Mr. Longdon recognizes Nanda's feelings for Van and understands that constant exposure to her mother's circle will lessen her marriageability by compromising her innocence, he proposes to Van that he, Longdon, put up a dowry for the girl. But Van still hesitates. If Mrs. Brook could simply wait in silence, she could keep Van on the terms she has always held him. But perceiving her daughter as a friend, she also recognizes her as a rival and so is too nervous to wait.

As James develops Mrs. Brook's rivalry with her daughter, he reveals the viciousness inherent in a society based on free talk and so uses a popular novel form for a new critical purpose. By casting a forty-one-year-old mother in a role conventionally held by a younger woman, James has given us a heroine whose behavior and attitudes can only be immature and inappropriate. Mrs. Brook shows her immaturity when she betrays Van's confidence and tells Mitchy, in Van's presence, that Mr. Longdon has offered to provide a dowry for her daughter. She characterizes the dowry as a bribe in order to discourage the scrupulous Vanderbank from accepting it. Her behavior recalls Van's earlier comment to Longdon that London life is "tit for tat," a process of "giving each other away." She is even more childish toward the end of the novel when her entire circle of friends gathers at Tishy Grendon's house. She is rude to everyone and at the end of the evening succeeds in forcing her daughter to admit publicly to having read a scandalous French novel. The admission is intended to make Nanda appear so worldly that Van will not take her and so endangered by her mother's circle that Mr. Longdon will adopt her. Ultimately, Mrs. Brook achieves both her objectives. But in the process she has talked too rudely, too bluntly, and too much; Van drops her as well as her daughter. Mrs. Brook is among the few heroines of dialogue novels whose flirtations end in failure. In meting out his punishment, James passes judgment on her and by implication on the society in which she had played a central role. Her defeat is James's condemnation of a society in which youth, modernity, and wit have taken the places formerly held by tradition, maturity, and wisdom.

The New Woman, as I noted in connection with *The Bostonians* began appearing in American fiction in the eighties. By the nineties, she was a staple of both English and American fiction, appearing often as a major character and even more often as a minor one, a sop to popular tastes, like the occasional aesthete. William Dean Howells, in a "Life and Letters" essay in *Harper's Weekly* in 1894, considered reasons for her frequent appearance in fiction. He suggested her present attraction was less that she enabled the writer to describe social change than that she had become a thoroughly conventional type: "I have my doubts of the existence of the New Woman on any extended scale, outside of the fancy of the writers and readers of certain books; the writers seem to have created her, and the readers believe in her. . . . The New Woman is the type of woman whom fictive art is just now dealing with, because she amuses, and because she is easier to do than the woman with less salient characteristics." By the end of the essay, Howells recanted somewhat, admitting that contemporary women "wish to know rather more of all sorts of things than they used," but he still insisted that her fictional counterpart had a distinguishable and conventional identity conferred on her by her self-dramatizing poses:

> She is distinguished, among those who have imagined her, from former phases of the eternal womanly. She is not what used to be called the woman of the period, she is by no means what used to be called fast, even in the less reproachful sense of the word. She is supposed to have certain views of marriage; she is supposed to have asked herself what her status would be if there was no marriage, in rare and extreme cases she is supposed to have tried to find out. Whether she is for the enlargement of her civic rights or not, as a rule, it would not be easy to say; but she takes herself seriously, and she wishes to be thought serious when she does not take herself seriously.[13]

One vehicle for the exhibition of the New Woman's views was the dialogue novel, for the genre gave her the opportunity to express herself at length. We see her as a major character in Hunt's books and as a minor character in Anstey's *Lyre and Lancet*—a novel about the social complications that occur when a poet and a veterinarian are each assumed to be the other. Another form in which the New Woman could be exhibited was the novel that contrasted the New Woman and her traditional sister. The form doubtlessly owes much to such earlier pairings as the Good and Bad Heroines, the Light and Dark Ladies, the Spiritual and Sensuous Women, but in the nineties the contrast is distinguished by the fact that the author thinks of his (or more usually her) characters as exponents in the contemporary discussion of the role of women. The first novel to use this contrast was a somewhat earlier book: Olive Schreiner's *The Story of an African Farm*, published in 1883 and an international best seller by 1887.[14] Although there is no evidence that James read this novel, it inspired similar works of fiction, and he probably knew some of them. A somewhat cryptic reference to Sarah Grand (Frances Elizabeth MacFall) in one of James's "London" columns in *Harper's Weekly* suggests that he was familiar with her best seller of 1893, *The Heavenly Twins*.[15] And it would have been difficult for him to escape knowledge of the work of an old friend, Eliza Lynn Linton. As a journalist, Linton had addressed herself to feminist subjects from the sixties on. In the nineties, she dealt harshly with the New Woman, castigating her in periodical articles (where she appears as "the Wild Woman") and in several novels, of which *The New Woman: In Haste and at Leisure* is representative. By combining a sensational topical issue with a conservative moral viewpoint, Linton attracted a large following and merits our attention now as, according to one modern critic, "a sound and faithful register of the times in which she lived."[16]

These novels of contrasting women illuminate *The Awkward Age* by presenting character types against which James's young heroines, Aggie— the ward of one of Mrs. Brook's friends—and Nanda, can be profitably evaluated. In spite of the fact that Schreiner and Grand, unlike Linton, considered themselves feminists, all three depict the traditional woman as a passive, suffering individual and the New Woman as a bold but tormented person who must come to terms with marriage whether she wishes to or not—thus giving substance to Howells's generalization. Schreiner's Em is limited by an "idea of love [that] was only service"[17] and so accepts a loveless marriage; her New Woman, Lyndall, refuses marriage on principle but having done so finds no place for herself in society and symbolically dies after the birth of her child. Grand's heroines both marry men who had been rakes in their youths. Edith Beale, who does not understand her husband's past, innocently believes that if he has been a bad man she can reform him, discovers she cannot, and dies after having given birth to a syphilitic child. Evadne Frayling, on the other hand, is a self-educated feminist, though more domestically inclined than Lyndall. When she learns of her husband's past, she refuses conjugal relations with him and is finally freed by his death to marry a good man whom she loves. Linton's New Woman, Phoebe Barrington, joins a radical feminist club and refuses to live outside London with her husband, Sherrard. He falls in love with Edith Armytage, a "maiden born for love and duty and purity,"[18] and she too comes to love him. But both respect his marriage, both keep silent about their love, and both suffer. Phoebe eventually returns to Sherrard and learns to respect him and to accept her role as wife. It is worth remarking that none of these three authors depicts the New Woman as a career woman. Career women appear in the fiction of this period, but they are George Gissing's Odd Women who do not marry or Grant Allen's Woman Who Did who find work an economic necessity.[19] The New Woman who is relevant to *The Awkward Age* is the woman inspired by Schreiner's work, the woman with leisure and education and a sense that she is different from the women of the past.

James's young heroines significantly vary the pattern established by their predecessors. Aggie is a type sometimes found in English society of the period but in stunning contrast to her fictional sisters. Whereas Edith Beale's innocence results from a well-intended but foolishly principled up-bringing, Aggie is the product of much calculation. Her guardian the Duchess explains that had the girl's parents lived, "She would have been brought up . . . under an anxious eye—that's the great point; privately, carefully, tenderly, and with what she was *not* to learn—till the proper time—looked after quite as much as the rest. I can only go on with her in that spirit . . ." (IX, 55). But laudable as the Duchess's fidelity to Aggie's parents and their traditions sounds, her interests are more practical. By raising her ward in the Continental manner as a *jeune fille*, the Duchess provides a public distraction from her own immorality. And even more important, in a society where a double standard exists, Aggie is the more attractive for her carefully cultivated innocence. In revealing metaphors, James has Longdon reflect that Aggie "had been deliberately prepared for consumption" by "being fed from the hand with the small sweet biscuit of unobjectionable knowledge" (IX, 238–39).

Given the "fast" society that Aggie lives in, her behavior after her marriage to Mitchy is not surprising—though it is both a funny and cynical comment on James's part. With the loss of innocence that her marriage brings comes also a loss of restraint and propriety. While the traditional woman passively accepts a loveless marriage, Aggie openly flirts with Lord Petherton, her guardian's lover and husband's friend. Mrs. Brook's set is both surprised and amused; the Duchess argues that this is what is to be expected when a sheltered girl marries; and only Nanda responds humanely: "Aggie's only trying to find out . . . what sort of a person she is. How can she ever have known? It was carefully, elaborately hidden from her. . ." (IX, 528). As Nanda's words bring home, Aggie has been cruelly used by those around her. Comparison with her fictional counterparts is instructive. Grand's and Linton's Ediths are simply counters that give their creators an opportunity to express the views they hold on the proper behavior of women: in one case, passive acceptance is pronounced wrong; in the other, proper. In contrast, James's Aggie, as Nanda helps us to see, is an implicit criticism of a society whose methods are manipulative, whose standards hypocritical. Although the Duchess speaks at length about how one should raise a girl, Aggie's plight speaks of more than what is proper female education and deportment. By treating a conventional type as expressive of specific social needs, James goes beyond the question of desirable female behavior and examines the corrupt values of the society he is depicting.

Nanda, too, is a contrast to her fictional counterparts. She is a New Woman in both her social awareness and her freedoms—to come and go as she likes, to visit whom she wishes, to conduct herself as she pleases. She does not have any kind of programatic sense of what woman's role should be as do Lyndall and Phoebe Barrington; instead, she is closer to Evadne Frayling and Moderna Maskelyne in simply understanding the social circle around her. But Lyndall, Phoebe, Evadne, and Moderna are what they are because they have chosen to be so. Nanda, like Aggie, is a passive victim of society and specifically of her mother.[20] Mrs. Brook's virtual abandonment of her daughter by her refusal to accept her maternal role has left Nanda without guidance or shelter. Tellingly, Nanda accounts for herself as one who has been victimized, and her tone as a result, is always apologetic. She explains to Longdon, "One's just what one *is*—isn't one? I don't mean so much . . . in one's character or temper—for they have, haven't they? to be what's called 'properly controlled'—as in one's mind and what one sees and feels and the sort of thing one notices" (IX, 230); to Van, "I can't help it any more than you can, can I?" (IX, 344); and to Mitchy, "Doesn't one become a sort of a little drain-pipe with everything flowing through?" (IX, 358). It is no wonder the Van concludes that "Little Aggie's really the sort of creature she [Nanda] would have liked to be able to be" (IX, 310). Yet in a sense, Nanda is what Aggie seems—a passive, accepting young woman, a traditional Victorian lady—just as Aggie, finally, is what Nanda seems—a modern young woman, heedless of all propriety.

Nanda's fate further bears out Van's observation. She is rejected by the finicky Van himself, and in turn rejects the nouveau riche Mitchy. She refuses his unvoiced proposal of marriage by directing him to Aggie, and she declines his hinted proposition that they become lovers in her last interview with him. Her values are indeed traditional, although her circumstances have made her "The modern girl, the product of our hard London facts and of her inevitable consciousness of them just as they are . . ." (IX, 312). At the very end of the novel, she is preparing to leave London society and live with Mr. Longdon. Adoption, not marriage, will be her lot. In this respect, too, she differs from her fictional peers. At the ends of their stories, the other New Women, with the exception of Lyndall, affirm the value of marriage and thereby the social structure, and Lyndall's death reflects Schreiner's inability to envision a career for her New Woman outside of marriage more forcefully than it suggests a rejection of society. But James is hardly posing a radical alternative to the plight of the New Woman, for Nanda is not to be counted with the defiant "rare and extreme cases" Howells mentioned. Midway through the novel, she senses what will become of her and tells Longdon, "I shall be one of the people who don't. I shall be at the end . . . one of those who haven't" (IX, 232). And she acquiesces to this fate as passively as she has accepted all else in her life. In her unsought, undesired celibacy, Nanda testifies to the power of her society.

Leon Edel has sentimentalized the end of *The Awkward Age*, seeing in it the culmination of James's self-therapy: "it seems in *The Awkward Age*, that in removing Nanda from her mother's drawing room, Mr. Longdon can now do what Henry James had done all his life—harbor within his house, the house of the novelist's inner world the spirit of a young adult female, worldly-wise and curious, possessing a treasure of unassailable virginity and innocence and able to yield to the masculine active world-searching side of James an ever-fresh and exquisite vision of feminine youth and innocence."[21] Without going so far as to see in Nanda evidence of her creator's androgyny, we can agree that the conclusion of *The Awkward Age*—almost by sleight of hand—serves James's private ends. While Nanda's retirement is a grim social commentary, it is also a fairy-tale ending. Mr. Longdon, described by Mrs. Brook as the *oncle d'Amérique*, the eccentric benefactor, the fairy godmother" (IX, 181) is the deus ex machina who will take Nanda out of the circumstances that have shaped her. Her new life will be the antithesis of the life she has known. Its keynote will not be talk but silence. "Oh but when *have* we talked?" Longdon asks Nanda in their last interview; "When haven't we?" she responds (IX, 542–43). Having, in the words of one of the few contemporary critics who did justice to the novel, provided "a study of certain phases of London society to which other novelists of late years have borne awkward and incomplete testimony. . . . [so that] There now remains nothing to be told about the conversation and the complications in those circles where vast moral indifference is united to extreme intellectual acuteness,"[22] James thus grants Nanda the escape he earlier denied Maisie. It is appropriate to recall that he had given up London life for the relative solitude of Rye shortly before he wrote *The Awkward Age*.

Notes

1. Critics concerned with social history in relation to *The Awkward Age* are William F. Hall, who in "James's Conception of Society in *The Awkward Age*," *Nineteenth-Century Fiction* 23 (1968–69):28–48, discusses the novel as a reflection of contemporary society and as implying an "ideal of society" in which intelligence and sincerity are particularly valued (p. 36); and Elizabeth Owen, who in " 'The Awkward Age' and the Contemporary English Scene," *Victorian Studies* II (1967–68):63–82, draws on a wealth of historical information to show the novel to be a relatively accurate and detailed reflection of its time, and offers a reading of the novel in which she concludes that James's final stance is one of "detached, complex irony" rather than affirmation of any positive values (p. 79). Owen also notes James's familiarity with E. F. Benson's dialogue novel *Dodo*. She observes that "James . . . was always ready to consider public taste, provided he could turn out a first-quality article" and suggests that the tight structure of *The Awkward Age* was James's attempt to "stiffen a slack popular genre" (p. 65).

2. Clarence Rook, "Anthony Hope," *Chap-Book*, 15 March 1897, p. 355, describes the evolution of the dialogue novel from the weekly periodical feature, although he mistakenly assumes that *Black and White* ran the first dialogues.

3. *The Awkward Age* was serialized in *Harper's Weekly* from October 1898 to January 1899.

4. A confirmatory sign of the popularity of dialogue was its use for serious topics. Vernon Lee used it to present her views on philosophical and social issues in *Baldwin: Being Dialogues on Views and Aspirations* (1886) and in *Althea: A Second Book of Dialogues on Aspirations and Duties* (1894). James, too, used the form for presenting his ideas on literary and social issues in "After the Play" and "An Animated Conversation."

5. Cruse, *After the Victorians*, pp. 186–88, discusses *Dodo* as a roman à clef. Margot Asquith, *The Autobiography of Margot Asquith*, ed. Mark Bonham Carter (Cambridge, Mass.: Houghton Mifflin, 1962), pp. 117–53, gives an account of the "Souls." The account includes a letter from James to Margot Asquith commenting on a diary that she had sent him: she had shed light, he says, on a group of people he had watched with interest from the outside (p. 152).

6. *Our Family Affairs: 1867–1896* (London: Cassell, 1920), p. 282. In spite of James's reservation, *Dodo* was popular enough to merit Benson's writing an additional Dodo dialogue, ironically called "The Taming of Dodo," printed in the *Chap-Book*, 15 May 1897, pp. 11–16, an issue that included two chapters of James's *Maisie*.

7. Cruse, *After the Victorians*, p. 189.

8. *Letters of Henry James*, p. 333 (1899).

9. Ian Gregor, "The Novel of Moral Consciousness: 'The Awkward Age' (1899)," in *The Moral and the Story*, by Ian Gregor and Brian Nicholas (London: Faber & Faber, 1962), pp. 151–84, offers a fine discussion of this aspect of the novel. He shows how the characters who are a part of London society in the book use a language which is divorced from moral values and as a result think of other people as objects to be manipulated. Margaret Walters, "Keeping the Place Tidy for the Young Female Mind: *The Awkward Age*," in *The Air of Reality: New Essays on Henry James*, ed. John Goode (London: Methuen, 1972), pp. 190–218, shows how all the characters, through both their language and their behavior, are a part of their society and concludes that James "no longer tries to envision a non-social self" (p. 217). Isle, *Experiments in Form*, pp. 165–204, shows how the symmetrical form of the novel and the extensive use of dialogue effectively portray a sterile society in which talk has replaced action.

10. "Gyp's" heroines, in contrast, are rather pleasant women but are not particularly clever. The heroine of her widely popular and many times translated *Chiffon's Marriage* (1894; first English trans. 1895) is a representative example. As my discussion of James will suggest, he seems to have responded to specific elements in the English versions of the dialogue novel and the New Woman novel in writing *The Awkward Age*.

11. The conflict between mothers and their "revolting daughters" was a subject of widespread interest in the nineties. This topical issue also entered into the composition of *The Awkward Age*, in, as I will indicate, an unusual form. Hamlin Hill, " 'The Revolt of the Daughters': A Suggested Source for 'The Awkward Age,' " *Notes and Queries* 206 (1961):347–49, notes the likelihood of James's knowledge of contemporary magazine articles dealing with the behavior and roles of mothers and daughters.

12. *The Maiden's Progress* (New York: Harper, 1894), p. 166.

13. "Life and Letters," *Harper's Weekly*, 4 May 1895, p. 417. Also see Lloyd Fernando, "The Radical Ideology of the 'New Woman,' " *Southern Review: An Australian Journal of Literary Studies* 2 (1967): "Many problem-novelists, enamoured of the 'advanced implications of the woman's movement, rapidly sacrificed the artistic potential of the novel as a literary form for the sake of illustrating particular views or theses on such topics as woman's role in society, the double standard of morality, and free love. The characterisation of the 'New Woman' suffered most" (p. 217).

14. Colby, *The Singular Anomaly*, p. 61.

15. "London," *Harper's Weekly*, 21 August 1897, p. 834. James is deploring the inappropriate use of classical references and he comments on the "strange colloquies in which Euripides gives an arm to Sarah Grand." I am not sure what he is referring to. In *The Heavenly Twins*, however, there is some discussion of the disregard the classical authors, including Euripides, had for women, and the name "Evadne" is from Euripides' play, *The Suppliants*.

16. Colby, p. 22.

17. *The Story of an African Farm* (1883; reprint, Harmondsworth, England: Penguin, 1971), p. 180.

18. *The New Woman: In Haste and at Leisure* (New York: Merriam, 1895), p. 315.

19. See George Gissing, *The Odd Women*, 1893, and Grant Allen, *The Woman Who Did*, 1895.

20. Krook, *The Ordeal of Consciousness*, pp. 135–66, also deals with Nanda's victimization. She attributes Nanda's situation to her social milieu and does not single out Mrs. Brook, as I do, as a particularly harmful influence.

21. *The Treacherous Years*, p. 259. Edel continues: "For this was the androgynous nature of the creator and the drama of his novels: innocence and worldliness, the paradisiacal America and the cruel and corrupt Europe—or in other variations, youthful ignorant America and wise and civilized Europe."

22. *Critic*, August 1899, p. 755.

James's *The Sacred Fount:* The Phantasmagorical Made Evidential   James W. Gargano*

I

The easiest way to account for the difficulties of Henry James's *The Sacred Fount* is to pronounce the narrator a near madman who converts the flux and heterogeneity of life into a world ruled by a simplistic psychological formula. Indeed, Jean F. Blackall has devoted a book to an exposé of the narrator's inconsistencies and self-indulgent, witless flights into airy theorizing. Two very recent essays make almost the same point: William F. Hall ends by tracing the "craziness" of James's observer to the "crucial error of confusing what he has made with the reality, the true experience, out of which he has made it"; Patricia Merivale accuses the narrator of turning his friends and acquaintances "into the characters of his own fiction." Such views reiterate, with emphasis, those of F. O. Matthiessen, who declares that *The Sacred Fount* betrays James's consciousness "of how preoccupation with nothing but personal relations might pass into insanity."[1]

Two of the most perceptive students of James's fiction find less madness and more ambiguity in the portrait of the restless, endlessly probing center of consciousness. In a fine introduction to the novel, Leon Edel sees the narrator's problem as stemming from the inevitable limits to human in-

*Reprinted with permission from the *Henry James Review* 2 (Fall 1980): 49–60.

quiry encountered by even the most clairvoyant analyst: *"The Sacred Fount,* in its rather madly obsessed way, states the dilemma of the extra-sensitive observer who can never be sure that he is fathoming the mystery whole." In a brilliant essay, Tony Tanner explores the manner in which James directs the reader to an "ambivalent assessment of the narrator." He concludes, however, by conceding that the artistic mind, as analyzed in *The Sacred Fount,* may well be distinguished by a touch of madness: "It is James's peculiarly modern insight—think of Mann's *Dr. Faustus*—to allow the suggestion that the activities of the artist might be allied to insanity."[2]

Probably the most cogent defense of *The Sacred Fount* as altogether sane and lucid is conducted by Alan W. Bellringer, who attributes to the narrator a "sense of honour" and a high degree of intelligence.[3] I agree with Bellringer that James's observer arrives at "truth" rather than delusion and that decency and the special nature of his knowledge keep him from making embarrassing disclosures. Edel, Tanner, and Bellringer have effectively challenged the widespread critical notion that the narrator's fantasticalities are destroyed by the hard "facts" produced by Mrs. Briss at the end of the novel. Is it not time to lay to rest at last the reputation of *The Sacred Fount* as an irresponsible, if not crazy, web of psychological absurdities? The web is indeed subtle and intricate, but it does make sense to the careful and sympathetic reader.

A short summary of the narrative action shows its impressive economy, its more than Wildean wit, and its mixture of the phantasmagorical and the real. On his way to a weekend sojourn at Newmarch, the narrator encounters Mrs. Brissenden, a friend who, instead of having aged since their last meeting, has become mysteriously youthful and radiant. The simple cause of this arresting phenomenon turns out to be her marriage to a man younger than herself, a man who appears to grow older as he supplies his wife with youth and vitality. Reflecting on this first of many bizarre occurrences, the narrator concludes that in all intimate relations one partner thrives at the expense of the other. Another meeting propels the narrator into the psychological research he will relentlessly pursue during his stay at Newmarch: he encounters Gilbert Long, once known for his dullness and boorishness but now conspicuously vivacious and amiable. This second transformation prods the narrator, abetted by the sprightly Mrs. Briss, to speculate on the identity of the victim who, it seems, has surrendered her wit and energy to "remake" Long. Part of the high comedy consists in Mrs. Briss's support of a theory she does not immediately recognize as deriving from her own marital situation. Always knowing less than the narrator, she accepts her role with the commitment and quick responsiveness of an ideal accomplice.

As one expects from James, the quest soon changes from a mere intellectual pastime to a complex, human drama. When Mrs. Briss "discovers" Long's sacred fount to be May Server, the narrator's detachment is compromised by his love and pity for the unfortunate woman. His scientific curiosity is overruled by his desire to protect Mrs. Server, who, if his original theory holds true, will be reduced to idiocy as Long grows brighter and more poised. Extending his sympathy to Briss as well as to May, the narrator helps the victims in the only way he can, by bringing them together and thus giving them a respite from their predatory partners. His interference on behalf of Briss and May alarms the others, who, the narrator concludes, join forces to frustrate him. Once his ally, Mrs. Briss finally turns against him, attacks him as a fabricator of insane theories, and produces "facts" which seem to topple his "house of cards" and to cause him to flee from Newmarch.

Even a cursory summary of *The Sacred Fount* indicates that it is a very special kind of novel. Ironically, its genteel characters and opulent setting are made to support the theme—described by one character as a "horror"—that men and women, in their inevitable interdependence, exploit and are exploited by one another in almost cannibalistic fashion. Readers familiar with Jamesian incongruities know, of course, that beasts and jungles can be found in his drawing-rooms, but in its indirect presentation of its theme *The Sacred Fount* may be one of the most elaborately ingenious fictions in American literature. In a letter to Mrs. Humphrey Ward, first made available to scholars by Leon Edel, James uses two words that may illuminate his idiosyncratic narrative method.[4] Commenting on the concluding episodes of the novel, he declares that, in order to dramatize his idea, he had to give an *evidential* basis to an essentially *phantasmagorical* action. In other words, the narrator's undertaking during his weekend at Newmarch should not be thought of in terms of strict realism but in terms of a phantasmagorical exploration of scenes and persons that change, fade, or dissolve into one another. The narrator's mind and intuitions confront the flux of a reality in which men and women exchange ages, personalities, and intellectual powers. In addition, the observer himself reverses *his* attitudes and roles: as will be seen, he changes from pursuer to protector, from an amused and heady analyst to a gentle, defeated man who surrenders his inner vision because of external pressures. The world of Newmarch, then, is an assemblage of images projected as if, like the original phantasmagoria, from a magic lantern: intrigues abound, men and women meet and separate with mysterious inconsequence, portraits "turn into" people, and scenes shift with remarkable rapidity and without cause. The actual constantly betrays its instability; the real is heightened into the surreal.

Yet it is the narrator's peculiar role to find order and meaning in what Emerson earlier called the "evanescence and lubricity of life." Obviously, the narrator must see what others cannot, or refuse to, see. Radically different from the naturalistic drama of physical action, *The Sacred Fount* has as its principal events the narrator's mental actions—the guesses, partial visions, revisions, self-doubts, and inspired insights that give organization to the maddening flux. In a sense, the objective world is refined into thought and speculation, and human couplings and disengagements are converted into the laws that govern them. Even James's setting, like T. S. Eliot's "streets that follow like a tedious argument of insidious intent," exists to provide the narrator an entrance into states of mind and being. The protracted and maze-like conversations, too, are less important for what they say than for the unspoken assumptions and the unarticulated needs they may reveal to the hypersensitive observer and listener.

Of course, such a phantasmagorical drama of the voracious and stricken consciousness runs the risk of vagueness and incoherence unless it receives support from the realm of objective fact and evidence. Because the external world is full of deception and ephemera, however, James must somehow confirm the visionary wisdom of his narrator without making it too dependent upon untrustworthy appearances. Nor can he, without destroying the subtle fabric of his novel, introduce the sort of irrefutable evidence that is the stock-in-trade of detective fiction. Indeed, it is clear that the one character who resorts to unassailable facts to uphold her conclusions invents them. The evidential must be surordinate to, even while it buttresses, what the mind and feelings have discovered and half created. James tells all the truth, but he tells it slant. After all, he is interested in the triumph of vision, not the triumph of proof, logic, or dialectics: clairvoyance needs corroboration for what it has already seen, not "exhibits" that will persuade a jury. In *The Sacred Fount*, then, the evidential may seem unsubstantial to readers who, distrusting revelations, demand signed confessions and—that curiously contradictory thing—a fiction of unimpeachable facts. Nevertheless, James's letter to Mrs. Ward asserts, as I hope to show, that he intended the evidence he produces to give his vision completeness and credibility.

Still, the letter was written to explain a sophisticated work that had grown beyond James's original projection, developing, in the organic process of its becoming, many strange qualities. Two early notebook entries, however, shed light on the novel in embryo, before it had been embodied in scenes and characters and before a controversial narrator had been invented. Obviously fascinated by a fanciful idea offered him by Stopford Brooke in 1894, James focuses his attention on how that idea can be elaborated into an interesting narrative:

> The notion of the young man who marries an older woman and who has the effect on her of making her younger and still younger, while he himself becomes her age. When he reaches the age that *she* was (on their marriage), she has gone back to the age that *he* was.—Mightn't this be altered (perhaps) to the idea of cleverness and stupidity? A clever woman marries a deadly dull man, and loses and loses her wit as he shows more and more. Or the idea of a *liaison*, suspected, but of which there is no proof but this transfusion of some idiosyncrasy of one party to the being of the other—this exchange or conversion? The fact, the secret, of the *liaison* might be revealed in that way. The two things—the two ele-

ments—beauty and "mind," might be correspondingly, concomitantly exhibited as in the history of two related couples—with the opposition, in each case, that would help the thing to be dramatic.[5]

This private memorandum is obviously marked by questions, by tentative expressions like "might" and "perhaps," and by an unresolved search for fictional possibilities. Brooke's germinal idea is at one point in danger of being completely transformed; then, as if with the rapidity of an inspired second guess, James conceives a new and supporting incident and a larger pattern. Moreover, the marriage of the clever woman and the dull man is altered to a secret *liaison* that will introduce mystery into the evolving narrative. Yet, although written with all the frankness of a private note, James's memorandum reveals that as of 1894 he does not regard as outlandish the notion that one person can tap and use, perhaps even use up, the vital resources of another; in addition, he is interested, as his narrator will be, in an investigation that will be resolved not by proof or definitive evidence but by someone's observation of a transfusion given by one person to another. Even at this point, the novel promises to avoid explicitness and to celebrate "vision." Lastly, James believes that his idea will be strengthened by being dramatized in two parallel situations, one of which is a "*liaison* suspected" that will become the focus of the novel. As of 1894, no hint of the theme of madness or the fatuity of Brooke's idea surfaces.

Five years later (February 15, 1899), James reminds himself of his earlier notebook entry:

> Don't lose sight of the little *concetto* of the note in former vol. that begins with fancy of the young man who marries an old woman and becomes old while she becomes young. Keep my play on idea: the *liaison* that betrays itself by the *transfer* of qualities—qualities to be determined—from one to the other of the parties to it. They *exchange*. I see 2 couples. One is married—this is the *old-young* pair. I watch *their* process, and it gives me my light for the spectacle of the other (covert, obscure, unavowed) pair who are *not* married.[6]

Clearly, such words as "little concetto" and "fancy" indicate that James appreciates the element of witty extravagance, the phantasmagoric quality, in his projected narrative; building on his conceit, he sees nothing absurd about the notion of an old woman who devours her husband's youth. Nor has he radically revised his original conception that the recognition of a "transfer of qualities" will be revelatory. Moreover, he continues to insist on a plot with two couples involved in two separate but interlocking adventures. The new ingredient in James's second notebook entry is his emphasis on "process" and on an observing presence peering into the "covert, obscure, unavowed." This presence is not endowed with any distinctive traits of character; for all practical purposes, he seems, at this stage of development of the novel, to be little more than a stand-in for the author himself.

The word "unavowed," however, implies that the covert and obscure elements have objective existence and are not invented by the observer. Of course, it may be concluded that, once James invented a narrator, the alteration in point of view and perspective may have compelled him to observe not only through his main character's eyes but also through that character's mind in its minutest operation. Such an insight could have led to the unexpected discovery that the mind may run amuck while it appears to be logically sifting, sorting, and judging; a mental odyssey begun with perfect self-control may turn into a misadventure made up of straying and self-deception. It may thus be argued that *The Sacred Fount* should be interpreted as an extended irony only superficially concerned with the holy waters that two deficient persons drain from others' vital depths; its real subject could become, instead, the study of how the narrator draws his intellectual sustenance and inspiration from the fountain of fantasy and delusion.

If James's notebook entries are suggestive rather than decisive, the question of the narrator's sanity must be answered by resort to the text of *The Sacred Fount* and by the sense of what James says in his letter to Mrs. Ward. I believe that my examination of the novel will support the implicit view of the notebooks that, once the whole narrative is accepted as a "little concetto," there is nothing deranged in what the narrator does at Newmarch. The letter to Mrs. Ward, I am also persuaded, confirms my thesis that the fantastic elements are intrinsic to the special nature of the novel and are designed to exhibit the phantasmagorical qualities of life and not the delusions of a runaway imagination. Moreover, although it may not be flattering to human vanity, the narrator's theory that men and women flourish and decline through a series of interdependent relationships is never challenged by James in his explicit advice to Mrs. Ward on how his story should be read. Where many critics go wrong, I think, is in reading James's novel as pure realism rather than as an account of the actual heightened by a plausible surrealism. In *The Sacred Fount*, Briss grows old in the sense in which Young Goodman Brown in Hawthorne's famous tale meets the devil or in which Beatrice in *Rappaccini's Daughter* lives in the garden of poisonous flowers. In some of his fiction, notably in "The Private Life," "Owen Wingrave," "Sir Edmund Orme," "The Jolly Corner," *The Turn of the Screw*, and *The Sense of the Past*, James has no little affinity to Poe, Hawthorne, and Melville in his mingling of realistic detail and imaginative hyperbole. *The Sacred Fount* belongs, I maintain, to the fictional genre in which wonders invade the real scene and become a necessary part of it.

II

As I have already indicated, James felt a compulsion to make his phantasmagorical novel evidential. In his letter to Mrs. Ward, he points out that one way of furnishing evidence for the narrator's perceptions is by having another character corroborate them. Without doubt, the three arresting conceits needing support are the exchange of ages between Briss and his wife, the surprising metamorphosis of Long into a polished and intelligent man, and the related loss of May Server's poise and sanity. The first conceit is made evidential many times in the course of the narrative. For example, the narrator fails to recognize Mrs. Briss at their initial encounter because her youthfulness belies her more than forty years; not much later, Gilbert Long confesses that he was equally mystified: " 'I didn't place her at first myself. She had to speak to me.' "[7] Still later, when the youthful Briss strikes the narrator as having turned into an old man, Ford Obert, a clear-sighted artist and not a visionary, confirms his insight by wondering why "so fine a young creature" as Mrs. Briss—really more than ten years older than her husband—should have married "a man three times her age." Moreover, the narrator's casual comment to an old lady, who is not privy to his "obsession," that Mrs. Briss looks like a girl of twenty elicits this remark: " 'Yes, isn't it funny?' " Finally, the narrator's conviction at the end of the novel that Briss has reached the limits of old age is shared by Obert, who laments that the poor victim " 'looks a hundred years old.' "

The idea of Long's change from bad manners and stupidity to gracious-ness and cleverness, though originally put forth by the narrator, soon receives objective support. Mrs. Briss not only acknowledges that a transfor-mation has taken place, but she traces it to the influence of a bright woman. Although she mistakenly identifies the woman as Lady John, she sees that Long has become a new man: " 'If she hasn't made him clever, what has she made him? She has given him, steadily, more and more intellect' " (p. 23). Obert agrees that Long now has the gift of tongues and speaks well even about aesthetic matters, and May Server pays tribute to his acuteness and wit. Clearly, James has taken more than a few pains to give a solid foundation to what might otherwise appear to be unsubstantial and suspect speculation. If the narrator sees extraordinary things, the world of *The Sacred Fount* is one in which strangeness is normalized by the insis-tent evidence that it exists.

Indeed, one of the notions on which the narrator bases his less demon-strable, later deductions derives from the insights of other persons. Obert, who has had the advantage of painting a portrait of May Server and of thus studying her closely, first detects her extreme nervousness; once a calm sit-ter for him, she suddenly rushes about in an agitated manner that leads him to conclude that something is the matter with her. Describing May as " 'all over the place' " and as " 'on the pounce,' " Mrs. Briss singles her out as Long's harried mistress. Only after such "evidence" is presented to him does the narrator comment on the rapidity with which May flits from one male partner to another. Even then he remains reasonably skeptical and looks for arguments against his own belief that she is losing her sanity in providing imagination and power of speech to Gilbert Long. Once he has

made up his mind, however, his opinion of May's condition is strongly reinforced by the symapthetic Briss, who confides that she "terrifies" him because she has "something to hide" in her "false appearance of happiness."

In a larger sense, James provides a firm evidential base for his novel
by underscoring his main character's prudence and humanity. Consistently,
the narrator wins the reader's respect and confidence by tempering cerebration with kindness. Far from being a nasty voyeur without a decent
scruple, he quickly reacts against Mrs. Briss's propensity to jump to conclusions and to incriminate. Her uncritical enthusiasm for peering and prying
makes him question the validity of his own investigation. He admits to feeling "a kind of chill—an odd revulsion—at the touch of her eagerness. Singular perhaps that only then—yet quite certainly then—the curiosity to
which I had so freely surrendered myself began to strike me as wanting in
taste" (p. 44). When Mrs. Briss accuses him of wishing to shield May, he
sees that his original adventure has markedly changed direction because his
heart has overruled his head. His early zest for discovery has been supplanted by a desire to keep his collaborators from arriving at a truth with
which they cannot be trusted. The man whom many critics denigrate as
infatuated and "possessed" acts from conspicuously humane and sentimental motives when once he sees the seriousness of May Server's destructive
relationship with Long. Aware that she may be personally destroyed and
socially compromised, he undertakes to be her champion against both Obert and Mrs. Briss:

> Had I myself suddenly fallen so much in love with Mrs. Server that the
> care for her reputation had become with me an obsession? It was of no
> use saying I simply pitied her: what did I pity her for if she wasn't in
> danger? She *was* in danger: that rushed over me at present—rushed over
> me while I tried to look easy. . . . She *was* in danger—if only because
> she had caught and held the searchlight of Obert's attention.
>
> (p. 54)

The critical failure to recognize the narrator's shift from mere investi-
gator to protector has, I believe, contributed to the persistent misreading
of his character and of *The Sacred Fount*. The novel is not only, or even
primarily, concerned with the search for the identity of the woman who
keeps Long socially and intellectually afloat. The narrator leaves little
doubt that he believes May Server to be Long's provider and victim. The
real movement of the novel—much more flattering to the narrator—can be
described as a counter-movement, a steady denial of what he knows to be
true in an effort to help May—and, not incidentally, Briss—to cope with
their problems. Dust must be thrown in Obert's eyes when, upon observing Long and May together, he suspiciously asks, " 'What's the matter with
them?' " The narrator's ingenious responses are designed to mislead the
artist, to suppress the emerging evidence. Cleverly, resourcefully, he tries
to dismiss Obert's question by attributing Long's and May's condition to
their being young, attractive, affluent, and in command of leisure. When

Obert continues to press and probe, the narrator parries with remarkable skill and tenacity until the artist has been induced to follow an erroneous trail: "If, accordingly, I was nervous for Mrs. Server, all I had to do was to keep him [Obert] on this false scent" (p. 56). The narrator is so successful that he soon induces Obert to disregard the plainest evidence, to discontinue the search, and to give up the " 'psychologic' glow" he feels in exercising his detective talents. For the moment at least, the artist concedes that May's personal affairs are, after all, none of " 'one's business.' " Unmistakably, the narrator practices the most egregious deception in his manipulation of his friend, but his deviousness serves a good cause. Most of his seeming inconsistency, then, does not derive from his fanatical sniffing out of clues but from his urgent wish to protect a vulnerable woman. His head has not been weaving congenial fictions; instead it has been craftily working in the interests of the heart and, in the process, has been transforming the whole man.

The narrator's reversal of roles, from detective to protector, is one of the major ironies in a novel illustrating that men and women pay for their human involvements by suffering radical psychological changes and by acquiring new selves. After all, the narrator is part of the phantasmagoria he observes with such astuteness and generosity. A second important irony can be found in Mrs. Briss's change from the narrator's ally and abettor to his determined foe. Naturally, the question arises as to whether or not her reversal of roles is due to her awareness of having been led into preposterous theorizing by a madman. Can her new attitude toward her former colleague be satisfactorily explained by her reiterated declaration that, once she is away from him, his lunacy becomes evident? Perhaps her disarming explanation needs to be explored in terms of her own character rather than as an indictment of the narrator. At the outset of the novel, she exuberantly follows his hints, anticipates some of his "discoveries," and strikes out boldly on her own. As an apt disciple, she first agrees with his evaluation of Long. Soon, however, without guidance, she has the uncanny intuition that Long, as a predator, enjoys his benefits with perfect unconsciousness; she sees that he relishes his new state without any awareness that he is draining May Server of life and sanity. She exultantly proclaims to the astounded narrator that " 'the man's not aware of his own change.' " Again, she elaborates, " 'Mr. Long finds his improvement natural and beautiful. He revels in it. He takes it for granted. He's sublime' " (pp. 66–67). Obviously, Mrs. Briss is intoxicated by her own sudden sharpness, her transformation into a person blessed with second sight. Rhapsodically praising the narrator as a benefactor who has made her capable of feeling and looking deeply into the human psyche, she acknowledges to him, " 'You've *made* me sublime. You found me dense' " (p. 67).

Of course, the supreme irony in all this pride cannot be missed: in assessing Long's condition, Mrs. Briss is unwittingly describing her own relation with her husband and asserting a principle of human intercourse she does not fully understand. An unconscious affinity with Gilbert Long enables her to speak from the fullness of personal experience; without knowing the source, she too revels in her improvement and finds it "natural and beautiful." The narrator thus has a more comprehensive vision of the phantasmagoria than his co-worker because he can fit her into the drama she is bent on analyzing. Naturally, personal delicacy prevents him from exposing her, but it does not keep him from relishing his superiority. Occasionally, he even comes close to telling her that she, like Long, is an unconscious predator; whenever Mrs. Briss begins to feel uncomfortable at his sharp-edged suggestiveness, however, he retreats into a sort of safe vapidity. He wants to enjoy his clairvoyance and power without arousing her full consciousness and thus spoiling his intellectual game. More to his credit, he fears that an aroused Mrs. Briss might be dangerous enough to injure both May Server and her own husband.

To grasp the reason for Mrs. Briss's rebellion against the narrator, it is important to note that in spite of her early rapport with him she remains ignorant for a long time about much that he has accumulated by flashes of insight and intense concentration on his problem. First, sublime as she thinks herself, she does not suspect that her brilliance and zest derive from her husband's expenditure of youth. Next, she entertains no idea of the narrator's complex vision of her as a counterpart of Gilbert Long. Neither can she know that her husband, like May Server, is aware of his personal deterioration in his service to her. Finally, she cannot perceive, as the narrator does, that the two victims find solace in each other's company and share a subtle sense of a common fate. In short, as a pupil of the narrator she has much to learn, and it can be assumed that, with her intellectual keenness, she will become conscious of all he has puzzled out. In a way, she follows the track of his inspiration, as she did in accepting his view of Long's transfiguration and in undertaking the search for the missing woman. Once she has discovered what the narrator has discovered, she can be expected to fight for her endangered vitality. Contrary to her stated objections to him and his theory, her real reason for opposing the man who made her sublime is her new awareness of her own predatoriness.

In a scene extraordinary for its delineation of how the intuitive process operates, James establishes the fact that Mrs. Briss has "caught up" with her teacher and is ready to counterattack. Worried about his now obvious interference in protecting May Server and her husband, she determines to discredit her former accomplice by "proving" his speculations to be mere fabrications; she shrewdly guesses that the only evidence he can adduce to support his position would be scorned as nonsense by the world they inhabit.

The scene which culminates in her decision to attack the narrator begins with the latter's description of Newmarch as a place of sumptuous banality, of glittering wealth and smartness unallied to the critical imagination. Not fully satisfied by lavish accommodations and a certain smug intactness of spirit everywhere visible, the narrator tells himself that "these were scenes in which a transcendent intelligence had after all no application" (p. 114). Everything, he feels, insists on being prized for its surface and luster: "We existed, all of us together, to be handsome and happy, to be really what we looked" (p. 114). A formal dinner is followed by the equal formality of a piano concert at which the auditors are "Felicitously scattered and grouped." Clearly, elegance and arrangement, as the paramount values of society, must cover up all human emotions, even such extreme anguish as May Server's; the covert, the obscure, and the unavowed do not exist. Disturbed by what he sees, the narrator dwells on the "salient little figure of Mrs. Server" as the focus in this "affluence of fine things." His sympathy reveals to him a suffering woman forbidden by the prevailing decorum to express her grief: "What, for my part, while I listened [to the music], I most made out was the beauty and the terror of conditions so highly organised that under their rule her small lonely fight with disintegration could go on without the betrayal of a gasp or a shriek, and with no worse telltale contortion of lip or brow than the vibration, on its golden stem, of that constantly renewed flower of amenity which my observation had so often and so mercilessly detached only to find again in its place" (p. 121). James compels his reader to wonder if artifice has become society's self-protective answer to humane appeals for help. Yet in the midst of this wellbred, ultimate indifference, the narrator keeps up his probing: "so it was that, while our pianist played, my wandering vision played and played as well" (p. 122). Little does he know, at this moment, that Mrs. Briss will present herself as a spokesman for this world, as a defender of appearances and a foe of the imagination.

Still the narrator discovers at this juncture something crucial to the denouement of *The Sacred Fount*. As he develops his theory to an appropriate musical accompaniment, he finds it lacking the symmetry of perfect art. The picture he projects contains two couples, each consisting of a thriving predator and a nearly depleted victim. The flaw in this seemingly balanced equation is, however, that while the victims gravitate toward each other by some unconscious necessity, their more fortunate partners remain conspicuously apart. Although he assures himself that life cannot be as tidy as art, he is evidently looking for the missing detail that will complete and give authority to his picture. After the concert, his intellectual readiness is suddenly rewarded as he catches sight of Mrs. Briss and Gilbert Long sitting closely and, it appears, conspiratorially together. This illuminating incident dramatizes the kind of mental action that James delights in; reality merges with thought and thought becomes reality as Mrs. Briss and Long compose, artistically, into a tell-tale unity: "For that was it—they *were* as one; as one, at all events, for *my* large reading" (p. 130). The narrator leaps, as if by inspiration, to the conclusion that the two exploiters have "begun to find themselves less in the dark and perhaps even directly to exchange their glimmerings." Simply put, the narrator's revelation is that the others have had *their* revelation—that they have sounded his depth and share his vision. Glossy, exploitative members of their society, Long and Mrs. Briss have lost the unconsciousness that made them "sublime"; their place in the world is threatened by their awakening into recognitions that must be unpleasant. Indeed, the narrator pities them, questioning the values of the full consciousness that will now give them access to the "imagination of atrocity" that Lady John accuses him of possessing. He sees them as having been arrogant and healthy—grossly lacking any guilt that might threaten their security. Now, having "fallen" into knowledge, they will no longer be able to escape the truth that all excess creates impoverishment. Aroused perception can, then, be a personal and social affliction: "To be without it was the most consistent, the most successful, because the most amiable, form of selfishness; and why should people admirably equipped for remaining so, people bright and insolent in their prior state, people in whom this state was to have been respected as a surface without a scratch is respected, be made to begin to vibrate, to crack and split, from within?" (p. 131).

The narrator's hypothesis that Mrs. Briss and Long have communed about their new knowledge and are ready to oppose him is made evidential by her immediate desire to meet him and to invalidate the theory she once gladly embraced, and by Long's nervous retreat into privacy and thoughtfulness. Mrs. Briss's manner as she requests a meeting with the narrator foreshadows her final magnificent imposture and her adherence to Newmarch's values. By her defiance, she does not disprove the narrator's theory but only demands a right to live as she has been living, as Newmarch lives, as—she might add—the world lives. Her assurance strikes him as "saying straight *at* me, as far as possible, 'I *am* young—I am and I *will* be; see, *see* if I'm not; there, there, there!' " (p. 138). It is important to remember that Mrs. Briss does not speak these words; instead her whole appearance—including her eloquent back—conveys these sentiments for herself and her society. In a sense, she admits her "guilt" but leaves the narrator a "little defeated," as if he has no defense against her desperate will; with almost preternatural foresight he has already guessed that his encounter with her will end in his surrender. Neither she nor Newmarch will make concessions to their victims. Why, their manner asks, should they forfeit their advantages?

Although it contrasts with Mrs. Briss's grandness, Long's dismal mood is also evidential. Clearly, however, the narrator has no incontrovertible evidence that Long has sought to think about his exploitation of May Server; no incriminating words are spoken, no revelatory action is performed. With an astonishing faith in the sensitivity of the heightened consciousness, James makes the point that only the grossest intelligence—the police or detective mentality—requires factual evidence in the presence of illumination. The things his observer sees cannot be proved in the usual courtroom fashion. As the narrator declares, "I couldn't have said what [these things] proved, but I was affected by them as if they proved everything. The proof simply acted from the instant the vision of [Long] alone there in the warm darkness was caught." As so often with him, the vision is the proof.

I suspect that those critics who consider the narrator "mad" cannot accept James's *donnée:* that the human mind, at its subtlest pitch of development, can leap to sound conclusions from an aggregation of hints, guesses, and happy accidents. For James the finely tuned sensibility can perform miracles of induction from an inspired examination of the bits and pieces that seem in permanent fluctuation in the vast phantasmagoria of life. For the narrator of *The Sacred Fount*, everything finally relates, coheres, and directs the alert intelligence to the principles underlying the existential flux. He hovers over the actual as if awaiting epiphanies with bated mental breath. Since his reserach concerns itself with such psychological intangibles as moods, looks, and gestures, however, he runs the risk of being thought downright obsessed and lunatic. He can be accused of "imagining" things into existence, of over-interpreting trifles, and of fabricating connections that support his theories. The narrator's admission that "my imagination rides me" and that his inner life keeps him inordinately keyed up may be taken as supporting Mrs. Briss's charge that he is insane. Still, it must be remembered that the Mrs. Brisses, with their secret lives and solid social support, have good reasons to be afraid of the disclosures of the penetrating imagination. In demanding proof and irrefutable evidence for every one of the narrator's insights, some Jamesian critics unconsciously adopt Mrs. Briss's quite conscious literalism and condemn the inner vision as flagrant solipsism.

III

Still, external and decisive proof does exist that James considered his narrator to be both sane and uncommonly perceptive. His letter to Mrs. Humphrey Ward explains, with an exasperated "of course," that the concluding scene of *The Sacred Fount* exposes Mrs. Briss and not the narrator. No matter what certain critics may assume, James indubitably intended her final triumph to have a hollow, unconvincing appearance; indeed, he bluntly tells Mrs. Ward that the final episode must be read ironically: "Mrs. B's last interview with the narrator being all an ironic *exposure* of her own false plausibility, of course." In one of James's most masterful ironies, the "facts" produced by Mrs. Briss are fictitious and the narrator's intuitions and illuminations emerge as truths. Her manufactured evidence seems plausible because she invents an eye-witness to the events she concocts: she insists that May Server is not Long's mistress because Briss discovered Long and Lady John in sexual intimacy; moreover, May is not a poor, heroic victim but a "horrid" woman who offered to be Briss's mistress. James's letter to Mrs. Ward expresses impatience with the gullibility of a reader who, taken in by Mrs. Briss, does not see the "terror" of an awakened consciousness behind her performance. He must have felt that he had given his readers the key, in direct statement after direct statement by the narrator, to Mrs. Briss's "success." Behind every word she utters, the narrator feels a "new consciousness" which "was full of everything she didn't say, and what she said was no representation whatever of what was most in her mind. . . . Just this fine dishonesty of her eyes, moreover—the light of a part to play, the excitement . . . of a happy duplicity—may well have been what contributed most to her present grand air" (p. 170). In the next to the last chapter of the novel, the narrator perceives in a climatic moment the extremes she will go to in order to save herself and Long: "It was an instant that settled everything, for I saw her, with intensity, with gallantry too, surprised but not really embarrassed, recognise that of course she must simply lie" (p. 183).

The letter to Mrs. Ward completely supports the narrator's vision of what happens at Newmarch and disproves Mrs. Briss's contention that he is crazy. Specifically, James confirms two of the narrator's views: that Briss is drained of his youth by his wife and that Mrs. Briss becomes conscious of what she is doing to her husband. As James lucidly puts it, Obert's agreement with the narrator provides the hard "evidence" needed to give concreteness to an obviously "phantasmagoric" novel: "As I give but the phantasmagoric I have, for clearness, to make it *evidential,* and the Ford Obert evidence all bears (indirectly,) upon Brissenden, supplies the motive for Mrs. B's terror and her re-nailing down of the coffin." Overwhelmed by the terror of consciousness, Mrs. Briss makes an impressive defense of herself and Long by abusing May Server as a loose woman who made love to Briss. Once again, however, James's letter sustains the narrator's belief that the two victims are drawn to each other because of their strangely similar destinies and not by an adulterous relationship: "I had to testify to Mrs. S's sense of a common fate with B." by having Obert comment on her as "temporarily pacified." In addition, the letter leaves no doubt that Long's solitariness after the piano concert is due to his sense of responsibility for having ruined May. Indeed, her apparent detachment from Long at this moment, her seeming recovery as he lapses into thought, convincingly reveals their fatal connection: "I had to give a meaning to the vision of Gilbert L. out on the terrace in the darkness, and the *appearance* of a sensible detachment on her [May's] part was my imposed way of giving it."

Finally, the letter refutes Mrs. Briss's declaration that May Server can be dismissed as a calculating woman perfectly in command of her senses. In James's unequivocal words, "Mrs. S. is back in the coffin at the end, by the same stroke by which Briss is." Both victims are surely headed for destruction, and yet Mrs. Briss uses both of them to strengthen her attack against the narrator's sanity: the gentle and enduring Briss is turned into an informer, and the frightened but loyal Mrs. Server—whose name indicates her "service" to Long—has her reputation blackened. In spite of Mrs. Briss's brilliance in her last interview with the narrator, his account of things remains reliable even though it may seem fantastic, and her account falls to pieces even though it makes an appeal to "facts." Perhaps the impatience with which James's letter deals with Mrs. Briss's condemnation of Mrs. Server derives from his feeling that May's fate had been made explicit enough in *The Sacred Fount*. Indeed, one passage from the novel is almost as explicit as the letter itself: in commenting on his desire to leave the scene of May's courageous but pathetic attempt to conceal her distress, the narrator "prays" that he will not see her again. He sadly confesses, however, that after the events at Newmarch, and thus after Mrs. Briss's castigation of her, his "prayer has not been answered. I did see her again; I see her now; I shall see her always; I shall continue to feel at moments in my own facial muscles the deadly little ache of her heroic grin" (p. 140). This confession should lay to rest the view that the narrator surrenders his "crackpot" theories at the end of the novel and that all the misfortunes and suffering at Newmarch can be charged to one mad mind.

My reading of *The Sacred Fount* requires an unorthodox view of the narrator. Above all, I regard him as a sane, self-doubting, and patient analyst of the human psyche who suffers from what he learns. He sees with a frightening keenness and clarity, and he is naturally exhilarated by his discoveries. Yet he carries on his psychological inquiries in neither a cynical nor a coolly experimental manner: capable of affection and restrained by social decorum, he resists the impulse to hurt his "subjects" or to expose them; he has a recurring fear of the consequences of his research and even worries about the damage he may cause by making Gilbert Long and Mrs. Briss conscious of their "roles"; he sympathizes with and helps the disintegrating Briss, and he protects May Server, even going so far as to lie for her; and even in the intensest moments of his quest, he never looks through keyholes, breaks into a room (as the narrator of *The Aspern Papers* does), or uses other disreputable means to learn the truth. For him, the search must be a challenge to the refined intuition and intellect, and his discoveries must be essentially moral and psychological. He wishes to get behind facades, to find the truths that are hidden behind the sophisticated accommodations of Newmarch and the polite, permissive routines of genteel life. With the perspicacity of someone used to exercising the critical sense, he can criticize in his social world "the grossness of our lustre and the thickness of our medium, our general heavy humanity." He can characterize himself and his elegant companions in unsparing terms: "We were all so fine and formal, and the ladies in particular at once so little and so much clothed, so beflounced yet so denuded, that the summer stars called to us in vain. We had ignored them in our crystal cage, among our tinkling lamps; no more free really to alight than if we had been dashing in a locked railway-train across a lovely land" (pp. 141–42).

The man who sees so acutely into the sterility of his society surely knows what he is doing when he permits Mrs. Briss to "get off" with a splendid but hollow victory. In fact, his resignation to defeat is the highest proof of his sanity, for he knows that his wisdom cannot save the world and, even more fundamentally, that the world will not accept his knowledge as wisdom. The thought of having to exteriorize and defend his inner vision appalls him: he can foresee that he will be pronounced a madman who erects preposterous structures out of dreams and fancies: "I suddenly found myself thinking with a kind of horror of any accident by which I might have to expose to the world, to defend against the world, to share with the world, that now so complex tangle of hypotheses that I have had for convenience to speak of as my theory" (p. 125). Yet, in describing how his theory came into being, the narrator ironically compares himself to a child who, in reading a fairy tale, feels an enchanted world spring into reality. His hypotheses impress him as having the pristine truth of the fable, the solid substantiality that inheres in fantasy. What he conceives of as phantasmagoric cannot be dragged into the courts as evidence: though possibly superior to facts, inspired perceptions and epiphanies cannot be touted as facts. So, in a sense, the narrator is a lunatic because he can make no appeal to common sense or the logic of the law. What he sees, he must keep to himself.

Indeed, the narrator's final refusal to confront Mrs. Briss with the truth is prefigured by an earlier example of his restraint. In one of the finest scenes in a novel filled with masterfully wrought scenes, James presents the narrator as gripped, in one of his frequent changes of mood, by the passion to trick May Server into betraying her love of Gilbert Long. At the end of a beautiful day, the narrator finds himself adrift in the walks and recesses of Newmarch, thinking with an "extraordinary elation" of his "indiscreet curiosity" and his "underhand process." At her loveliest, nature seems to beguile the senses and stimulate the imagination: "There was a general shade in all the lower reaches—a fine clear dusk in garden and grove, a thin suffusion of twilight out of which the greater things, the high tree-tops and pinnacles, the long crests of motionless wood and chimnied roof, rose into golden air. The last calls of birds sounded extraordinarily loud; they were like the timed, serious splashes, in wide, still water, of divers not expecting to rise again. I scarce know what odd consciousness I had of roaming at close of day in the grounds of some castle of enchantment" (pp. 96–97). Into this wonderful landscape, where the physical world enhances the mental journey, May Server appears like a lost princess, as if in answer to the narrator's unconscious summons. He suddenly "felt almost as noiseless and guarded as if I were trapping a bird or stalking a fawn." When he detects May's hesitation in approaching him, however, he acts with encouraging solicitude; and, once they are together, he treats her with kindness and succeeds in putting her at ease. Sensitive to her distress, he sees her "tragedy" as that of a person who has been "wrung dry" and deprived of all inner resources. At this point, instead of taking advantage of her helplessness, he commiserates with her and, becoming "more tender," excuses her as the type of an errant humanity that includes himself. It is difficult to brand as insane a man capable of his magnanimity: "Who of us all could say that his fall might not be as deep?—or might not at least become so with equal opportunity. I for a while fairly forgot Mrs. Server, I fear, in the intimacy of this vision of the possibilities of our common nature" (pp. 101–102). As she sits before him, "the absolute wreck of her storm," he pays tribute to her courage in trying to remain afloat and accords her a "wan little glory" and a "small sublimity."

Nevertheless, his humanity is soon put to the test by a rare, accidental chance to extract a confession from her. Having said that he has just left a " 'man' " who " 'wanted to find you,' " he immediately detects that May thinks he is referring to Gilbert Long rather than to Briss. Sorely tempted to apply an "objective test" to his theory, he declares that "There would be excitement, amusement, discernment in it." He confesses himself "dazzled by my opportunity": "She had had an uncertainty . . . as to whom I meant, and that it kept her for some seconds on the rack was a trifle compared to my chance. She would give herself away supremely if she showed she suspected me of placing my finger on the spot—if she understood the person I had not named to be nameable as Gilbert Long" (p. 105). A not altogether explicable impulse, however, curbs the narrator's desire to manipulate, in the interests of science, a pliable human being. With a sudden gush of feeling, he looks at her and wonders "how much the extraordinary beauty of her eyes during this brevity of suspense had to do with the event" (p. 106). Admitting her moral frailty, he responds to her with pity and love; acknowledging her beauty at the moment of her breakdown, he concedes that this beauty "caused me to be touched beyond even what I had already been, and I could literally bear no more of that" (p. 106). Unequivocally, he puts aside temptation and simply states that "I therefore took no advantage." Certainly, this is a moral triumph, a proof that in giving up his opportunity to arrive at conclusive proof he is capable of renunciation, a virtue that James attributes to some of his most admired and sane heroes and heroines.

Of course, the narrator's knowledge stops none of the world's predations. In fact, his doom is to suffer for his vision: to feel in his own "facial muscles the deadly little ache" of May Server's "heroic grin" and to allow Mrs. Briss and Newmarch the righteous satisfaction of deriding him as insane. The polite, scared society that will have nothing to do with "horrors" discovers a simplistic formula to account for him, and, surprisingly, many of James's readers have been taken in by it.

Notes

1. Jean Frantz Blackall, *Jamesian Ambiguity and The Sacred Fount* (Ithaca: Cornell Univ. Press, 1965); William F. Hall, "The Meaning of *The Sacred Fount:* 'Its own little law of composition,' " *Modern Language Quarterly*, 37 (1976), 178; Patricia Merivale, " 'The Esthetics of Perversion: Gothic Artifice in Henry James and Witold Gombrowicz," *PMLA*, 93

(1978), 994; F. O. Matthiessen, *American Renaissance: Art and Expression in the Age of Emerson and Whitman* (London: Oxford Univ. Press, 1941), p. 365.

    2. Leon Edel, Introduction to *The Sacred Fount* (London: Rupert Hart-Davis, 1959), pp. 13–14; Tony Tanner, "Henry James's Subjective Adventurer: 'The Sacred Fount,' " in *Henry James's Major Novels: Essays in Criticism* (East Lansing: Michigan State Univ. Press, 1973), edited by Lyall Powers, p. 240.

    3. Alan W. Bellringer, "*The Sacred Fount:* The Scientific Method," *Essays in Criticism*, 22 (1972), 244–64.

    4. Edel, Introduction to *The Sacred Fount*. The whole of the letter is contained on page 9.

    5. *The Notebooks of Henry James*, ed. F. O. Matthiessen and Kenneth B. Murdoch (New York: Oxford Univ. Press, 1961), pp. 150–51.

    6. *The Notebooks of Henry James*, p. 27.

    7. Henry James, *The Sacred Fount*, ed. Leon Edel (London: Rupert Hart-Davis, 1959), p. 19, hereafter cited parenthetically in my text.

Lambert Strether's Renaissance: Paterian Resonances in Henry James's *The Ambassadors*

Barton Levi St. Armand*

That Henry James was "steeped" in Walter Pater's *Studies in the History of the Renaissance* of 1873 has been proved in abundant detail by Adeline Tintner and George Monteiro.[1] Tintner observes that although "by 1881 James had fundamentally abandoned the Pateresque point of view," he still "continued his dialogue with Pater all through his life."[2] And Monteiro has demonstrated how a tale as late as "The Beast in the Jungle" of 1903 "can be read as a trenchant critique of Pater's ethic of aesthetics."[3] Briefly stated, the facts are that on 31 May 1873, James wrote from Florence to his brother William, who seems to have made some reference to Pater's newly published work, that "I saw Pater's *Studies* just after getting your letter, in the English bookseller's window: and was inflamed to think of buying it and trying a notice. But I see it treats of several things I know nothing about."[4] As Tintner points out, James's professed modesty did not prevent him from including a mini-review of the book in a piece on "Old Italian Pictures" that he published in the *Independent* on 11 July 1874, and incorporated into his *Transatlantic Sketches* of a year later. Having seen in Florence's Pitti Palace and Uffizi gallery many of the paintings by Sandro Botticelli that Pater discussed in his chapter on that artist in *The Renaissance*, James characterized Pater as "an accomplished critic," but felt that he had spoken of the artist's achievements "on the whole more eloquently than conclusively." "Putting aside whatever seems too recondite in Mr. Pater's interpretation," he adds, "it is evidence of the painter's power that he

*This essay was written specifically for this volume and is published here for the first time by permission of the author.

has furnished so fastidious a critic so inspiring a theme. A rigidly sufficient account of his genius is that his own imagination was active, that his fancy was audacious and adventurous" ("Germ," 16–17). Pater is praised rather equivocally, then, not so much as a sensible scholar as a scholarly sensibility, as one of those on whom nothing is lost.

James's ambivalence toward Pater—especially symbolized by the images of phosphorescence and fire derived, as we shall see, from a famous passage in Pater's conclusion to the book which had so "inflamed" him when he first saw it in the English bookseller's window—worked itself out in his fiction more than in his critical prose. Tintner demonstrates that Pater and Paterian thinking influenced a remarkably large number of James's works, from short stories like "The Author of Beltraffio" to novels like *The Portrait of a Lady* and *The Golden Bowl*, while Monteiro surmises that "Pater's brave and challenging conclusion caught his full attention. Indeed, it seems to have stung, stimulated, and haunted him for the rest of his creative life" (103). "Haunted" is an apt word, because although James was drawn to Aestheticism, he also feared the egotism, solipsism, and amoral passivity that seemed inextricable with its practice. Perhaps in Pater he even saw (à la "The Jolly Corner") a possible imaginary portrait of himself as an exquisite but empty connoisseur, just as Nathaniel Hawthorne had fashioned an unflattering and irredeemably narcissistic self-image in the Miles Coverdale of *The Blithedale Romance* of 1852. In any event, Pater was a potent presence whom James was forced to both appreciate and to exorcise, and I would maintain that the greatest act of mingled praise and dismissal came finally in *The Ambassadors* of 1903, the same year as "The Beast in the Jungle."

Here James at last worked out his own equivocal attitude toward Pater in his fictional treatment of the figure of Lambert Strether. Indeed, as early as 1894, in refusing a request by Arthur Symons to contribute to a memorial volume on Pater, James remarked that "the only thing I can fancy writing about Pater would be a thing for which absolute freedom of literary portraiture would be indispensable" ("Pater," 80). In another letter to Edmund Gosse he refers to "faint, pale, embarrassed Pater," and compares him to a glowing matchbox which "shines in the uneasy gloom—vaguely, and has a phosphorescence, not a flame" (81). Even more praise with faint damns is evident in another letter to Gosse two years later, in 1896, when, commenting on Pater's unfinished *Gaston de Tour*, James writes that "reading him always gives—that kind of illusion that some refined, pathetic object or presence is *in the room* with you—materially—and stays there while you read." James adds that "He has too little point, and a kind of wilful weakness, but he's divinely uncommon" (81–82).

This latter sentence strikes me as a bit of dialogue lifted bodily from *The Ambassadors*, where there are so many niggling, qualifying conversations about, paradoxically, the virtues of the protagonists' faults. Take, for example, this exchange between Chad Newsome and Strether:

> "There are certainly moments," said Chad, "when you seem to me too good to be true. Yet if you are true," he added, "that seems to be all that need concern me."
> "I'm true, but I'm incredible. I'm fantastic and ridiculous—I don't explain myself even to myself. How can they then," Strether asked, "understand me? So I don't quarrel with them."[5]

Strether's Pierrot-like conception of himself as a comic figure also recalls James's 1906 comment to A. C. Benson, Pater's authorized biographer, that in the case of figures like Pater, "It's a matter altogether independent of the mere possession of genius or achievement even of 'success' . . . it's a matter almost of tragic or ironic (or even comic) felicity; but it comes here and there to the individual—unawares—and leaves hundreds of the eminent alone" ("Pater," 82). Lambert Strether is just such an intriguing "matter," in the same sense that James refers to Pater as "a *case* if ever there was one," with the tragic, the ironic and the comic modes all mingled and melded together in a wonderfully Pateresque expression of "a strong and painful identity" which yet "presents itself . . . as one of the successful, felicitous lives and the time and manner of the death a part of the success" ("Pater," 80). What all of this boils down to is Strether's ambiguous character in the novel, and his achievement of aesthetic, as opposed to worldly, success, for failing miserably as the ambassador of American moral values, he achieves, like Pater as James saw him, an epiphanic yet self-destructive identity as Aestheticism's double-agent.

If anyone ever burns with, and is burnt out by, a "hard, gem-like flame,"[6] it is "poor Strether," who indeed even evokes this lapidary and quintessentially Paterian image in thinking of the city of Paris as "a vast bright Babylon, like some huge iridescent object, a jewel brilliant and hard, in which parts were not to be discriminated nor differences comfortably marked. It wrinkled and trembled and melted together, and what seemed all surface one moment seemed all depth the next" (64). This is an apt description of the "method" of *The Ambassadors*, in which Strether's consciousness constantly shifts in attempting to gauge what is "real" and what is "ideal," what is spiritual and what is material, what is superficial and what is deep. It is also the very formula for refined perception first enunciated by Pater in the famous "Conclusion" to *The Renaissance*. With its seductive theory of sensuous and self-indulgent impressionism, Pater excised this "Conclusion" from the second edition of his book, at the urging of John Wordsworth, the Chaplain of Brasenose College, and others, fearful that "it might possibly mislead some of those young men into whose hands it might fall." Strether is a middle-aged, indeed "elderly" man when he arrives in Paris for the second time after many years in order to carry out his patroness Mrs. Newsome's injunction to rescue her son Chad from the entanglement of a supposedly evil relationship, but he is misled nevertheless by precisely this kind of narcissistic, youth-oriented Aestheticism. Pater's painful plea in his "Conclusion" is for the cultivation of momentary and serendipitous sensual delights culled from a chaos of transient events, which are then crystallized into "relics," or we might say today, "collectibles," of consciousness. "The service of philosophy," Pater writes, "of speculative culture, towards the human spirit, is to rouse, to startle it to a life of constant and eager observation" (188). To read the whole of the "Conclusion" to *The Renaissance* is to read the plan of action, or rather, of passive connoisseurship, that Strether puts into operation after his climactic conversion in Gloriani's garden. Forbidden by his Puritan upbringing and his idealistic temperament from becoming an active Decadent, Strether must settle, like Pater, for the infinite pleasure of sensuous discrimination. It is for this kind of spiritual "success" he aims, because—to quote Pater in the entirety of his ecstatic peroration—

> To burn always with this hard, gem-like flame, to maintain this ecstacy, is success in life. In a sense it might even be said that our failure is to form habits: for, after all, habit is relative to a stereotyped world, and meantime it is only the roughness of the eye that makes any two persons, things, situations, seem alike. While all melts under our feet, we may well grasp at any exquisite, passion, or any contribution to knowledge that seems by a lifted horizon to set the spirit free for a moment, or any stirring of the senses, strange dyes, strange colours, and curious odours, or work of the artist's hands, or the face of one's friend. Not to discriminate every moment some passionate attitude in those about us, and in the very brilliancy of their gifts some tragic dividing of forces on their ways, is, on this short day of frost and sun, to sleep before evening. With this sense of the splendour of our experience and of its awful brevity, gathering all we are into one desperate effort to see and touch, we shall hardly have time to make theories about the things we see and touch. What we have to do is to be for ever curiously testing new opinions and courting new impressions, never acquiescing in a facile orthodoxy of Comte, or of Hegel, or our own.
>
> (189)

In *The Ambassadors*, facile orthodoxy originates in Woollett, Massachusetts, rather than in alien philosophers, and initially, in his struggle against this orthodoxy, which is "The failure to enjoy" (25), Strether regains part of his lost youth. Ultimately, however, he becomes even more old and tired than when he arrived in Europe, a genteel Dorian Gray literally consumed by his "desperate effort to see and to touch." It is in this state that, defeated by the cynical and worldly Chad, who looks forward to a career in advertising back in the States, since "Advertising scientifically worked presented itself thus as the great new force" (39)—no doubt a Comtean and Hegelian one—, he finds the younger man taking "his arm to help and guide him, treating him if not exactly a little as aged and infirm, yet as a noble eccentric who appealed to tenderness, and keeping on with him, while they walked, to the next corner and the next" (338). Strether's sense of himself as "a perfectly equipped failure" is only reinforced by his expansive experience in Europe; quite literally he is "stretched" beyond his former bounds and limits and left only with his rare, precious, but ultimately ephemeral impressionist sensations, his incalculable "accumulations" (337). He is also, when we first meet him, a man at the end of his "tether," that tether being the very short leash held by Mrs. Newsome ("Newsy," "Nosey," "Nuisance," and—at last—"Noisesome") as the emblem of Puritanical New England. The supreme irony is that Strether himself becomes both a relic of, and a reliquary for, Pater's flitting lights and shades, anticipating T. S. Eliot's wasteland image of "the empty chapel, only the wind's home."[7]

The fact of being part of an aesthetic elite is no compensation, since as even Maria Gostrey admits, "The superiority you discern in me . . . announces my fulitily" (40), but Strether has been educated even beyond this superiority to a higher and more remote level of appreciativeness, connoisseurship, and futility. Whereas at one time he could conceive of Maria Gostrey's apartment as the inmost shrine of a "temple" filled with objects of "high rarity," his experience of Mme. de Vionnet's rooms in the Rue de Bellechasse causes him to regard these former treasures as a "little museum of bargains." Now he recognizes, with a newly-acquired Burkean or "European" sense of organic and inherited tradition, that Mme. de Vionnet's objets d'art are not merely "possessions" but a collection of heirlooms "founded much more on old accumulations that had possibly from time to time shrunken than on any contemporary method of acquisition or form of curiosity. Chad and Miss Gostrey had rummaged and purchased and picked up and exchanged, sifting, selecting, comparing; whereas the mistress of the scene before him, beautifully passive under the spell of transmission—transmission from her father's line, he had quite made up his mind—had only received, accepted, and been quiet" (145–46). His final impression of Maria Gostrey's "Dutch-looking dining-room," with its "ideally kept pewter" and "vivid Delft" (340) is a signal that he has passed far beyond her pedestrian tastes, for Dutch art was on the lowest rung of the hierarchy of nineteenth-century painting sacred to Aesthetes like Ruskin and Pater: indeed, the latter found the "pure line" of Dutch painting "quite independent of anything definitely poetical in the subject it accompanies" (103).

Thus Strether is a superannuated man in more than one sense: he has nothing to retire to but his beautiful memories; nothing to live with but his cultivated perception; nothing to live on but a vaguely-promised pension from the caddish Chad. Even when admitting to Maria Gostrey that his situation "makes—that's what it comes to in the end—a fool of me," he keeps his eyes fixed "on a small ripe round melon" (341), a symbol of his visual avariciousness as well as of his insatiable curiosity, which amounts to a latent scopophilia. Austin Warren has observed that "the aesthete is one kind of hedonist" who eschews gluttony or debauchery for "the Epicure's pleasures, those of the gourmet in any form." He also adds that "Sexually the aesthete generally proves to be a lover, passive or active, of his own kind—

a lover of young men,"[8] for even though James takes pains to detail the fact that Strether has married and sired a child, eventually losing both his son and wife in tragic illnesses, there is no doubt that he is to some extent "in love" with the handsome and charismatic Chadwick Newsome. In his fascination with the blond-beastly (or rather, since his hair is described as an unexpected "strong young grizzled crop" [97], gray-beastly) capitalist go-getter Chad, Strether both Americanizes and elevates Pater's taste for "a certain kind of almost dumbly inarticulate and unconscious young Englishman of character" (Warren, 646). He finds Chad to be neither inarticulate nor unconscious, but surely there is a question of character involved, though it reflects more on his own ineffectual idealism than on the young man's very able and effective pragmatism. Indeed, Strether's relationship with Chad's powerful mother has so ennervated him that he is on the verge of a nervous breakdown when he is sent to Europe, "a plain tired man taking the holiday he had earned" (171), a burnt-out case who is on an ambassadorial mission which is also a standard rest-cure through travel.

In a massive reversal of sex roles, Europe—and Europe's emissary, Mme. de Vionnet—becomes the Pygmalion who carves the elegant new Chad from the rough block of the old. Yet Strether himself also becomes the only connoisseur who can truly appreciate this "brown and thick and strong" figure (97). He is affected "almost with awe" by Chad's "palpable presence and his massive young manhood," which also harbors "some sense of power, oddly perverted; something latent and beyond access, ominous and perhaps enviable" (99). Even though Chad is an unadulterated American, he appears "Greek" to Strether in the sense that Greece and the image of Grecian youth had become a firm code for homosexual attraction in the Victorian underworld known to Pater (the author of *Greek Studies*) as well as to James. As Oscar Browning—an active homosexual—later wrote of the period, "Few people know that the aesthetic movement which had so much influence in England from Ruskin to Oscar Wilde had as one of its characteristics a passionate desire to restore 'Greek Love' to the position its votaries thought it ought to occupy. They believed that bisexual love was a sensual and debasing thing and the love of male for male was in every way higher and more elevatory to the character."[9] Hence it comes to Strether "in a flash" that what he is "really dealing with" is "an irreducible young pagan" (99). In spite of the fact that he is nonplussed by Chad's maturity and feels himself all the younger for this unforeseen experience, what Strether admires and craves in Chad, who admits that "I always had my own way" (101), is the young man's solid aura of success—hard, brutal and aggressive Social Darwinian success—which, as an irredeemable failure, he can never hope to match with his own more diaphanous, Aesthetic kind of achievement. As Strether muses, "The fact that he had failed, as he considered, in everything, in each relation and in half a dozen trades, as he liked luxuriously to put it, might have made, might still make, for an empty present; but it stood solidly for a crowded past" (61). Chad, then, represents lost possibilities, but his "experience" and poise, which make him so "marked out by women" (98) and also so alluring to the "innocent" Strether, are precisely what excite in the latter that most Paterian of passions, an insatiable and all-consuming "curiosity."

I

"Curiosity" is one of the key words used by Pater in his *Studies in the History of the Renaissance;* in his chapter on Leonardo da Vinci, for example, he even refers to death as "the last curiosity" (101). This is integral with Pater's assertion that "nothing which has ever interested living men and women can wholly lose its vitality" (38), a statement that justifies the critic looking into such obscure and esoteric by-ways of knowledge as the occult studies which so absorbed Pico Della Mirandola. Tintner points out that in revising his references to painting in the 1909 edition of *Transatlantic Sketches,* James became "more enthusiastic about both Botticelli and Pater," affirming that in his passionate appreciation Pater paid Botticelli "the tribute of an exquisite, a supreme curiosity" ("Germ," 17). Lambert Strether's sublime and sublimated curiosity is also *his* "constant tribute to the ideal" (241). But "curiosity" is, as well as "A desire to know or learn, especially about something new or strange," also "That which arouses interest because of novelty or rarity; singular; odd" *(American Heritage Dictionary).* Curiosity may not only be a noun describing the desire to know, but the object of that desire, the material result of acquisitiveness or possession, as in the antique phrase, "Cabinet of Curiosities." With the Aesthete, curiosity as desire can be Pater's urge "to discriminate every moment some passionate attitude in those about us," to assemble relics of fine consciousness, or it can lead to the kind of avaricious and indiscriminate collecting exemplified by Chad and Maria Gostrey. In the highest type of Aesthete, the mania for collecting is tempered by a remote connoisseurship, a reverence for the object as a pure work of art that must be cherished and even hidden or secreted away, not flaunted as a museum piece that is vulgarly owned, labelled, and publicly exhibited. The mediating term here is Pater's own use of the idea of discrimination, of judging between or among the objects of desire without distorting them by self-interjection; the resulting delight inheres in the process of perceiving or discriminating itself, and not in the material stimulus of that perception or discrimination. In an "Introduction" to Pater's *Renaissance,* his disciple Arthur Symons (who corresponded with James about the Lessons of the Master) fixes on this characteristic attitude, claiming that what is "most wonderful" in Pater's style "is precisely its adaptability to every shade of meaning or intention, its extraordinary closeness in following the turns of thought, the waves of sensation, in the man himself."[10] This is of course also James's strategy in *The Ambassadors,* but as Symons (and James) further observed, part of Pater's "secret" was due to his personal presence or aura as well as to his felicity of verbal expression, for the lyrical yet measured cadence of his prose flowed from "the gift and cultivation of a passionate temperance, an unrelaxing attentiveness to whatever was rarest and most delightful in passing things" (xiii).

Symons admits that he "caught" from Pater "an unlimited curiosity, or, at least, the direction of curiosity into definite channels" (xv). Most of all he stresses the detachment and blasé attitude that was so much a part of this Aesthete's manner, for so anti-Victorian was he that "He looked upon undue earnestness . . . in a world through which the artist is bound to go on a wholly 'secret errand,' as bad form, which shocked him as much in person as bad style did in books" (xvi). Here we return full circle to both the character and "secret errand" of Lambert Strether, for while his ostensible mission is to save Chad from the Babylonish captivity of Paris and Mme. de Vionnet, his "secret errand" is to cultivate his own consciousness and to perfect himself as an Aesthete. Indeed, even after his ostensible mission has failed and the Pococks, Mrs. Newsome's new ambassadors, are charging full steam ahead to Europe in order to redeem Chad, Strether answers Maria Gostrey's taunt that "so your idea is—more or less—to stay out of curiosity?" with the supremely diffident reply that "Call it what you like! I don't care what it's called—" (192).

Strether finally becomes his own work of art, recalling Yeats's admonition that we must chose either perfection of the life or of the work; in effect, Strether abandons his work, as the editor of an elite, fruitless, high-toned journal funded by the extremely earnest "moral swell" Mrs. Newsome, for perfection of the abbreviated life of the complete Aesthete. But as brief as is his personal "Renaissance," he does not accomplish rebirth without a struggle, for he has to do constant battle against his own desire to transform a sublime curiosity into a vulgar prying (and here the figure of Hawthorne's Miles Coverdale, a "spiritualized Paul Pry," peeps in again). He must also steel himself against his own reawakened collecting instincts, akin to the materialistic desires of Chad and Maria Gostrey. As Strether cultivates his sensibility, he has to learn to renounce the material while bringing all the forces of a sensuous consciousness into that fragile equilibrium of "passionate temperance" which Symons ascribed to Pater.

Part of Strether's renunciation of Maria Gostrey at the end of James's novel is thus the rejection of a life "charged with possession," as his had started to become when, "giving the rein for once in a way to the joy of life" (173), he broke down and bought a seventy-volume set of Victor Hugo's works bound in red and gold. But it is not mere physical accumulation that constitutes the joy of the aesthetic life; it is those other intangible "accumulations" that make the most of the passing moment. As Strether says to his fellow American traveller, the dyspeptic Waymarsh, "*Let* yourself, on the contrary, go—in all agreeable directions. These are precious hours—at our age they mayn't recur" (273). He himself resolves to "live all he can" in the amount of time that is left to him, which is little enough, for as he assures Chad's friend Little Bilham, "I shan't live long" (258). Strether's final strategy, then, is to follow the path of passionate temperance outlined by Pater in his "Conclusion," which significantly begins with a relevant quotation from Victor Hugo:

> Well! we are all *condamnés* as Victor Hugo says: we are all under sentence of death but with a sort of indefinite reprieve—*les hommes sont tous condamnés à mort avec des sursis indéfinis:* we have an interval and then our place knows us no more. Some spend this interval in listlessness, some in high passion, the wisest, at least, among the "children of this world," in art and song. For our one chance lies in expanding that interval, in getting as many pulsations as possible into the given time.
>
> (190)

The notion of living under sentence of death inescapably conjures up, in James's Romance of Modern France, those aristocrats who suffered under the guillotine, and indeed Mme. de Vionnet's apartment is filled with exquisite mementoes of Napoleon's First Empire, while on his last visit to her Strether's extraordinarily sensitive cultural antennae, "subject to sudden gusts of fancy in connection with such matters as these—odd starts of the historic sense, suppositions and divinations with no warrant but their intensity," pick up vibrations that "were the smell of revolution, the smell of the public temper—or perhaps simply the smell of blood" (317). Immediately after this "impression" he finds that "His hostess was dressed as for thunderous times, and it fell in with the kind of imagination we have just attributed to him that she should be in simplest coolest white, of a character so old-fashioned, if he were not mistaken, that Madame Roland must on the scaffold have worn something like it" (317). Madame Roland, born Marie Jeanne Philipon, was a precocious 18th century French intellectual who, as *Chambers's Encyclopaedia* informs us, was arrested on trumped-up charges in June of 1793, and

> spent the period of her imprisonment in study, in the composition of her political *Memoires*. Summoned before the Revolutionary Tribunal in the beginning of November, she was condemned, and on the 9th was guillotined, amid the shoutings of an insensate mob. It is said that while standing on the scaffold, she asked for a pen and paper that she might "write down the strange thoughts that were passing through her head." Only a genuine child of the French Republic could have been so ostentatiously speculative at such a moment.[11]

But if Strether can conjure up such a determinedly romantic figure as Madame Roland, it is only because he has earlier conceived of himself also as a *condamné*, in this case, as Dickens's fictional Platonic hero, Sidney Carton. Debonairly "dressed in the garments of summer . . . save that his white waistcoat was redundant and bulging," Strether muses that "Yes, he should go to the scaffold yet for he wouldn't know quite whom. He almost, for that matter, felt on the scaffold now, and really quite enjoying it" (268-

69). In defending Mme. de Vionnet against Woollett's murderous ambassadors, Strether does "a far, far better thing than he has ever done"; like Sidney Carton, he at last discovers a pure and self-sacrificial love in the immolation of the scaffold. Moreover, he remains to the end Mme. de Vionnet's lugubrious white knight, devoted to an outworn romantic chivalry that looks back to Don Quixote as much as it looks ahead to "The Love Song of J. Alfred Prufrock."

Yet Pater had admonished that it was the wisest and not the most foolish of the children of the world who spent their last moments in art and song. Lambert Strether—the innocent lamb brought to slaughter as well as a sensibility stretched beyond its natural limits—is as much the perfect and perfected Aesthete as he is the failed lover and unsuccessful ambassador of materialistic values. Like Sidney Carton, his virtues had been there all along but had simply not been developed by circumstance; as James warns us at the beginning of *The Ambassadors*, "He was burdened, poor Strether—it had better be confessed at the outset—with the oddity of a double consciousness. There was detachment in his zeal and curiosity in his indifference" (18). These are precisely the qualities which, when properly energized and cultivated, lead to Pater's own "passionate temperance."

II

How these qualities are cultivated by Strether brings us to another portentous word which occurs with disturbing frequency in both James and Pater. This is the word "virtue," which takes on a very special meaning in the latter's "Preface" to *Studies in the History of the Renaissance*, for in discussing the idea of aesthetic criticism, Pater chooses an older philosophical resonance of the term which dates back to alchemy, the occult sciences, and the ancient pharmacopoeia. "The aesthetic critic," he writes:

> . . . regards all the objects with which he had to do, all works of art, and the fairer forms of nature and human life, as powers or forces, producing pleasurable sensations, each of a more or less peculiar or unique kind. This influence, he feels, and wishes to explain, by analysing and reducing it to its elements. To him, the picture, the landscape, the engaging personality in life or in a book, *La Gioconda*, the hills of Carrara, Pico of Mirandola, are valuable for their virtues, as we say, in speaking of a herb, a wine, a gem; for the property each has of affecting one with a special, a unique, impression of pleasure. Our education becomes complete in proportion as our susceptibility to these impressions increases in depth and variety.
>
> (xx)

A little later, speaking of the "great nicety" required "to disengage this virtue from the commoner elements with which it may be found in communion," Pater declares that "Few artists, not Goethe or Byron even, work quite cleanly, casting off all *débris*, and leaving us only with what the heat of their imagination has wholly fused and transformed" (xxi). Leonardo da Vinci becomes the epitome of this semi-magical search for the divine essence of things, since "he brooded over the hidden virtues of plant and crystals" (81), and in his capacity as "sorcerer or magician" produced works of art that made "the alchemy complete" (89). Although in his passivity Lambert Strether is no Leonardo, still he is pulled onward by the two conflicting passions that animated this Renaissance master, since:

> Curiosity and the desire of beauty—these are the two elementary forces in Leonardo's genius; curiosity often in conflict, with the desire of beauty, but generating, in union with it, a type of subtle and curious grace.
>
> (86)

Strether's fatal gift of a double consciousness, with its detached zeal and indifferent curiosity, causes him to analyze the relationship between Chad and Mme. de Vionnet as if it were an "herb, a wine, a gem," and he extracts from his imaginative sorcery a wide variety of precipitates and residues. But as an alchemist of sensibility what concerns Strether most of all is whether or not this connection is, as the intense Little Bilham assures him, a "*virtuous* attachment" (112) [emphasis mine]. Much of Strether's mingled delight and anguish has to do with his investigation of the sexual reality behind this euphemistic phrase, but also with his extraction of the essence, Platonic power, or transforming property that lies concealed behind its material manifestation.

This transforming essence, like the Philosopher's Stone, is the paradoxical "virtue" that has metamorphosed Chadwick Newsome from an uncouth, awkward youth into a modern, sophisticated version of a polished Greek Adonis. As Strether apprehends with "every throb of his consciousness" when he first sees the "improved" Chad in Maria Gostrey's box at the Théâtre Français, what he has to deal with is "an absolutely *new* quantity . . . represented by the fact that Chad had been made over" (95–96). But Strether continues to deal with this quantity, which is based in turn on a secret quality, a mysterious "virtue," in a subtle Leonardian way that contrasts markedly to the bluff, austere manner of Waymarsh, whom Little Bilham calls "Michelangelesque," a "Moses, on the ceiling brought down to the floor; overwhelming, colossal, but somehow portable" and a decided "success" (125). According to Pater, who devoted a chapter of *The Renaissance* to "The Poetry of Michelangelo," Leonardo found that "the way to perfection is through a series of disgusts" (81), and it is through a series of just such disgusts—of recoils from the flesh—that Strether reaches the self-destructive apex of his aestheticism. As James writes, "He was building from day to day on the possibility of disgust, but each day brought forth meanwhile a new and more engaging bend of the road" (152).

It is one bend of that road that causes Strether to question whether Mme. de Vionnet has in fact given Chad "an immense moral lift" (168), when, at a country inn, to complete the delicious landscape he has been contemplating, he thinks he sees "exactly the right thing—a boat advancing round the bend and containing a man who held the paddles and a lady, at the stern, with a pink parasol" (307). "It was suddenly as if these figures," he muses, "or something like them, had been wanted in the picture, had been wanted, more or less, all day, and had now drifted into sight, with the slow current, on purpose to fill the measure." But what perfects one picture shatters another, for the man turns out to be Chad, and the woman Mme. de Vionnet, and their evasion of Strether's casual scrutiny causes the idea of a "virtuous attachment" to vaporize entirely. That is, they become more than "staffage" in the lyrical landscape painting that Strether has been part creating, part viewing; rather than giving scale to the scene, they shock Strether into deromanticizing the supposed Platonism of their relationship. The pink parasol, which otherwise would have been the ideal color contrast in an over–all "special-green vision" (301), suddenly assumes the hue of a shame-faced blush.

It is important to realize that James, in spite of the fact that he emphasizes the initial "idyllic" quality of "the very moment of the impression" that briefly absorbs Strether, is making pointed reference not to a French Impressionist style but to the works of the Barbizon school, the more literal forerunners of the impressionists. Strether's previous description of "a certain small Lambinet that had charmed him, long years before, at a Boston dealer's" (301) makes this patently clear, for Strether's "impressionism" is not the objective, scientific matter of optics that it often was with Monet and Renoir, but a subjective, Paterian impressionism that results from contemplation of an empirical scene rather than an already altered vision.[12] As James wrote disparagingly of Whistler, "His manner is very much that of the French 'Impressionists,' and, like them, he suggests the rejoinder that a picture is not an impression but an expression—just as a poem or a piece of music is."[13] Hence James's preference here for the subdued tonalities of the Barbizon school—"the poplars, the willows, the rushes, the river, the sunny, silvery sky, the shady, woody horizon"—which, in contrast with the riotous Impressionist palette, were often dark, cloudy, and moody, and so in need of just such a reddish color-note as Mme. de Vionnet's pink parasol provides.[14]

"Impression" is another Paterian noun that, if we discount its allied codewords "consciousness" and "sensation," becomes nearly the leitmotif of *The Ambassadors:* "the place itself was a great impression" (119); "an impression that—whatever else you take—you carry home with you" (152); "At the end of the ten minutes he was to spend with her his impression— with all it had thrown off and all it had taken in—was complete" (155); "The short interval had, in the face of their complication, multiplied his impressions" (228); "He was doubtless not to know till afterwards, on turning them over in thought, of how many elements his impression was composed" (249). The word almost drops out of Strether's interior discourse after the incident at the country inn, when the awkwardness and vulgarity of

Chad's relationship to Mme. de Vionnet is revealed, and Strether reverts back momentarily to his old Puritanical ways, to the "odious inbred suspicion of any form of beauty" (119). Yet this "disgust," like that of Leonardo, cannot prevent the onward and upward movement of his idealizing imagination, nor retard the development of his Aesthetic education, because as Pater had writen in his Preface, "Our education becomes complete in proportion as our susceptibility to these impressions increases in depth and variety." The alchemizing action of Strether's sensibility manages to extract the quintessential "virtue" out of even this ultimate betrayal of his incorruptible idealism; here is how he defends Little Bilham's dissimulation about the "virtuous attachment" to Maria Gostrey:

> "Well," said Strether, "it was but a technical lie—he classed the attachment as virtuous. That was a view for which there was much to be said—and the virtue came out for me hugely. There was of course a great deal. I got it full in the face, and I haven't, you see, done with it yet."
>
> (330)

The magical alembic may have blown him up, when the whole alchemical experiment exploded in his face, but it has still blown him sky high. Therefore when Maria claims that "you dressed up even the virtue," Strether maintains that he has distilled a real substance and not a vapory nonentity. "Yes, but things must have a basis," she insists, to which he replies that "A basis seemed to me just what her beauty supplied." When again suggesting that Mme. de Vionnet's beauty is superficial, that it is a mere "beauty of person," Maria at last wins from Strether a statement that, with its final insistence on the primacy of "impressionism," becomes a Paterian justification for the depth, significance, and "success" of his whole Parisian experience. Thus he unequivocally affirms the other Marie's "beauty of everything. The impression she makes," adding that "She has such variety and yet such harmony" (30). Indulgently, Maria covers her "irritation" with the equivocal epithet, "You're magnificent," but what is really magnificent is not Strether's dense foolishness but his grand conception of womanly beauty as a potent "virtue" composed of infinite variety and harmony. This brings us finally to Pater's similar conception of female charisma in The Renaissance.

III

The most trenchant example of Pater's fascination with a deeply disturbing yet strangely harmonious female beauty is his well-known passage on the Mona Lisa, La Gioconda, in the chapter on Leonardo; for "the presence that rose thus so strangely beside the waters, is expressive of what in the ways of a thousand years men had come to desire" (98). The passage is far too famous, or rather, notorious, for me to quote it entirely, but suffice it to say that Pater's focus on a "subdued and graceful mystery," mixed with a "sinister quality," makes for a prose poem that creates an archetype of eternal sexual potency, mixing the pagan with the Christian, the familiar with the exotic, the saint with the vampire:

> The fancy of a perpetual life, sweeping together ten thousand experiences, is an old one; and modern philosophy has conceived the idea of humanity as wrought upon by, and summing up in itself, all modes of thought and life. Certainly Lady Lisa might stand as the embodiment of the old fancy, the symbol of the modern idea.
>
> (199)

Mme. de Vionnet is also described as one of those "women who are for all your 'times of life' " (140); "as polyglot as a little Jewess" (138); as "brilliant," "various," the component of "fifty women" (157). Long ago F. O. Matthiessen noted that "though Mona Lisa is not mentioned," through such descriptions "James is evoking something very like Pater's spell."[15] Yet modern women themselves, in general, are described in *The Ambassadors* as "abysses" by one of their own sex (141), and it comes to Strether after seeing the Pococks that "the society, over there, of which Sarah and Mamie—and, in a more eminent way, Mrs. Newsome herself—were specimens, was essentially a society of women" (213). As Jim Pocock says of the "prostrate" Mrs. Newsome, "they're never so lively, you know, as when they're prostrate" (217), and at this point in the novel we seem very close to Ann Douglas's description of "The Feminization of American Culture"[16] as well as to some of the ideas about the repression or reversal of nineteenth-century sexual roles expounded by James's bitterly critical friend, Henry Adams.[17] Just as Adams sought for the soothing and salvific presence of femininity in the thirteenth-century Virgin of Chartres, so does Strether seek in Mme. de Vionnet some salvation from the energetic moral dynamo of the modern American female.[18] Tellingly, however, it is not in the Middle Ages but in the Renaissance that he finds his most propitious archetype. At Gloriani's sumptuous garden party, his liege lady appears dressed in a metallic "silvery gray" with the added "green note" of a collar of emeralds, while

> Her head, extremely fair and exquisitely festal, was like a happy fancy, a notion of the antique, on an old precious medal, some silver coin of the Renaissance; while her slim lightness and brightness, her gaiety, her expression, her decision, contributed to an effect that might have been felt by a poet as half mythological and half conventional. He could have compared her to a goddess still partly engaged in a morning cloud, or to a sea-nymph waist-high in the summer surge. Above all, she suggested to him the reflexion that the *femme du monde*—in these finest developments of the type—was, like Cleopatra in the play, indeed various and multifold.
>
> (160)

Although Strether's closing reference to Shakespeare's Cleopatra conjures up a dark chiaroscuro that once more relates back to Pater's sinister Mona Lisa, the half mythological, sea-borne character of Mme. de Vion-

net's icy apparition is actually closer to a less well-known but just as striking
Paterian word-painting from *The Renaissance*, his description of Botticelli's
"Venus Rising from the Sea" in the Uffizi gallery:

> The light is indeed cold—mere sunless dawn; but a later painter would
> have cloyed you with sunshine; and you can see the better for the quiet-
> ness in the morning air each long promontory, as it slopes down to the
> water's edge. Men go forth to their labors until the evening; but she is
> awake before them, and you might think that the sorrow in her face was
> at the thought of the whole long day of love yet to come. An emblemati-
> cal figure of the wind blows hard across the grey water, moving forward
> the dainty-lipped shell on which she sails, the sea "showing his teeth,"
> as it moves, in thin lines of foam, and sucking in, one by one, the falling
> roses, each severe in outline, plucked off short at the stalk but em-
> browned a little, as Botticelli's flowers always are. Botticelli meant all this
> imagery to be altogether pleasurable; and it was partly an incompleteness
> of resources, inseparable from the art of that time, that subdued and
> chilled it. But this predilection for minor tones counts also; and what is
> unmistakeable is the sadness with which he has conceived the goddess of
> pleasure, as the depository of a great power over the lives of men.
>
> (46–47).

Mme. de Vionnet turns out, too, to be a sad, even a pathetic "goddess
of pleasure," in spite of her "great power over the lives of men," and James
paints her in appropriately "minor tones." After Strether's "vision" is "dark-
ened for the moment" by the revelation of the purely exploitive relationship that binds her to Chad, she even seems common, a "creature" who
spoke a language "beautifully easy for her, yet of a colour and a cadence
that were both inimitable and matters of accident" (310). Still, Pater writes
of Botticelli that his "peculiar character" was the fact that "His morality is
all sympathy; and it is this sympathy, conveying into work somewhat more
than is usual of the true complexion of humanity, which makes him, visionary as he is, so forcible a realist" (44). Interested neither in "untempered
goodness" nor "untempered evil," Pater's Botticelli ultimately concerns
himself with "men and women, in their mixed and uncertain condition, always attractive, clothed sometimes by passion with a character of loveliness
and energy, but saddened perpetually by the shadow upon them of the
great things from which they shrink" (43). Strether's morality, too, is at the
last, "all sympathy" and he deals with Chad's brutal "energy" and Mme. de
Vionnet's shrinking "loveliness" in the same terms of a visionary realism, a
"passionate temperance." Even when realizing that Mme. de Vionnet
adores the unworthy Chad in a way remarkably similar to his own unthink-
ing adoration of her, Strether notes at their final interview that "She was
older for him to-night, visibly less exempt from the touch of time; but she
was as much as ever the finest and subtlest creature, the happiest apparition, it had been given him, in all his years, to meet; and yet he could see
her there as vulgarly troubled, in very truth, as a maidservant crying for
her young man" (323).

Strether may have outgrown the vulgar creature who is Mme. de Vionnet, but this dark night of his impressionist soul only prepares him to revere even more the ideal and sublime type she represents, as Aphrodite Porne or Pandemos is elevated at last to Venus Urania. This "type" still has something of the vampirish in it; that predatory "smell of blood" that Strether senses outside her apartment, or the "something in the great world covertly tigerish, which came to him across the lawn, as a waft from the jungle," at Gloriani's party (133). After all, according to Hesiod, Aphrodite arose from the sea only because Chronos castrated his father Uranus and threw his genitals into the ocean. Venus was born of the foam they created, and just as Botticelli suppressed ("subdued and chilled," in Pater's words) the underlying violence of this myth by painting its aftermath in cool tones and severe outlines, so did James transform Strether's maiming into a more subtle social and intellectual decapitation. For Strether is destined quite literally to lose his head, whether it be at the hands of Mrs. Newsome, who "looked, with her ruff and other matters, like Queen Elizabeth" (43), that queen who sent her lover Essex and so many others to the block for defying her regal authority, or on the scaffold with the bewitching Mme. de Vionnet, who is a real aristocrat—a countess, no less. Like Madame Roland, Strether savors his "impressions" till the very moment the blade falls; this is what makes him, in all senses of the term, an incurable romantic. It is Maria Gostrey who ironically, even contemptuously speaks his epitaph: "But with your wonderful impressions you'll have got a great deal" (345), since by any objective standards Strether has been shamelessly used, had, bamboozled, and taken. Still that "great deal" also includes the subjective "great passions" which Pater urges on all of us, as *condamnés* crowded into the tumbril of time:

> Great passions may give us this quickened sense of life, ecstacy and sorrow of love, the various forms of enthusiastic activity, disinterested or otherwise, which come naturally to many of us. Only be sure it is passion—that it does yield you this fruit of a quickened, multiplied consciousness. Of such passion, the desire of beauty, the love of art for its own sake, has most. For art comes to you proposing frankly to give nothing but the highest quality to your moments as they pass, and simply for those moments' sake.
>
> (190)

Strether is "sure it is passion" he has experienced, though his creator, Henry James, leaves it up to his reader to decide whether we have witnessed the white heat of a vital flame, or a mere weak and "lambent" phosphorescence. Just as he has slipped into our consciousness as readers, so is it Strether's fate to fade away into the delights of his own multiplied consciousness. For as Pater reminds us about any group of impressions, "Every one of those impressions is the impression of the individual in his isolation, each mind keeping as a solitary prisoner its own dream of a world," subject to "that continual vanishing away, that strange, perpetual, weaving and unweaving of ourselves" (187–88). Yet in the character of Lambert Strether, James at last achieved that "absolute freedom of literary portraiture" that had always tempted him in connection with Pater's name, art, and intentions. Of "Two Early French Stories" in the first chapter of his central work, Pater wrote: "The history of the Renaissance ends in France, and carries us away from Italy to the beautiful cities of the country of the Loire. But it was in France, also, in a very important sense, that the Renaissance had begun" (1). The same can be said for the short, happy Renaissance of that quintessential American Aesthete, Lewis Lambert Strether.

Notes

1. In honor of his wide-ranging scholarship on American and European Literature, I dedicate this essay to my longtime friend and mentor, Austin Warren.

2. Adeline Tintner, "Pater in *The Portrait of a Lady* and *The Golden Bowl*, including some unpublished Henry James Letters," *Henry James Review* 3, no. 2 (Winter 1982):94. This essay, 80–95, will hereafter be referred to in the text by the short title "Pater." See also her "Another Germ for 'The Author of Beltraffio': James, Pater, and Botticelli's Madonnas," *Journal of Pre-Raphaelite Studies* 1, no. 1 (November 1980):14–20. This essay will hereafter be referred to in the text by the short title "Germ."

3. George Monteiro, "Henry James, Great White Hunter," *Modern Language Studies* 13, no. 4 (Fall 1983):104.

4. *Henry James Letters*, 1, ed. Leon Edel (Cambridge: Harvard University Press, 1974), 391.

5. Henry James, *The Ambassadors*, ed. S. P. Rosenbaum (New York: W. W. Norton, 1964), 286. Hereafter all references will be to this edition.

6. Walter Pater, *The Renaissance: Studies in Art and Poetry: The 1893 Text*, ed. Donald L. Hill (Berkeley: University of California Press, 1980), 189. Hereafter all references will be to this edition. I am assuming, with Tintner and Monteiro, that James renewed his acquaintance with Pater's work shortly after Pater's death on 30 July 1894, and so would have been familiar with both the first 1873 edition of this work and the revised fourth edition of 1893, the last published during the author's lifetime. Only the first edition was entitled *Studies in the History of the Renaissance*, but I will take the liberty of using both titles in the text, the shorter one *(The Renaissance)* to emphasize the book as a manifesto of Aestheticism, the longer one *(Studies in the History of the Renaissance)* to indicate its scholarly nature. It is pertinent that the motto which Pater selected to preface his work, "ye shall be as the wings of a dove" (Psalms 68:13) was one that James also used for the title of the novel that James wrote after *The Ambassadors*, even though through a publishing fluke the latter came out in 1903 and *The Wings of the Dove* in 1902.

7. T. S. Eliot, "The Waste Land," in *The Complete Poems and Plays: 1909–1950* (New York: Harcourt, Brace and World, 1952), 49.

8. Austin Warren, "Pondering Pater: Aesthete and Master," *Sewanee Review*, 91, no. 4 (Fall 1983):644.

9. Oscar Browning, quoted by Ian Anstruther in *Oscar Browning: A Biography* (London: John Murray, 1983), 59. For an exploration of this subject, see Anstruther's entire chapter, "Greek Love and George Curzon," 55–66, and Richard Jenkyns, *The Victorians and Ancient Greece* (Cambridge: Harvard University Press, 1980).

10. Arthur Symons, Introduction to *The Renaissance*, by Walter Pater (New York: Boni and Liveright, 1919), xiii.

11. *Chambers's Encyclopaedia* (New York: Collier, 1886), 6:685.

12. In his introduction to James's *The Painter's Eye: Notes and Essays on the Pictorial Arts* (Cambridge: Harvard University Press, 1956), John L. Sweeney claims that "The landscape in which Strether finds himself reflects the ascendency of Impressionism" (29), and in *Person, Place, and Thing in Henry James's Novels* (Durham: Duke University Press, 1977), Charles R. Anderson, while recognizing that Lambinet was a Barbizon school painter rather that one of the new Impressionists, still asserts that "Consciously or not, James made dramatic use of a special Impressionist technique, the color-spot to focus the eye of the beholder" (274). Yet long before the advent of Monet and Renoir, Barbizon school painters like Corot had utilized red-clad peasants to counterbalance, highlight, or relieve the prevalent silvery-gray-green tones of their compositions. Viola Hopkins Winner is on firmer ground when she points out, in *Henry James and the Visual Arts* (Charlottesville: The University of Virginia Press, 1970), that "this was the French landscape school that discerning Bostonians were beginning to collect in the 1860's," that James reviewed some specimens of the school in 1872, and that the Tremont Street gallery in which Strether first sees the Lambinet was most probably that of Mssrs. Doll and Richards (76). The other major Boston dealer in Barbizon painters was Seth Vose, but his gallery was on Washington Street, and Doll and Richards were also the agents for the works of William Morris Hunt, the main propagandist for French art in America. Hunt had studied with, idolized, and bought the paintings of Millet, a leader of the school, and it was Hunt with whom James and his brother William studied painting in Newport in 1860. Yet Winner, too, claims that once Strether enters the village, James changes from a Barbizon to a frankly Impressionist technique. I would maintain that there is a marked unity of tone here, and that James's character continues looking at a series of pictures at the same Barbizon exhibition rather than bolting for a far too-distant *Salon des Refusés*. As James himself writes of Strether, "he was moving in these days, as in a gallery, from clever canvas to clever canvas" (316). Sweeney makes it clear that James's actual comments on Monet, Degas, and Manet were more the fruit of a sudden confrontation with these artists in America in 1904 than of any earlier rumination on their virtues or vices. Moreover, if one examines a large number of Impressionist paintings, one finds that their prevailing tonality is decidedly blue in color. As Joris-Karl Huysmans wrote of Armand Guillaumin's work, "the eye of most [of the Impressionists] was monomaniacal; this one saw hairdresser's blue in all of nature; that one saw violet; earth, sky, water, flesh, everything in their work borders on the color of lilac and eggplant." Quoted by Pierre Courthion in *Impressionism* (New York: Harry N. Abrams, 1977), 102. The natural contrast to this blue tone is white or cream, which is in fact the color of most women's dresses in Impressionist works, not the characteristic pink or the red of the Barbizon school.

13. Henry James, "The Grosvenor Gallery" (1878), in *The Painter's Eye*, 165.

14. In his *American Art in the Barbizon Mood* (Washington: Smithsonian Institution Press, 1975), Peter Bermingham writes that "Lambinet's favorite subject, the fields along the upper Seine, usually painted in a restricted, cool palette of middle grays and blues with deep green . . . may well have eased the later success in America for Corot and Daubigny, just as the silvery, vaprous landscapes of the Hudson River painter Thomas Doughty would later remind many Americans of the late style of Corot" (46).

15. F. O. Matthiessen, "*The Ambassadors*," from *Henry James: The Major Phase* (1944), reprinted in Rosenbaum, 437.

16. See Ann Douglas, *The Feminization of American Culture* (New York: Knopf, 1977).

17. For Adams's opinion of women in American society, see his chapter entitled "The Dynamo and the Virgin" and "Vis Inertiae" in *The Education of Henry Adams* (1918) (Cambridge: Riverside Press, 1961); for his worship of the Virgin and his admiration for the power of thirteenth-century women in general, see the chapters entitled "The Virgin of Chartres"

and "The Three Queens" in *Mont-Saint-Michel and Chartres* (1905) (Princeton: Princeton University Press, 1981). Interestingly enough, although Adams regards the Renaissance as a time which saw the disastrous ascendency of science and secular humanism, of "modernity" in general and the attendant destruction of "unity" by "multiplicity," he devotes chapter twelve of *Mont-Saint-Michel and Chartres* to the "chant-fable" of "Nicolette," which Pater also discusses in the first chapter of his revised *Renaissance*.

18. Richard Chase writes that:

> By the end of the novel Strether has come to resemble James' friend Henry Adams more than he resembles Howells. Like the aging Adams, Strether had completed his education by worshipping at the shrine of the goddess . . . Like the Virgin herself, Mme. de Vionnet is unity, humanity, culture, the ideal culmination of history.

"James' Ambassadors" (1958), reprinted by Alfred Kazin in "Critical Supplement" to James, *The Ambassadors* (New York: Bantam Books, 1969), p. 550.

The Wings of the Dove   Sallie Sears*

The central situations in most of James's novels are very similar: conflict is brought about by two characteristics shared by protagonists and antagonists alike—a greediness or hunger to have everything that life might offer, coupled with an unwillingness to accept or possibly even to acknowledge limitations to the realization of their desires. And yet there always are limitations: the execution *is* confined, and in the Jamesian fictional world with more formal rigor even than in life itself. In this world, experience is limited by being polarized, most often into the extremes represented by the European and American ways of life. And this European-American antithesis is as much a symbolic construct of impossibilities as it is of possibilities. If the face of the American coin is innocence and energy, fortune and freedom, "old heads and . . . young morals," as Christopher Newman reflects, its back is unworldliness and washtubs, a general bewilderment at the arithmetic of art, culture, and taste. Similarly, if to be a European is to be, in contrast to this, "a master of all the distinctively social virtues and a votary of all the agreeable sensations," it is to be at the same time corrupt, to be a possessor of "morals the most grizzled and wrinkled."[1]

In the early novels (*Roderick Hudson, The American, The Europeans*) someone always tries—and always fails—to annex the virtues of both civilizations without paying the price of the vices of each; in other words, to remake the conditions of his world.[2] Such an effort, attended by such a failure, is also the paradigm of the dramatic situation in the late novels. In these, however, the antitheses are more complex, the "goods" and "bads" more manifold. But the same hunger and yearning for the best of all possible worlds continue to provide the motivating principle for the interaction

*Reprinted from Sallie Sears, *The Negative Imagination*. © 1968 by Cornell University. Used by permission of the publisher.

of the characters. In *The Wings of the Dove*, for example, both Merton and Kate defy the logical and moral restrictions that seem to be inherent in their situation. Merton will have Kate and his honor too; Kate will have Merton and a fortune too. Yet in each case circumstances decree that the choice of one of these precludes the other. The plot issues from the characters' defiance of this dictate, from their yearning and greed for both alternatives, which set into motion the deepest concerns of the novel: pursuit and possession, perjury and blame, the ultimate despising of what one has sought because of what one has done to oneself in seeking it.

In the broadest sense the novel is an anatomy of guilt; of the causes, then the consequences, of deliberate, conscious violation of another human being's existence for the sake of personal gain. Each half of the book deals in a general way with one of these two aspects of the subject, so that the major structural break that takes place at the end of Book V corresponds with the shift in thematic focus from the genesis of guilt to its consequences.

James's own image for the novel's subject is a medal hanging free so that "its obverse and its reverse, its face and its back, would beautifully become optional for the spectator." The medal's face is the "stricken state" of Milly Theale, its back "the state of others as affected by her"[3] and, one might add, as affected by themselves in relation to her. As the events of the novel play themselves out, the word "stricken" takes on new meaning, referring finally not so much to the peril to her health as to the blow given to her will to live in spite of it when she discovers the real connection between Kate and Merton. Similarly, the way in which others are "affected by" Milly means one thing at the outset of the story, quite another as she begins in fact to be deceived. In the beginning Kate and Merton are affected by the possibility of using her, in the end by the actuality of having done so and the nightmarish difference that this makes. The emotional complex is shifting and varied, moving for them from greed to remorse, from activity to paralysis and, for Milly, from ignorance to knowledge—which in this context is to say from hope to agony.

The real subject of the book in other words is a dynamic one. It is neither the deceived nor the deceiver who is studied but rather the changing relationship between the two and the phenomenon itself of manipulation; of the circumstances that give rise to it and of the effects it has upon both victim and victimizer. This is what James means, I think, when he speaks, in reference to his narrative method, of scarcely remembering "a case . . . in which the curiosity of 'beginning far back,' as far back as possible, and even of going, to the same tune, far 'behind,' that is behind the face of the subject, was to assert itself with less scruple."[4] So he writes that "though my regenerate young New Yorker, and what might depend on her, should form my centre, my circumference was every whit as treatable. . . . One began, in the event, with the outer ring, approaching the centre thus by narrowing circumvallations."[5]

His "outer ring" then is the state of the other characters as affected by Milly and by what she represents at the outset of the novel. It is what he begins with, even though Book I ostensibly deals just with Kate and her family. From the ground laid in that book Milly is only, in James's words, "superficially" absent. Kate is shown under the pressure of various circumstances creating for her a series of dilemmas, all of which, however different in certain respects, have one thing in common: they would not exist if Kate had a fortune like Milly's. These circumstances weave into a web of considerable precision, and if the moth is superficially absent, the spider is waiting; one might say that a general invitation has been issued. Something of the sense of this is what James means when he speaks of having intended Milly's predicament to be created "promptly" and built up "solidly, so that it should have for us as much as possible its ominous air of awaiting her."[6]

The predicament is certainly solid. There is an inexorable and formal irony in the very confluence of events operating on and within Kate that is reminiscent in its way of Hardy. By various vague and nameless deeds Kate's father has brought the family, which includes the four small children of her widowed sister, into dishonor and financial collapse. Her wealthy aunt is willing to rescue Kate on the explicit condition that she renounce all contact with her father and on the unspoken condition that she marry a man of the aunt's choice. Kate herself is beautiful, proud, poor but covetous of wealth, and in love with a penniless man not of her aunt's choice. She is also painfully conscious of the responsibilities and obligations, the silken cords of familial relations, and "the part, not always either uplifting or sweetening, that the bond of blood might play in one's life."[7] She is not free from this bond—as Milly so pre-eminently is—either in fact or, more important, in feeling. "That's all my virtue" she murmurs to Densher, "—a narrow little family feeling. I've a small stupid piety—I don't know what to call it" (XIX, 71). Finally, she occupies a unique position within the family complex: with her youth, her pride, her presence, and the magnetism that makes her appear "more 'dressed,' often, with fewer accessories, than other women, or less dressed, should occasion require, with more" (XIX, 5), she is the one piece of solid collateral the disgraced and distressed family possesses, the one tangible asset whose worth to them is the price it will bring at barter. And she knows it. Lionel Croy has few pleasures. Like Gilbert Osmond in *The Portrait of a Lady*, he is concerned with appearances and wears the mask of propriety but feels almost nothing. Yet he does take pleasure, she realizes, in the fact "that she was handsome, that she was in her way a tangible value" (XIX, 9). And later she repeats to Densher, "My position's a value, a great value, for them both. . . . It's *the* value—the only one they have. . . . It makes me ask myself if I've any right to personal happiness, any right to anything but to be as rich and overflowing, as smart and shining, as I can be made" (XIX, 71).

So the theme of manipulation, of tampering, of regarding a fellow human being not as a person but as an object for use is present from the beginning of the novel, more horrifying perhaps because of its context within the family setting, where the distortion and reversal of roles are so severe, the primary responsibility of who nurtures whom so askew, that the situation takes on almost cannibalistic overtones: a family party feeding off the younger daughter.

The purpose of these opening chapters according to James was to "account" for Kate: "The image of her so compromised and compromising father was all effectively to have pervaded her life, was in a certain particular way to have tampered with her spring; by which I mean that the shame and the irritation and the depression, the general poisonous influence of him, were to have been *shown*." "They weren't shown," James feels; instead the author's "poor word of honour has *had* to pass muster for the show."[8] And it is true that Lionel Croy's compromising influence does not really seem to have very much to do with Kate's deepest possibilities and energies. But it does not matter; it is not a serious flaw. When we first view Kate gazing into the mirror, the impact of her beauty, vitality, and power speaks for itself. She does not need "accounting for." Her personality with both its resources and its susceptibilities, its passion and its narcissism, is one of the givens of the novel, the concern of which as a study of human guilt is phenomenological rather than psychological. To the extent that the novel is concerned with causes, it is as they exist in the combination of character and circumstance, not as they relate to the origins of character itself. And though James is one of the great scholars of human motives, his interest is in their processes: in the effects, the implications, the reverberations of self-interest and not in its psychodynamics.

Some guilt by association does touch Kate: her sister is abject, her father is full of "folly and cruelty and wickedness" (XIX, 64), her aunt is "unscrupulous and immoral" (XIX, 31). It is sufficient for the evil of the day that Kate exists in contiguity with them, that she is the prime object of their various desires, and that she recognizes this and even partially acknowledges its justice. By so doing of course she accepts not only their right to use her but also, by extension, anyone's right to use anyone who might be in a position to be useful. The acceptance of this principle is the primary distortion of human values in the novel, and it operates on a number of levels,[9] reversing the meaning even of ordinary terms of moral discourse. Thus Kate is under pressure from all the members of her family not to be "selfish," that is not to marry a penniless man or, to put it another way, not to marry the man she loves since he not only is penniless but also feels that the "innermost fact . . . of his own consciousness" is his "private inability to believe he should ever be rich" (XIX, 62).

It is not merely through the eyes of her family, however, that Kate regards herself as an object to be put to use, but through her own eyes as well. Looking at herself in the mirror, she meditates upon the possibility of at least a partial escape from ruin—escape implicit in the fact that she is "agreeable to see." And she is aware of her power: "If she saw more things than her fine face in the dull glass of her father's lodgings she might have seen that after all she was not herself a fact in the collapse. She didn't hold herself cheap, she didn't make for misery" (XIX, 5–6). To an extent her vision of herself is one with that of her family: they don't judge her cheap either. The difference is in her intense personal pride, which is reflected in an extension of her self-identification to the "precious" family name, the debasing of which causes her shame and a quality of remorse they themselves do not share. With a certain horror, Kate sees her sister's abjectness, watches her "instinctively neglect nothing that would make for her submission to their aunt" (XIX, 34), realizes that Marion's lust for profit is "quite oblivious" of dignity, honor, and pride.

One of the most characteristic traits of James's imagination is to see life in terms of mutually exclusive possibilities and negative alternatives. The typical problem faced by his characters is not so much a choice as a dilemma, in which any decision means some major sacrifice, capitulation, or surrender. And for Kate the dilemma rapidly becomes acute; she has accepted her position, even to the extent of questioning her own right to personal happiness, as the family pawn. At the same time it is only she who can or cares to preserve their collective dignity. To preserve it means not to be abject, but not to be abject means in turn "to prefer an ideal of behavior—than which nothing ever was more selfish—to the possibility of stray crumbs for the four small creatures" (XIX, 34). So that any way she turns, something, and something important, stands to be lost.

Her one attempt to maintain her spiritual freedom, her integrity, literally her wholeness, of self is her initial offer to her father to stick by him, with or without Densher, and renounce Aunt Maud. This is the first and last unequivocally moral gesture Kate makes in the course of the novel, and part of the inexorability of the patterning of circumstances spoken of earlier lies in its never being allowed to become a genuine option for her. The irony is intensified by the fact that of all the various pressures operating upon and within her, not the least is that of her own "dire accessibility to pleasure" from material things, from "trimmings and lace . . . ribbons and silk and velvet . . . charming quarters" (XIX, 28).[10] It is an accessibility that makes her feel in danger; in the face of the temptation offered by Aunt Maud, Kate likens herself to "a trembling kid . . . sure sooner or later to be introduced into the cage of the lioness" (XIX, 30). Yet the source of the danger is internal not external, and Aunt Maud's imagined ferocity is an image for Kate of some possibility within herself that she dreads and that Milly too is soon to dread, recognizing after an interview with Kate that "she had felt herself alone with a creature who paced like a panther" (XIX, 282).

The intensity of the temptation Kate feels is a measure of the meaning of her gesture to her father. It is no empty offer, but an effort to redeem herself in advance from herself, from what she so clearly senses she might do, and by doing, become. "I did it," she cries to Densher, "to save myself—to escape" (XIX, 69). To save herself and "the precious name" she is willing at this juncture to give up both love and a possible fortune—a willingness, perhaps understandably, she never demonstrates again.

Given, then, the nature of her own character in the context of circumstances that surround it, there is no set of alternative actions that does not represent a dilemma for Kate. She does not want to give up Densher, yet she does not want to be poor, and she would be poor if she married him. She especially does not want, after the example of the Misses Condrips' who spend their days sniffing out dregs of gossip that might somehow be turned to their financial advantage, to be both poor and unmarried. She does not want to be dishonorable. She does not want to see her family's fortune and honor remain in the mud. She does not want to sacrifice her personal—and familial—dignity to regain that fortune, yet she does not want to have to maintain that dignity at the cost of taking crumbs away from babes. If she maintains her integrity she sacrifices her family to poverty and, equally to the point, herself as well. So that the choice of any one alternative means the surrender of the other possibilities. And that in turn means the renunciation of her ideal self-image, because that image is precisely a composite of all the possibilities: it is Kate wealthy, dignified, of proud name, charitable in her munificence, and married to Merton Densher.

The one sacrifice on the altar of this vision is her morality. Not the appearance of it, since to seem untouchable and beyond scandal, to have the aura of propriety, is an intrinsic part of her ideal portrait of herself. But certainly the fact of it. So she tells Densher she sees as her one danger the possibility "of doing something base" (XIX, 72). It is not the danger of "chucking him," as he suggests: "I *shan't* sacrifice you. Don't cry out till you're hurt. I shall sacrifice nobody and nothing, and that's just my situation, that I want and that I shall try for everything" (XIX, 73).

Kate's cry of yearning is to be echoed in one form or another by all of the characters, "good" and "bad" alike, in the late novels. Her situation, that of a person whose longings will recognize no limits and yet who is caught up in circumstances that are unusually limiting, is a microcosm of the fundamental situation James deals with again and again. His imagination so orders reality that the possibilities for happiness that face each character inevitably have an either-or quality about them, and yet the characters are all the kind of people for whom the alternative to the fulfillment of their desires is an empty, pointless existence. And it is in terms of these two extremes that James persistently examines the meaning and significance of "morality." For Kate, the pendulum has swung full swing: if initially she was willing to renounce everything to preserve her spiritual safety, she is now willing to surrender that safety to preserve everything else. In a sense what she does is simply to reject the logical premise of her situation—the premise that she is in a dilemma, that she must choose between one thing and another. But her one peril, that of doing something base, is by definition also a peril to someone else. The shifts in her feeling and attitudes toward herself can be reduced to a series of propositions about the nature of the relationship between self-gratification and morality, and the limits on each imposed by the other. Kate's situation, as she sees it, is such that the price of absolute morality is absolute self-renunciation; the price of partial morality is partial self-renunciation; and finally, the reward of immorality is total self-gratification. It is the novel's concern to disprove this last proposition, but the rigor of her "logic" is nonetheless one of the forces motivating the subsequent events.

This fact, together with the fact that the possession of a fortune is the *sine qua non* of her vision, constitutes the basis of Milly's predicament, and is why it has indeed "its ominous air of awaiting her." Milly has a fortune, Kate needs one; Milly is passive and gentle—a dove; Kate is restless and ruthless—a panther. In addition not only is Milly mortally ill while Kate is vibrantly alive, but also Milly's one English acquaintance happens to be Merton Densher, and she happens to be susceptible to his attractions. Thus every element in Milly's situation has its opposite correspondence in Kate's, and the predicament of the former is a function or extension of the predicament of the latter; it is its logical outgrowth.

One could indeed say that much of the energy of the novel is logistical, rhetorical, dialectical. And clearly both the strengths and the weaknesses of the book are in some important way tied up with this fact. The structuring of the plot, for example, the way the initial dramatic situation is conceived and set up, is characterized by a high degree of formal balance and antithesis, correspondences and oppositions. The way in which what Milly needs and what Milly has to offer so neatly dovetail with what Kate needs, and also has to offer, is almost too good to be true. Or too painful to be bearable, which is the effect James intended. The "soul of drama," he writes, ". . . is the portrayal, as we know, of a catastrophe determined in spite of oppositions. My young woman would *herself* be the opposition— to the catastrophe announced by the associated Fates."[11]

That is, the effect of the remorseless logic of the combined circumstances of the two girls is precisely the feeling of impending catastrophe— and catastrophe that is inevitable, unavoidable, inexorable. Whatever one might argue about the apparent improbabilities, coincidences, even patnesses of the initial situation in the novel, the result is one of ironic contrast, of heightened tension and expectation. There is something ruthless in the manipulation of the events, to be sure, but that very fact contributes to the intensity of the emotional effect, the sense of dread and pity, the feeling of the inevitable mockery and destruction of the deep yearning for life that is so profound a part of Milly's makeup.

The effect is not merely dramatic; it is almost diabolic. There is something reminiscent of a hellish chess game in the book's presentation of the mathematics of narrowing alternatives, in which the loser of the game not only does not know she is losing, she does not even know she is playing.

James has an almost Satanic instinct for situation; indeed much of his power as a novelist lies in his remorselessness in this respect.

Remorseless in his delineation of character too, he is one of the great pathologists of human nature we have in modern fiction. His ability to cast a cold eye on a whole spectrum of moral sickness and to present it without flinching is one of the paradoxes of a sensibility that in many respects evaded the direct confrontation of powerful emotion. In the midst of the yearning and separation that are characteristic motifs of his imagination is this preoccupation with the darker aspects of the human psyche, a preoccupation characterized by the degree to which the author seems close to and unfearful of its concerns rather than detached or distant from them. "What bothers Gide most in James' characters," writes Matthiessen, "is the excessive functioning of their analytical powers, whereas . . . 'all the shaggy, tangled undergrowth, all the wild darkness [is absent.] . . .' But in works as different as *The Turn of the Screw* and *The Wings of the Dove*, James showed an extraordinary command of his own kind of darkness, not the darkness of passion, but the darkness of moral evil."[12]

The characters in *The Wings of the Dove* form a spectrum ranging from evil to moral mediocrity: Lionel Croy, who had "no truth in him. . . . He dealt out lies as he might the cards from the greasy old pack for the game of diplomacy to which you were to sit down with him" (XIX, 7); Aunt Maud, "Britannia of the Market Place," who, in addition to her "florid philistinism . . . fantastic furniture and heaving bosom, the false gods of her taste and false notes of her talk," was "unscrupulous and immoral" (XIX, 30–31); Marion, "grown red and almost fat" (XIX, 37), and whose abjectness and desire to profit are oblivious of any dignity; the Misses Condrips, who "lived in a deeper hole than Marion, but . . . kept their ear to the ground . . . spent their days in prowling" (XIX, 43); Susan Shepherd, who "had now no life to lead; and she honestly believed that she was thus supremely equipped for leading Milly's own" (XIX, 113), and in whose view "it was life enough simply to feel her companion's feelings" (XIX, 115); Lord Mark, "bald . . . and slightly stale" (XIX, 151), to whom Milly remarks, "You're *blasé*, but you're not enlightened. You're familiar with everything, but conscious really of nothing. What I mean is that you've no imagination" (XIX, 162), and who "pointed to nothing; which was very possibly just a sign of his real cleverness, one of those that the really clever had in common with the really void" (XIX, 178); the "great" Eugenio, "recommended by granddukes and Americans," who was "a swindler finished to the fingertips . . . for ever carrying one well-kept Italian hand to his heart and plunging the other straight into her pocket, which, as she had instantly observed him to recognise, fitted it like a glove" (XX, 132–33); Sir Luke Strett of the "thousand knives": "What *was* he in fact but patient, what was she [Milly] but physician, from the moment she embraced once for all the necessity, adopted once for all the policy, of saving him alarms about her subtlety?" (XX, 125).

This, aside from the protagonists, constitues the cast of *The Wings of the Dove:* the vulgar and the vicarious, the abject and the empty, the snoopers and swindlers, the relentless and the helpless. It is on the whole a considerably tamer list of characters than is to be found in that problematic group of novels that immediately precede the major works: *What Maisie Knew, The Awkward Age,* and *The Sacred Fount,* and furthermore the comic and satiric note[13] in the mode of their presentation is obvious. Still, it is a society less of fools than of knaves, most of whom, to the degree of their talents, have in common the fine art of calculated self-gain.

It is the society in which the gentle dove, the princess, the heiress of all the ages finds herself, small wonder, a "success." Its keynote, a somewhat ravenous mutual parasitism (not symbiosis), is sounded almost from the beginning, when Lord Mark, at Milly's first London dinner party, after pronouncing her a success, "pleasantly" remarks that Mrs. Lowder will, however, get back her money: "He could say it too—which was singular—without affecting her either as vulgar or as 'nasty'; and he had soon explained himself by adding: 'Nobody here, you know, does anything for nothing.' " (XIX, 160). This explicit note of warning to Milly is sounded twice again, by Kate herself. The first instance is soon after the dinner, when Kate explains that Lord Mark himself is no more indifferent to himself than Aunt Maud is to herself," for he was working Lancaster Gate for all it was worth: just as it was, no doubt, working *him,* and just as the working and the worked were in London, as one might explain, the parties to every relation" (XIX, 178). And strangest of all, Kate adds, is the "happy understanding" that "the worker in one connexion was the worked in another" (XIX, 179). But on the subject of Milly's own paying role, Kate declines discussion: it is to be taken for granted that "Milly would pay a hundred per cent—and even to the end, doubtless, through the nose" (XIX, 180).

The *tone* of the remarks—which might mislead, even amuse, someone of much greater sophistication than Milly[14]—is of course calculated for amusement; first of all for the narcissistic amusement of the inner circle in which the question of anyone's being misled by it simply does not exist. The game of treating Milly as if she were a fully initiated member of the circle is an added refinement, the ironical contrast between their words and her response (or their awareness and her innocence) providing a source of mild sadistic pleasure. In itself this is not entirely heinous: there can be something extraordinarily irritating about total gullibility—especially in the possessor of an immense fortune, dazzled by her social "success" but unaware that it is a function of the fortune, and unaware too that in proper perspective it is she and not they who should be dispensing the favor of "acceptance." Her obvious and abysmal ignorance of the *kind* of society into which she has made her triumphant debut is a further irritant: Lord Mark is a penniless *inutile* aristocrat, Mrs. Lowder is a moderately well heeled, status-seeking Philistine. These two revolve in each other's orbits because of the obvious possibility of bartering goods to their mutual benefit. Yet of all this, Milly, with both status and millions (she is "the girl with the background, the girl with the crown of old gold" [XIX, 109]), is oblivious.

It is only in conjunction with the other complex functions it serves that the tone of the social intercourse of this group becomes sinister. It is geared toward the flattery, seduction, and deception of Milly. And the mask of frankness is a means to all these ends: it is flattering to be told what is "really" going on behind the glittering social facade; seduction is a process accomplished by effecting the substitution of one set of values for another, less rigorous and more "honest" to the infinitely varied nature of man; deception occurs when appearances are made misleading. In this case the logic roughly is that no one really so out for himself as Kate and Lord Mark describe would admit it, hence the admission is a kind of sophisticated joke, a "pleasantry."

And it is perfectly true that in a society which condemned stepping on others to advance oneself, no one would admit to it. But it is not that kind of society. It does not value honor and honesty and selflessness, but only their appearance. It does value material wealth and social status, and gives both tacit and open approval to any means utilized to obtain them.

Milly's fundamental error of judgment with respect to her English acquaintances is her failure to recognize this inversion of values, her assumption that she and they speak a common moral language. In fact nothing could be further from the truth: there are two separate grammars here and, as in any two widely different languages, different assumptions about the nature and significance of reality.

Up to a point, as we have seen, her error is the result of the deliberate deception practiced upon her, and she is therefore blameless. But with Kate's second warning to Milly, the complexion of events alters significantly: the panther reveals itself for a moment. To Milly's comment on the remarkable kindness of Aunt Maud, Kate exclaims: "Oh but she has . . . plenty of use for you! You put her in, my dear, more than you put her out. You don't half see it, but she has clutched your petticoat. You can do anything—you can do, I mean, lots that *we* can't. You're an outsider, independent and standing by yourself; you're not hideously relative to tiers and tiers of others. . . . We're of no use to you—it's decent to tell you. You'd be of use to us, but that's a different matter. My honest advice to you would be . . . to drop us while you can." She continues with a denunciation of Susan Stringham for having let Milly in to the mess, and when Milly protests, "And yet without Susie I shouldn't have had *you*," Kate flashes back, "Oh, you may very well loathe me yet!" (XIX, 281–282).

Milly's story is one of resisting until too late, and in spite of reiterated warnings, knowledge that she should have accepted; a story of not seeing. She is practiced upon by others "for interests and advantages, from motives and points of view, of their own," and these "promptings" from others,

James writes, consititute "contributively, her sum of experience, represent to her somehow, in good faith or in bad, what she should have *known*."[15] Of course, Milly's stake in not knowing is very great indeed. Part of James's dramatic genius consists of his diabolic sense for situations in which the negative significance of alternative choices for the characters is stronger than the positive. Either way for Milly now is a matter of life or death, or rather, death is the probability, life only a possibility. One of the most powerful things in the novel is the portrayal of her resistance to the insights that in fact she has again and again; long before Kate's outburst of frankness, Milly has sensed dangers, "sinister motives," "brutality," "the not wholly calculable" as well as the potent and magnetic beauty of her friend, the fact that she was "made for great social uses." But even worse, Milly has felt "the hint of pity," first from Kate, then from Sir Luke, then from Aunt Maud, as she is later to feel from Densher, Eugenio, Susie, Lord Mark—from everyone in fact with whom she comes into contact. When Aunt Maud displays it, independently, Milly takes it as "the charge of weakness. It was what every one, if she didn't look out, would soon be saying—There's something the matter with you!'" (XIX, 270).

The "matter" with her is a complex thing from the point of view of her London milieu. Kate perceives her stoicism, her struggle, her fierce pride, but the intense spiritual beauty, generosity, and hunger of the dying girl fully become clear only after her death. It is *after* her death that Merton falls in love with her. Her virtues are not of a sort to be recognized as such by her English friends; her innocence, as we have seen, is sport for them; what deeply interests them about her, what they "revere," is her fortune, not her inner being. The latter they cannot see clearly any more than she can see theirs; a blindness is at work here, to the ultimate woe of all the main actors. But before Merton, and Kate, are unblinded, Milly is (among other things) pitied by them; not merely for her illness but also for her lack of female, animal magnetism, really of sexuality. Kate, for example, has

> a feeling not analysed but divided, a latent impression that Mildred Theale was not, after all, a person to change places, to change even chances with. Kate, verily, would perhaps not quite have known what she meant by this discrimination and she came near naming it only when she said to herself that, rich as Milly was, one probably wouldn't—which was singular—ever hate her for it. . . . It wasn't obscure to her [Kate] that, without some very particular reason to help, it might have proved a test of one's philosophy not to be irritated by a mistress of millions . . . who, as a girl, so easily might have been, like herself, only vague and cruelly female.
>
> (XIX, 176)

So that part of what Milly is fighting is the knowledge of the way she is seen by the people closest to her. The reason she resists this, and resists correctly reading their motives, is that to do so would be to learn not so much that they do want her fortune as that they don't want her. Sir Luke has put the responsibility for her life in her own hands; she "could" live if she "would." His prescription against death is to live; he makes it sound simple. To "live" in turn means to fall in love and be loved. She already is in love of course, with the young man that many-splendored Kate keeps failing to mention. At this point, Milly is in possession of all the relevant facts: that Kate and Densher know each other; that Kate envies Milly's money and the freedom it brings; that Densher is poor; that he loves Kate; that Aunt Maud is concerned about their attachment. The one fact anyone actively bothers to deceive her about is the degree of Kate's interest in Merton, but then Milly has the option of drawing her own conclusions about that, except that if she acknowledges the obvious she passes sentence of death upon herself. In short, she can neither afford to see nor afford not to see what the situation really is.

This is an example of James's uncanny instinct for narrowing and negative alternatives, in which any move spells disaster. It is part of what makes him powerful as a dramatist; it is also what can make him nearly unbearable. In the very nature of the situations he constructs, the whole conception of human freedom of actions, choice, and hence responsibility, amounts to a bitter farce; it is practically nonexistent. It may be that one reason critics have accused him of "moral unsatisfactoriness"[16] is his almost violent rejection of the notion of free will. Recall his definition of drama as "catastrophe determined in spite of oppositions"—the word "determined" should not pass unnoticed. And what, for example, actually are the alternative courses of action open to the three protagonists? If Kate did not play her game the way she played it, her choices would be either to marry Densher and remain penniless or to marry Lord Mark and remain loveless; equal impossibilities, given her character. Merton has the option of refusing to play Kate's game. If he did, he would preserve his integrity but lose Kate. And the terror that speaks loudest to him is that possibility: "What if I should begin to bore this splendid creature?" Finally Milly as we have seen, has the option of consciously admitting the implications of what she has observed, sensed, and intuited all along. If she did, she would have spared herself the final humiliation, but she would have died sooner. Kate puts this succinctly to Merton at the end, " 'She never wanted the truth—' —Kate had a high headshake. 'She wanted *you*' " (XX, 326–327).

This is not to suggest that James is unconcerned with these very issues of freedom, will, and responsibility. On the contrary, he is obsessed with them. The concept of "freedom" is the pivotal point of Isabel Archer's character, for example, but the book is about how, thinking she is freely making the choice that will bring her the most freedom, she has in fact been beguiled into making the one that will bring her the least. Milly, too, is profoundly concerned with the question of responsibility, but she has a wider, more ironic vision of the various ways of viewing this issue than does Isabel. In a passage of great power, James describes her inward upheaval after she has been told by Sir Luke that whether she lives or dies is up to her:

"Grey immensity had somehow of a sudden become her element; grey immensity was what her distinguished friend had, for the moment, furnished her world with and what the question of 'living,' as he put it to her, living by option, by volition, inevitably took on for its immediate face" (XIX, 247). She drives through Regent's Park, and suddenly in her vision identifies her plight with the human plight in general:

> Here were benches and smutty sheep; here were idle lads at games of ball, with their cries mild in the thick air; here were wanderers anxious and tired like herself, here doubtless were hundreds of others just in the same box. Their box, their great common anxiety, what was it, in this grim breathing-space, but the practical question of life? They could live if they would; that is, like herself, they had been told so: she saw them all about her, on seats, digesting the information, recognising it again as something in a slightly different shape familiar enough, the blessed old truth that they would live if they could.
>
> (XIX, 250)

The real complexity of James's vision of life lies in the relationship between knowledge and action as these relate to the whole question of moral responsibility. Yet that question itself assumes alternative shapes in his imagination, with a kind of shadowy option suggested between real interior freedom and the mere illusion of it. Furthermore, though Milly's wilful blindness makes her one of the agents of the catastrophe, that catastrophe would have been inevitable even if she *hadn't* blinded herself to the facts. That is the terror of her position: she could not have avoided her doom by correctly seeing the situation around her. And again, what are our feelings at the end of the novel, when the disaster is an accomplished fact? Do we blame either Kate, the prime mover, for the results of practiced deception, or Milly for allowing herself to be practiced upon? *Merton* certainly blames Kate—in fact he goes to incredible lengths to see to what lengths she will go—but it is not at all clear that James does; besides, Merton has his own, rather unpalatable way of drawing ethical lines and splitting moral hairs.

On the other hand, the events of the novel do assert something about the outcome of certain forms of human behavior. All three of the protagonists are playing for the highest possible stakes: money, morality, love, life itself. And all three lose: their calculated risks collapse in a nightmare of death, dishonor, and distrust. What might be called Milly's suspension of disbelief betrays her just as certainly as Kate's and Merton's partnership in manipulation and deception betrays them. And these facts mean something.

It is possible, that is, to go through the novel and show that the principal agents are not responsible for what happens; it is also possible to show that they are. A paradoxical sense of things, antithetical modes of structuring and comprehending reality without granting authority to any one mode, is a fundamental characteristic of James's imagination. In many serious works of art, of course, one finds opposed assumptions about the nature and meaning of existence, assumptions whose value is expressive rather than explanatory. James, however, tends to systematize his structures, elaborate, juxtapose, and finally exhaust them. Without giving credence to any one—though each structure claims *for itself* absolute authority—he renders their inception, evolution, interplay, and destruction. The dreams of the characters are programs for existence, models to "better" reality. Each construct proposes itself to the character who fashions it as pre-emptive, inevitable, justifiable: a superior version of the conditions of life, designed for self-fulfillment. Only, the premises of the different models by definition exclude one another, and we are witnesses to the disintegration of the models that results when their conflicting premises are exposed.

On another level what we are given is the outcome, the end results, of certain forms of behavior, usually manipulation. The results are seen to destroy both those who practiced it and those upon whom it was practiced. James's tales in a way constitute cases in point from which it is possible to make certain inductions, usually about what will not work. We spoke earlier about his strange vision of the culpability of innocence as well as of knowledge. In relation to this matter, his novels are illustrations of the *practical* failure of both self-deception and the deception of others, and of the fact that the refusal to adjudicate between one's own needs and those of others simply does not work.

The question whether he sees greed and manipulation as *moral* failures is another matter altogether. In general, James utilizes moral constructs for the sake of the interest and intensity that result from their juxtaposition with other models for behavior. He is concerned with rendering the excruciation that results from exposing someone of a trusting, open, innocent nature to someone who, beneath a perfected social manner of grace and charm, hides deadly intents. Fascinated with his villains and with the general human capacity for destructiveness, he is often primarily involved in exploring the peripheral limits of that capacity in his characters. *The Awkward Age*, *What Maisie Knew*, and even the comparatively mild *Washington Square* are all, for example, studies of parental abuse of the young. As we saw in the first chapter, James has a tendency to be preoccupied with the process of victimization for its own sake, or for its sheer dramatic effect, by no means for its moral implications per se. In this sense, he has along with other American writers, an important kinship with Poe. D. H. Lawrence, in his *Studies in Classic American Literature*, recognizes a similar affinity between Poe and Hawthorne, and characterizes a tendency in American art that is at *least* as true of James (though Lawrence does not have a chapter on James) as it is of any of the writers the book deals with:

> "All the time there is this split in the American art and art-consciousness. On the top it is as nice as pie, goody-goody and lovey-dovey. Like Hawthorne being such a blue-eyed darling, in life, and Longfellow and the rest such sucking doves. . . .

"Serpents they were. Look at the inner meaning of their art and see what demons they were."[17]

The most obvious manifestations of this kind of duality in James are the studied contrasts between the manners and morals of America and Europe. Generally, James's treatment of manners has been much, if ambivalently, praised by critics, while his treatment of morals has caused dissatisfaction and been badly misinterpreted. He "knew . . . manners too well; he had penetrated too thoroughly," writes Leavis, who adds that it "is no doubt at first appearances odd that his interest in manners should have gone with such moral-intellectual intensity. But the manners he was interested in were to be the outward notation of spiritual and intellectual fineness, or at least to lend themselves to treatment as such. Essentially he was in quest of an ideal society."[18]

By "manners," Leavis means "the refinements of civilized intercourse" or "highly civilized" conduct. That of course is to narrow the possible meaning of the word from "a person's habitual behavior or conduct," or his "outward bearing" in general (to borrow one definition from *The American College Dictionary* and one from *The Oxford Universal Dictionary*), to a particular kind of behavior ("civilized"). The latter is a fair enough designation of one type of conduct James dealt with, but it certainly does not do justice to the range and complexity of his fascination with external behavior. In the broader sense of the term, the Pococks have "manners" too (though not refined ones) and ones that, however ironically, interest James greatly.

But a more important issue raised by Leavis is the nature of the relationship between a person's conduct in the world around him and his inner "self." According to Leavis, James intended a one-to-one correspondence between manners and morals, one's demeanor and one's "essence," one's mask and one's face. Sometimes this is the case: with Madame de Vionnet, pre-eminently. But by and large James's interest in manners is often exactly the opposite of the sort of equation Leavis posits. Most frequently, James's preoccupation lies with the profound *discrepancy* between the outward veneer of polish, wit, charm, "correctness," and the inward darkness of the human heart. Such a discrepancy is postulated for characters like Kate Croy, Madame Merle, Charlotte Stant, and the energy, interest—and horror—of the novels in which they appear are contingent upon it. Leavis has been beguiled too much by the goody-goody surface, the guise the serpent takes. The "outward notation" stands in deliberate ironic contrast to the inner spiritual reality and is intended as a disguise rather than a manifestation of the latter. Or the "manners" become a kind of muted, oblique language for concerns that lie far beneath their surface, regions of bliss and bale that have nothing to do with the drawing room:

> He can convey an impression, an atmosphere of what you will with literally nothing. Embarrassment, chastened happiness—for his happiness is always tinged with regret—greed, horror, social vacuity—he can give you

it all with a purely blank page. His characters will talk about rain, about the opera, about the moral aspects of the selling of Old Masters to the New Republic, and those conversations will convey to your mind that the quiet talkers are living in an atmosphere of horror, of bankruptcy, of passion hopeless as the Dies Iræ! . . . That, you know, is what life really is—a series of such meaningless episodes beneath the shadow of doom—or of impending bliss, if you prefer it. And that is what Henry James gives you—an immense body of work all dominated with that vibration—with that balancing of the mind between the great outlines and the petty details.[19]

It must be more clearly recognized that James's vision of human existence is first and last an ironic one, and that it is not he who is deceived by the glitter of the social facade he studies. He was in one sense in search of an ideal society, and the search took place in the two countries of his imagination that in effect constituted a mythological setting: America, the Pale Lady, the boring paradise, and Europe, the Dark Lady, seductive, sensual, totally attractive, totally wicked, the enchanting hell. His novels are all legends of the failure of the quest, because in *his* vision truth and beauty are not one. His Holy Grail is the golden bowl with the imperceptible flaw.

But the success of any ironic presentation depends first of all upon consistency of tone. Reuben Brower defines irony as "meaning . . . narrowed to opposition" and remarks that metaphor and irony "present two levels of meaning which the reader must entertain at once if he is to respond imaginatively to either of these forms of expression. . . . To experience the irony . . . we must entertain both of the clashing possibilities."[20] Even in works (the problem novels, for example) in which James deliberately renders reality from a multiplicity of perspectives, without giving authority to any one of them, each perspective is itself clear, and it is obvious that if either level of meaning (whether or not the clashing viewpoints are resolved ultimately) becomes obscured, or the author's attitude toward it is ambivalent or inconsistent, the ironic effect is lost in confusion. This is finally what happens with the figure of Merton Densher in *The Wings of the Dove*. Up to a point in the delineation of Densher, James's touch is sure and masterly as he keeps a fine and deliberate balance between Densher's increasingly distorted self-image and the more objective image of him held by others. Eugenio, for example, "took a view of him . . . essentially vulgar . . . the imputation in particular that, clever, *tanto bello* and not rich, the young man from London was—by the obvious way—pressing Miss Theale's fortune hard" (XX, 257). Densher's passivity, his self-deception and rationalization, his increasing helplessness and loss of freedom are superbly handled. One of the first consequences of his fall is the diminution in his power of "right reasoning": it is Kate's doing and not his. Or it is Milly's *and* his, freely, not Kate's at all; therefore he is not being manipulated, has not lost his manhood. His ethical position entails obedience to the law, not the spirit; action alone, and not intent or desire, is what is culpable. So long then as he doesn't *do* anything: tell a direct lie, propose marriage himself to Milly, he is blameless. The fact that he knows that both Kate and Aunt Maud have "told the proper lie" for him (that Kate doesn't love him) he passes over. And it will be all right if Milly proposes to him. He has, it is true, moments of clearer awareness, in which he wonders about the validity of his distinction between active and passive participation in the whole affair: "It was Kate's description of him, his defeated state, it was none of his own; his responsibility would begin, as he might say, only with acting it out. The sharp point was, however, in the difference between acting and not acting: this difference in fact it was that made the case of conscience. He saw it with a certain alarm rise before him that everything was acting that was not speaking the particular word" (that is, disabusing Milly of the notion that Kate is indifferent to him) (XX, 76).

He decides, however, that it would be "indelicate" to mention the matter to Milly when she would never dream of mentioning it to him, and that further there would be a kind of unnecessary "brutality" in shaking Milly off when she so clearly enjoys his company. At this point, he has not yet given Milly reason to believe that he has any kind of romantic interest in her, though that deception is imminent. The deception itself (what he calls "turning his corner") he perpetrates out of *politeness:* "Clearly what had occurred was her having wished it [that he accompany her on a drive] so that she had made him simply wish, in civil acknowledgement, to oblige *her*" (XX, 88). We are to take this extraordinary gesture at face value; he is quite sincere. It is extraordinary because, from here on out, he will not just disoblige but kill her if he does not keep up the pretense. This is the fateful moment, for *now* he would (so far as he knows) merely wound her feelings if he declines her invitation; *later* he would destroy her, as he himself quickly recognizes a few moments later: "If he might have turned tail . . . five minutes before, he couldn't turn tail now" (XX, 90).

His politeness is a matter of real concern: he sees she yearns for him, he is touched by her "shy fragrance of heroism" (XX, 81). But his displacement of perspective is incredible, particularly in view of his awareness, en route to this very visit, that he was "the kind of man wise enough to mark the case in which chucking [someone] might be the minor evil and the least cruelty" (XX, 71). And so the code of chivalry becomes the Law that Merton obeys: "The single thing that was clear in complications was that, whatever happened, one was to behave as a gentleman. . . . The law was not to be a brute—in return for amiabilities" (XX, 183–184).

To be a blue-eyed darling in appearance and a serpent in fact—and not to recognize it. The irony of the portrait is intense, deliberate, and in splendid control until the concluding portions of the book, when something goes askew and the man who has tried so hard not to be a brute becomes what is almost worse, a prig. This was not James's intent of course: Merton was to have gone through a spiritual transformation—literally a conversion—to have conceived a "horror" of the scheme in which he had become involved, as James puts it in his notebooks, and to have emerged morally reborn, "faithful to the [exquisite] image of the dead."[21]

But a conversion implies a degree of self-examination and valuation (rejection of the sinful self) that never takes place in Merton.[22] He dreads public exposure and feels "a dire apprehension of publicity" (XX, 391), but this is about the limit of any self-scrutiny that we are shown. Because of this, his conversion is not persuasive, in the sense that we do not feel moved, convinced of some radical spiritual growth. It is one of those cases where instead of being *shown*, as James would put it, we have to take the word of the "poor author" for it. About James's intention, there can be no question: the question is to what degree he realized it. He himself is the first to admit that sometimes an artist's plan is one thing, his result another. One reason we do not feel a sense of Densher's spiritual growth is that his concern is so little with himself, so exclusively and so harshly focused upon Kate. That he should feel a revulsion toward her is not, in itself, surprising, but the way in which he manifests it is very much unlike the "grace" Milly extended to him. He is nearly cruel. He sets little tests and traps for Kate like placing in her hands, to deal with at her option, both the letter from Milly and the envelope from her New York lawyers stating the amount she had left him. When Kate opens it—and who can conceive of her doing anything but—he confesses he is "disappointed": it wasn't the "handsome way" of renunciation he had hoped for; he had hoped she would return it unopened, accompanied by "an absolutely kind letter" (XX, 398) of refusal. When she points out that he neglected to express this hope in his letter to her, he explains, "I didn't want to. I wanted to leave it to yourself. I wanted—oh yes, if that's what you wish to ask me—to see what you'd do."

"You wanted to measure the possibilities of my departure from delicacy? . . ."

"Well, I wanted—in so good a case—to test you" (XX, 399). And test her he continues to do, up to the bitter end. "He had given poor Kate her freedom" (XX, 396), as he puts it: freedom to choose the money without him, or him without the money. So that once again she is in the very dilemma, caught between the same set of negative alternatives, that she was at the outset. There is nothing wrong with this degree of "poetic justice" descending on her shoulders, but there is something wrong with Merton's sanctimonious viciousness, especially when it is coupled with the comparatively gentle, forgiving attitude he has toward himself. He explains to Kate at one point that Sir Luke had understood that he had "meant awfully well"; at another, he senses that Mrs. Lowder gathered the "essence" of his situation: "The essence was that something had happened to him too beautiful and too sacred to describe. He had been, to his recovered sense, forgiven, dedicated, blessed" (XX, 343). But he does not extend to Kate the charity he, without tests, has received.

How then are we to understand these events with which the novel

closes? Are we intended to make a split judgment, in which Merton is finally exonerated, but Kate not? If this is the intention, it certainly is not
realized; in fact the emotional effect is just the opposite. There is a certain
beauty in the brave if somewhat harrowing consistency of Kate's character,
in her risking everything to gain everything. And this we feel right up
through the end, in spite of Merton. Perhaps it is partly due to the principle cited by E. E. Stoll, that readers tend to identify with the active agent
rather than the passive, whether that agent is morally acceptable to them
or not.[23] At any rate, the bravery of her risk coupled with her refusal to
rationalize her behavior, while most of Merton's energy is devoted to rationalization, helps to account for our greater sympathy for Kate. There is
something much more unpalatable about immorality when it is in the mask
of piety than when it is frank and open.

I suspect that James's *scheme* for the novel, which we have in the
notebooks, called for a kind of formal resolution of the plot that was incom-
patible with the profoundly paradoxical nature of his vision of the source
and meaning of human suffering. It was mentioned earlier that much of the
energy of the novel is logistical, rhetorical. James's concern with formal balance and opposition, and with fateful logic, is highly effective in the initial
portions of the book, where it creates the feeling of impending catastrophe
that is not to be eluded by any efforts on Milly's part. But James's preoccupation with the mathematics of situation badly weakens the ending. In a
way, one could say that the two deepest artistic impulses—concern for
shape, form, and aesthetic organization, and concern for truth—obtruded
upon each other in this novel at its conclusion. Densher's actions and reactions toward Kate are both harsher and simpler than those of the total
work, just as his reactions toward himself are kinder. But because this is
the case, the novel can end "neatly," with Densher scarred but beautified
and Kate plunged back into the original dilemma upon the altar of which
she sacrificed her morality: Kate given and refusing one last option to renounce her lust for money; Kate not spiritually transformed as Densher
supposedly is but in fact (that is in *effect*) is not. Kate is thus left formally,
though once again this is not the emotional effect, bearing the brunt of the
drama of pain that has been enacted. What the book makes so clear and
the ending does not is that all three of the principal agents played their
role in the events that took place, and that all three are at one and the same
time responsible and not responsible. It is this ambivalent sense of things,
constantly articulated throughout the book, that the ending does not, or
cannot rise to meet. The ending therefore undermines both the complexity
and the emotional intensity of the work as a whole. Densher's sudden access to piety is accomplished with too much ease; he does not suffer enough
in the sense that he escapes the self-confrontation that would be the symbolic recognition of and penance for some of the pangs Milly has endured
at his hands. This in turn means that the whole moral order of events that
centered around his figure has to be questioned: did James after all take

him at his own valuation, as a reluctant pawn who is to be exonerated for having tried to be chivalrous in the middle of a compromising situation? And if James did take him that way, what then are we to make of the central ethical problem that is the really interesting and really powerful circumstance of Densher's position: that "case of conscience" which lay in the difference between acting and not acting on his part? If we accept the ending, we must dismiss the case of conscience as a mere rhetorical murmur to himself in the middle of the gentlemen's plight. Yet the book, fortunately will not allow us to do that. In spite of the ending, Densher's passive involvement has implicated him deeply indeed. This at least is the effect, and it is a good thing that it is. If it were not, the whole novel would suffer from a superficiality, even sentimentality, of vision. But James explicitly consigned even to Milly responsibility for the outcome of events, and it is difficult to believe he did not intend at least the same burden of blame for Merton, if not quite a lot more. It does not seem convincing, that is, that James's intention was different from the effect created by the events of the novel up until the end. It is the ending that is unpersuasive, even unreal. The novel itself survives, but certainly at a cost to its integrity of effect and full realization of its own order of spiritual reality. In that order Merton *is* exonerated, but in a very different sense from that in which he exonerates himself, just as Kate is condemned on quite another level from that on which he condemns her: one considerably less legalistic, literal, and petty. He has of course applied the letter of the law to himself, earlier, so perhaps it is not surprising that he does so to Kate at the end. But the burden of the book rests upon violation not of the word but of the spirit. Is not the whole point that no "word" is spoken to Milly, that the crime and the woe are committed wordlessly but nevertheless absolutely? It is this central human fact of the novel that the ending betrays, and it is in spite of the betrayal that the novel survives.

Notes

1. Henry James, *The American*, New York ed., Vol. II (New York, 1907), p. 134.

2. See Chapter I for a more detailed discussion of this matter with respect to *The Europeans*.

3. Henry James, *The Art of the Novel: Critical Prefaces*, ed. R. P. Blackmur (New York, 1962), p. 294.

4. *Ibid.*, p. 295.

5. *Ibid.*, p. 294.

6. *Ibid.*

7. Henry James, *The Wings of the Dove*, New York ed. (New York, 1909), XIX, 32. Subsequent citations are to this edition.

8. *The Art of the Novel*, pp. 297, 298.

9. Most of the relationships in the book can be looked at from the point of view of who is using whom: Kate's father, sister, and sisters-in-law try to recover their ruined fortune

by pressuring her to accept Aunt Maud's offer to "do for" her; Aund Maud in turn has had Kate "marked from far back" as the means by which she can realize her own social ambitions if Kate under her tutelage marries properly; through Kate's countermanipulations and Densher's passive assistance, Aunt Maud herself becomes the one who is used; and everyone—including Lord Mark, the subtle parasite Eugenio, and even, it could be argued, Susie—uses Milly.

10. In respect to material things of course, her susceptibility is one with her family's; it is only their abjectness in the face of it that she loathes. There is a sense in which their whole relationship with her parodies the forces that in a subtler way most motivate Kate.

11. *The Art of the Novel*, p. 290.

12. *Henry James: The Major Phase* (New York, 1944), pp. 93–94.

13. Kate, in near despair over her father's rejection of her offer to forsake all others and go with him, exclaims: "I wish there were some one here who might serve—for any contingency—as a witness that I *have* put it to you that I'm ready to come." "Would you like me [her father asked] to call the landlady?" (XIX, 20–21).

14. The tone is summarized by Milly: "These were the fine facilities, pleasantries, ironies, all these luxuries of gossip and philosophies of London and of life, and they became quickly, between the pair, the common form of talk" (XIX, 180).

15. *The Art of the Novel*, p. 291.

16. F. R. Leavis, *The Great Tradition* (Garden City, New York, 1954), p. 205.

17. (Garden City, New York, 1953), pp. 92–93.

18. *The Great Tradition*, p. 198.

19. Ford Madox Hueffer, *Henry James: A Critical Study* (New York, 1916), pp. 153–155.

20. *The Fields of Light: An Experiment in Critical Reading* (New York, 1951), pp. 50–51. Brower adds, "So obvious a point needs stressing . . . because some definitions of irony imply that the reader finds the intended or true meaning beneath the apparent, a view that tends to destroy irony both as a literary experience and as a vision of life."

21. *The Notebooks of Henry James*, ed. F. O. Matthiessen and Kenneth B. Murdock (New York, 1955), pp. 173–174.

22. When Saul of Tarsus is on the road to Damascus and hears the voice of Christ saying "Saul, Saul, why persecutest thou me?" it is a private matter of conscience with respect to the implications in the stoning of Stephen. The behavior of the other Jews involved in the persecution is in no way relevant to his experience.

23. Elmer Edgar Stoll, "Give the Devil His Due," *Review of English Studies*, XX (April, 1944), 124.

The Difficulty of Ending: Maggie Verver in *The Golden Bowl*   Ruth Bernard Yeazell*

James's last completed novel ends with an embrace. "Close to her, her face kept before him, his hands holding her shoulders, his whole act enclosing her" (24, VI, iii, p. 369), the Prince clasps the Princess, and she buries

*Reprinted from Ruth Bernard Yeazell, *Language and Knowledge in the Late Novels of Henry James* (Chicago: University of Chicago Press, 1976), 100–130 and 139–140. Reprinted with permission of the University of Chicago Press and the author.

her head in his breast. It is a rare moment in Jamesian fiction—rare not only in the physical immediacy of the Prince's gesture, but in its conclusiveness. His act is one of literary as well as literal enclosure: embracing his wife, Amerigo brings *The Golden Bowl* to an emphatic finish. Maggie Verver's struggle to save her marriage has reached its fulfillment: "She knew at last really why—and how she had been inspired and guided, how she had been persistently able, how to her soul all the while it has been for the sake of this end" (p. 367). Unlike Isabel Archer in *The Portrait of a Lady*, Maggie does not end her story by fleeing from an embrace to an undefined future. James does not leave the Princess, like his earlier heroine, "en l'air,"[1] but in her husband's arms.

No other novel of the major phase comes to so apparently definite or victorious a conclusion. "Then there we are!" says Strether in the last line of *The Ambassadors* (22, XII, v, p. 327); but his desire "not, out of the whole affair, to have got anything for myself" (p. 326) makes "there" a very uncertain location needed. "To what do you go home?" asks Maria Gostrey twice. "I don't know," Strether can only reply. "There will always be something." Like so many Jamesian novels before it, *The Ambassadors* closes with a gesture of renunciation: we know that Strether is deeply changed, but we are told only what he will *not* do—that he will not stay with Maria in Paris and that he will not marry Mrs. Newsome in America. So too *The Wings of the Dove* concludes with a marriage that will not take place—unless we wish to think of Densher as joined in spiritual union with the memory of a dead girl. The last motion of the novel is a gesture of negation: Kate Croy shakes her head, speaking in words which are the tragic inversion of Strether's final statement: "We shall never be again as we were!" (20, X, vi, p. 405). Like Strether's, her last assertion is remarkably without concrete substance. *The Ambassadors* and *The Wings of the Dove* project undefined futures; in outward form, their resolutions are closer to the unfinished destinies of *The Ivory Tower*—a novel which is quite literally open-ended—than to the substantial reunion of Maggie and her Prince.

But the apparent finality of *The Golden Bowl* is in one sense terribly deceptive. With the possible exception of *The Turn of the Screw*, no Jamesian novel has left its readers themselves more *en l'air:* Maggie's reconciliation with her husband arouses many more unanswered questions than Isabel's return to hers.[2] For Maggie Verver is the first Jamesian innocent who confronts painful knowledge by choosing neither renunciation nor death; determining rather to live and to fight, she implicitly chooses instead the ultimate loss of her own innocence. Unlike Strether—and the long line of Jamesian heroes and heroines from whom he descends—Maggie wants very much to have something for herself "out of the whole affair," and she must risk inflicting pain on others as well as herself to achieve her ends. Struggling at once to understand her private world and to reshape it, Maggie Verver becomes James's strangest heroine: a character who combines Milly Theale's innocence, Densher's passive complicity in evil, and Kate Croy's active need for passion and control. It is a moving but uneasy combination: in this last Jamesian princess, the conflicting motives and desires of the central characters in the late fiction are compressed with an almost unbearable intensity. The resulting strains threaten to shatter not only the Princess herself, but the very coherence of the novel in which she finally rules.

The new elements in the design are of course Maggie's passion for her husband, her determination to win him back—and, perhaps less obviously, the Prince's apparent willingness to be won. Seven years before *The Golden Bowl*, James had written a novel in which a young girl, just emerging from childhood, makes an oddly similar choice: in her demand that the charming Sir Claude desert Mrs. Beale and run away with her—and in her own readiness equally to sacrifice Mrs. Wix—Maisie Farange is the youthful and quasi-innocent precursor of Maggie Verver. Despite endless talk about Maisie's "moral sense," her wish to be alone with Sir Claude—like Maggie's desire for her husband—seems to have very little to do with that faculty; certainly the tears which she wants to shed as the train to Paris pulls away from the station, leaving herself and Claude behind, "had nothing—no, distinctly nothing—to do with her moral sense" (11, xxxi, p. 354). If Maisie nevertheless remains with the relentlessly moral Mrs. Wix, it is not that she repents her original choice, but that Sir Claude finally shrinks from breaking his tie to Mrs. Beale (like Charlotte Stant, the heroine's stepmother). James does not allow his small heroine to have Sir Claude on her own terms; with his other heroines of the nineties, Fleda Vetch and Nanda Brookenham, Maisie must renounce the man she "loves."[3]

But in *The Golden Bowl* the Prince acquiesces in the betrayal of his mistress: the terms of the sexual equation are radically altered. The conflicting desires of *The Golden Bowl* demand that some sacrifice finally be exacted, and if Maggie is not to renounce her claim on the Prince, then Charlotte must be made to surrender hers. The critical debate over James's last novel usually shapes itself in moral terms—in arguments about whether Maggie's victory represents the triumph of a redemptive love or a "diabolic . . . geometry of destruction"[4]—but Maggie Verver finally conquers by what in *Maisie* James calls "something still deeper than a moral sense" (p. 354). In this obscurely compelling novel, James is most profoundly concerned not with the vexed question of morality, but with problems of knowledge, of passion, and of power.

For the reader of *The Golden Bowl*, the peculiar division in the novel's structure is itself problematic. Despite James's assertion in the Preface that "the Prince, in the first half of the book, virtually sees and knows and makes out, virtually represents to himself everything that concerns us" (*AN*, p. 329), the first volume moves freely through the minds of Adam Verver, Charlotte, Fanny Assingham, and even, briefly, of Maggie herself. When the Princess awakens to consciousness in the novel's second volume, her theories about the past have thus a special authority: having "gone behind" each of the members of her strange *menage à quatre*, we have already half known much of what Maggie now slowly and agonizingly discovers, and her interpretations have therefore the feel of truth. As she speculates on the relationship of Charlotte and the Prince, we need not suspect her of suffering, like the narrator of *The Sacred Fount*, from an excess of erotic imagination. And because the processes of her mind clarify much that has previously been obscure to us, Maggie's experience of discovery becomes ours as well. The novel is not a purely spatial form: though the two-part structure of *The Golden Bowl* might suggest that we are meant to sympathize equally with both "sides" in this passionate battle,[5] the fact that Maggie's interpretation is the last—and most comprehensive—inevitably draws us closer to her vision of events. The novel compels us to identify with Maggie not so much because she is the most virtuous inhabitant of her world, as because her knowledge of that world is nearest to our own.

And that knowledge is finally the source of the Princess's extraordinary power. Maggie triumphs not through moral purity, but through intelligence; she wins in the end because she possesses the sort of knowledge which Charlotte, despite all her worldly cleverness, lacks. "Ah for things I mayn't want to know I promise you shall find me stupid," Charlotte warns the Prince at Matcham (23, III, ix, p. 363). Of course in the first half of *The Golden Bowl* it has been Maggie herself who thus unconsciously desired, and achieved, stupidity: indeed at Matcham, "the extraordinary substitute for perception that presided, in the bosom of his wife, at so contented a view of his conduct and course" moves the Prince to "a strange final irritation" (23, III, vi, p. 333). But in the second half of the novel, Maggie becomes painfully conscious of her own abandonment and loss; if it is now Charlotte who has grown stupid, it is because she does not want to acknowledge that Maggie herself has left ignorance far behind. Ironically, therefore, Charlotte fulfills her own prediction of stupidity by failing to imagine her rival's capacity for growth. Speaking to his wife, the Prince delivers the verdict on his former mistress: "She ought to have *known* you. . . . She ought to have understood you better. . . . And she didn't really know you at all" (24, VI, ii, p. 347).

"She's stupid," the Prince finally declares (p. 348), and the structure of *The Golden Bowl* grants the reader no certain knowledge with which to refute that judgment, however harsh it may seem. Only for a brief space of time do we really penetrate Charlotte's consciousness and share directly in her vision of events: at the great diplomatic party, the height of her splendor and her triumph, we are accorded the power of seeing things through "the golden glow with which her intelligence was temporarily bathed" (23, III, i, p. 264). Beginning with her dramatic pause "half way up the 'monumental' staircase" (p. 245), the scene is all Charlotte's own—a demonstration from her point of view of "the *proved* private theory that materials to work with had been all she required and that there were none too precious for her to understand and use" (p. 246). But though we share her sense of triumph, her theory proves dangerously premature: the second half of the novel suggests that in Maggie there has indeed been material too precious for Charlotte's understanding and use. And we cannot know whether Charlotte herself comes to recognize her failure of imagination, for in the second volume of *The Golden Bowl* we are allowed no further access to Charlotte's private theories—proved or otherwise. To the reader, this woman of "exceptional radiance" (p. 264) becomes peculiarly opaque: for all we know, she may have grown quite dull indeed.

But if we are nevertheless reluctant to dismiss Charlotte's splendid intelligence so abruptly, our objections are surprisingly anticipated by Maggie herself. Amerigo's pronouncement draws from his wife a "long wail" of protest:

> "She's stupid," he abruptly opined.
> "O-oh!" Maggie protested in a long wail. It had made him in fact quickly change colour. "What I mean is that she's not, as you pronounce her, unhappy." And he recovered with this all his logic. "Why is she unhappy if she doesn't know?"
> "Doesn't know—?" She tried to make his logic difficult.
> "Doesn't know that *you* know."
> It came from him in such a way that she was conscious instantly of three or four things to answer. But what she said first was: "Do you think that's all it need take?" And before he could reply, "She knows, she knows!" Maggie proclaimed.
> "Well then what?"
> But she threw back her head, she turned impatiently away from him. "Oh I needn't tell you! She knows enough. Besides," she went on, "she doesn't believe us."
> It made the Prince stare a little. "Ah she asks too much!" That drew however from his wife another moan of objection, which determined in him a judgement. "She won't let you take her for unhappy."
> "Oh I know better than anyone else what she won't let me take her for!"
> "Very well," said Amerigo, "you'll see."
> "I shall see wonders, I know. I've already seen them and am prepared for them." Maggie recalled—she had memories enough. "It's terrible"—her memories prompted her to speak. "I see it's *always* terrible for women."
>
> (24, VI, ii, pp. 348–49)

The Prince's "logic" is simple: Charlotte's is the bliss of ignorance. It is the argument with which Kate and Densher defended to one another their use of Milly Theale, and it has been the stance of the Prince and Charlotte herself toward the Ververs (" 'They're extraordinarily happy.' Oh Charlotte's measure of it was only too full. 'Beatifically' " [23, III, v, p. 310]). But Maggie cannot so easily dismiss the possibility that Charlotte suffers. She knows that the other woman's unhappiness has been the necessary price of her own reunion with the Prince (p. 346)—that "it's *always* terrible for women" in a world which permits the existence of desires so passionately and so fatefully in conflict.

And it's always terrible, we might wish to add, for the reader as well. More fully conscious than any of her manipulative predecessors, Maggie Verver arouses in us at once an intenser sympathy and a more profound fear. And the tensions within Maggie which evoke our own deeply divided response make here for a dialogue of special impenetrability, a conversation whose premises seem continually to shift. Maggie tries, perversely, to make the Prince's logic "difficult" because she must deal with premises which are emotionally, if not logically, almost irreconcilable: acknowledging another's pain, she must nonetheless continue to act so as to inflict that pain. Unable to echo the Prince's complacent assertion of Charlotte's igno-rance—as Kate Croy or Charlotte herself might in a similar circumstance—the Princess proclaims her rival's consciousness: "She knows, she knows!" But when Amerigo probes further—"Well then what?"—Maggie turns, in a gesture reminiscent of Kate Croy, impatiently away: "Oh I needn't tell you! She knows enough." Maggie prefers to affirm her husband's other and more limited claim—not that Charlotte is actually happy, but that she won't let Maggie take her for unhappy. After those wails of protest and moans of objection, the Princess seems to greet this argument with eager relief: "Oh I know better than anyone else what she won't let me take her for!" Too aware of the possibility of Charlotte's unhappiness simply to assert that it does not exist, the Princess must depend on Charlotte's own power to assert saving fictions—on her mastery of an art much closer to Fanny Assingham's "new arithmetic" than to the Prince's bald logic.

By an emotional law of the excluded middle, Maggie's gain would seem to depend on the fact of Charlotte's loss, but the Princess conquers by a logic which bravely—or brazenly—defies such laws. Though Maggie is privately conscious that her victory has exacted a price, publicly she re-mains in that long line of Jamesian characters who want, as Charlotte her-self says, "everything" (23, III, ix, p. 363): the Princess's very definition of success demands, paradoxically, that even the defeated do not acknowledge failure. Only by granting the others the power to invent their own saving fictions can Maggie herself genuinely triumph. If her verbal coercion is fi-nally more effective than that of her manipulative predecessors, then, it is precisely because she does not always control the terms of the discourse. The Princess conquers by affirming the imaginative autonomy of her vic-tims.

Confronting Charlotte for the last time, Maggie thus allows her to as-sert—and perhaps to half-believe—that returning to America has been all her own idea. The scene takes place in the arbor at Fawns, where Char-lotte has apparently sought refuge from a cool house felt as even more op-pressive than the unusual heat of the day. Maggie comes in pursuit, but as she approaches her rival, she pauses—lingering "gravely and in silence" so as to give Charlotte time to choose her fiction: "Whatever she would, whatever she could, was what Maggie wanted—wanting above all to make it as easy for her as the case permitted. That was not what Charlotte had wanted the other night, but this never mattered—the great thing was to allow her, was to fairly produce in her, the sense of highly choosing" (24, V, v, pp. 309–10). Unlike "the other night"—the scene of that "prodigious kiss" in the drawing-room (24, V, ii, p. 251)—it is now Maggie rather than Charlotte who is physically the pursuer; but in verbal aggression Mrs. Verver remains outwardly supreme:

> "I'm glad to see you alone—there's something I've been wanting to say to you. I'm tired," said Mrs. Verver, "I'm tired—!"
>
> " 'Tired'—?" It had dropped, the next thing; it couldn't all come at once; but Maggie had already guessed what it was, and the flush of recognition was in her face.
>
> "Tired of this life—the one we've been leading. You like it, I know, but I've dreamed another dream." She held up her head now; her lighted eyes more triumphantly rested; she was finding, she was following her way. Maggie, by the same influence, sat in sight of it. . . . "I see something else," she went on; "I've an idea that greatly appeals to me—I've had it for a long time. It has come over me that we're wrong. Our real life isn't here."
>
> Maggie held her breath. " 'Ours'—?"
>
> "My husband's and mine. I'm not speaking for you."
>
> "Oh!" said Maggie, only praying not to be, not even to appear, stupid.
>
> "I'm speaking for ourselves. I'm speaking," Charlotte brought out, "for *him*."
>
> "I see. For my father."
>
> "For your father. For whom else?" They looked at each other hard now, but Maggie's face took refuge in the intensity of her interest. She was not at all events so stupid as to treat her companion's question as requiring an answer; a discretion that her controlled stillness had after an instant justified. "I must risk your thinking me selfish—for of course you know what it involves. Let me admit it—I *am* selfish. I place my husband first."
>
> "Well," said Maggie smiling and smiling, "since that's where I place mine—!"
>
> "You mean you'll have no quarrel with me? So much the better then; for," Charlotte went on with a higher and higher flight, "my plan's completely formed."
>
> Maggie waited—her glimmer had deepened; her chance somehow was at hand. The only danger was her spoiling it; she felt herself skirting an abyss. "What then, may I ask, *is* your plan?"
>
> It hung fire but ten seconds; it came out sharp. "To take him home—to his real position. And not to wait."
>
> (24, V, v, pp. 313–15)

The Princess consciously adopts the role of *ficelle* in Charlotte's drama: her questions serve to elucidate and extend the other woman's "idea," not to challenge it. "I've dreamed another dream," Charlotte triumphantly asserts, and by taking her verbal cues from her rival, Maggie affirms the force and dignity of that "dream." Though we may suspect that even in her dreams the desire to live with Adam in American City has for Charlotte no reality, we are still half moved to belief by the power of her verbal imagination. Hers is a dream which finally may be only a matter of words, not genuine feeling, but it nonetheless holds out to us a consoling possibility. And it is to this imaginative power in the other woman that the Princess temporarily surrenders. Despite all that has happened, despite even the crucial shift in actual power, this exchange recalls for a moment the old Charlotte Stant—that polyglot mistress of language, that woman in whose very first remark to the Prince ("It's too delightful to be back!") were a tone and attitude "as far removed as need have been from the truth of her situation" (23, I, iii, p. 51). "If she was arranging she could be trusted to arrange," the Prince thinks in those first few moments of reunion; and scenes such as this in the arbor at Fawns lend some truth to what might otherwise seem the terrible complacency of his final pronouncement on the fate of his ex-mistress: "She's making her life. . . . She'll make it" (24, VI, ii, p. 349).

Ironically, it is not Maggie, heiress to American candor, but the Italian Prince, with his heritage of discreet evasion, who at the last minute expresses a desire for brutal frankness. It is the day of Charlotte's and Adam's departure for America, and Maggie has suggested to her husband that he see Charlotte alone for the last time. Amerigo announces the use he intends to make of such an encounter; he will tell Charlotte the truth—that Maggie does in fact "know" all:

> "I shall tell her I lied to her."
> "Ah no!" she returned.
> "And I shall tell her you did."
> She shook her head again. "Oh still less!"
> With which therefore they stood at difference, he with his head erect and his happy idea perched in its eagerness on his crest. "And how then is she to know?"
> "She isn't to know."
> "She's only still to think *you* don't—?"
> "And therefore that I'm always a fool? She may think," said Maggie, "what she likes."
> "Think it without my protest—?"
> The Princess made a movement. "What business is it of yours?"
> "Isn't it my right to correct her—?"
> Maggie let his question ring—ring long enough for him to hear it himself; only then she took it up. " 'Correct' her—?" and it was her own now that really rang. "Aren't you rather forgetting who she is?" After which, while he quite stared for it, as it was the very first clear majesty

he had known her to use, she flung down her book and raised a warning hand. "The carriage. Come!"

(24, VI, iii, pp. 355–56)

"She isn't to know," says Maggie—but only that morning she has spoken quite differently: "She knows! She knows!" (24, VI, ii, p. 348). Hovering on the edge of a logical contradiction, her assertions leave us quite baffled: we know neither what Charlotte "knows" nor even what Maggie *thinks* she knows. But the resolution, if resolution there finally is, has little to do with logic. Affirming the power of Charlotte's intelligence, the Princess nevertheless knows that only the truth of desire, not of fact, will save both herself and her rival: Charlotte "may think"—indeed must think—"what she likes."

Maggie's logic may seem equivocal, and her refusal to be candid, frightening, but James so arranges the terms of this dispute that the Prince's desire for truth fails to arouse our deepest sympathies. Amerigo's language betrays him: by speaking not of being honest with his former mistress, but of his "right to correct her," he reveals a distressing arrogance. The more attractive we have found Charlotte in the past, the more we are moved to echo Maggie's question: " 'Correct' her—? . . . Aren't you rather forgetting who she is?" The exchange is thus profoundly disturbing, for its terms suggest that to be truthful to Charlotte in one sense is to be false, even cruel, in another. The language of *The Golden Bowl* refuses to grant us a simple conflict between truth and deception; it poses instead another, and far more difficult, choice.

Verbally, then, it is not her former lover who proves Charlotte's final champion, but her rival and her conqueror. "The very first clear majesty" which the Princess uses is paradoxically an affirmation of Charlotte's own regal nature: obeying Maggie's commands, the Prince "received Royalty, bareheaded, therefore, in the persons of Mr. and Mrs. Verver, as it alighted on the pavement" (24, VI, iii, p. 356). Charlotte is "great" (24, VI, iii, p. 364); she is "splendid" (p. 368); she is "incomparable" (p. 363): Maggie allows neither her husband, her father, nor the reader to forget who Charlotte is. The "beautiful" (p. 365) Miss Stant may finally be sacrificed to preserve the Princess's marriage, but Maggie speaks and thinks of that sacrifice almost as if it were a celebration. "They were parting," she thinks of her father and herself, "absolutely on Charlotte's *value*":

> —the value that was filling the room out of which they had stepped as if to give it play, and with which the Prince on his side was perhaps making larger acquaintance. If Maggie had desired at so late an hour some last conclusive comfortable category to place him in for dismissal, she might have found it here in its all coming back to his ability to rest upon high values. Somehow, when all was said, and with the memory of her gifts, her variety, her power, so much remained of Charlotte's! What else had she herself meant three minutes before by speaking of her as great? Great for the world that was before her—*that* he proposed she should

be: she wasn't to be wasted in the application of his plan. Maggie held to this then—that she wasn't to be wasted. To let his daughter know it he had sought this brief privacy. What a blessing accordingly that she could speak her joy in it! His face meanwhile at all events was turned to her, and as she met his eyes again her joy went straight. "It's success, father."

(24, VI, iii, pp. 365–66)

All this talk of Charlotte's "value" is not merely glib; if we feel more than a touch of complacency in the Princess here, we must also acknowledge "the fact of a felt sincerity in her words" (p. 363). For Maggie is genuinely able to imagine the magnificence which the Prince, and we ourselves, have sensed in Charlotte Stant. In the second volume of *The Golden Bowl*, we are granted no further access to Charlotte's consciousness, and it is Maggie alone who keeps alive for us the; memory of her rival's splendor. Mrs. Verver herself must perforce remain silent, but her stepdaughter sympathetically imagines her unspoken self-defense:

> She could thus have translated Mrs. Verver's tap against the glass, as I have called it, into fifty forms; could perhaps have translated it most into the form of a reminder that would pierce deep. "You don't know what it is to have been loved and broken with. You haven't been broken with, because in *your* relation what can there have been worth speaking of to break? Ours was everything a relation could be, filled to the brim with the wine of consciousness; and if it was to have no meaning, no better meaning than that such a creature as you could breathe upon it, at your hour, for blight, why was I myself dealt with all for deception? Why condemned after a couple of short years to find the golden flame—the golden flame!—a mere handful of black ashes?"
>
> (24, VI, i, pp. 329–30)

"The wine of consciousness," "the golden flame": in the mind of Maggie Verver, Charlotte's passion finds some of its most poignant images. When Maggie pronounces Charlotte "beautiful" and "splendid," then, we know that her words are not simply polite evasions, for we sense behind them a true imagination of Charlotte's value.

Drawn by the very brilliance of that "golden flame," however, we may also find ourselves echoing Charlotte's imaginary lament: something magnificent has indeed turned to ashes. But readers like F. R. Leavis, who deplore the cruel sacrifice of this "relation filled to the brim with the wine of consciousness," would do well to recall that at the very beginning of the affair, Charlotte has revealed the limits of her own imagination; "I can't put myself into Maggie's skin—I can't, as I say. It's not my fit—I shouldn't be able, as I see it, to breathe in it" (23, III, v, p. 311). Though Maggie comes very near to putting herself in Charlotte's skin, that lady cannot imagine herself in Maggie's.[6] Seduced by Mrs. Verver's "mastery of the greater style" (24, VI, iii, p. 368), the modern reader risks forgetting that the golden flame is finally Maggie's image, not her stepmother's—that by imagining the lovers' "wine of consciousness," the Princess reveals the vintage of her own.

But attractive as it is, it is also this very power of sympathetic imagination which makes of Maggie Verver so ambiguous and disquieting a heroine. While Charlotte delivers a museum-like lecture to a group of visitors at Fawns, her voice "high and clear and a little hard" (24, V, iv, p. 290), we hear through Maggie's "conscious ears"—ears imaginatively attuned to the unspoken—"the shriek of a soul in pain" (p. 292). The Princess's eyes fill with tears, yet the pain with which she so sympathizes is of course the pain which she herself has in large part caused. And the more intensely do we share her feeling for Charlotte's anguish, the more uneasy must we grow over Maggie's own acts. For unlike Fleda Vetch, unlike Milly Theale, the Princess does not finally choose to sacrifice herself to the imagined needs of others; her self-abasement is verbal only. Maggie's compassion does not radically alter Charlotte's fate: Maggie weeps, but Maggie wins.

While it is simply not true that, as one recent critic has argued, "nowhere does Maggie recognize the darker side of her behavior,"[7] the Princess's moments of recognition are not necessarily consoling. For the direct link between imaginative sympathy and self-sacrifice—that link so crucial to the moral vision of George Eliot and of the earlier James himself—is in *The Golden Bowl* strangely broken. Maggie Verver is no Maggie Tulliver: though Eliot's Maggie, like James's, implicitly chooses to sacrifice others to the demands of her own passion, in *The Mill on the Floss* full consciousness finally makes such self-indulgence impossible. Allowing herself to be "borne along the tide" with Stephen Guest (*The Mill*, VI, xiii), Maggie Tulliver brings pain to Lucy—Stephen's virtual fiancée—to Philip Wakem, and to her brother Tom. But her surrender to Stephen entails, in Eliot's words, "the partial sleep of thought":[8] it is a surrender to a dream. With Maggie's "waking" (xiv) comes the vivid image of the others' suffering ("could she ever cease to see before her Lucy and Philip, with their murdered trust and hopes?" [p. 413]) and the decision to return to St. Ogg's. In the psychology of *The Mill on the Floss*, full consciousness and conscience are one: a more intense imagination of others, Eliot suggests, would have made Maggie's act of betrayal impossible. "If we—if I had been better, nobler, those claims would have been strongly present within me," Maggie tells Stephen, "I should have felt them pressing on my heart so continually, just as they do now in moments when my conscience is awake—that the opposite feeling would never have grown in me, as it has done: it would have been quenched at once. . ." (p. 417).

But in *The Golden Bowl*, Charlotte's "claim" does not even hypothetically "quench" Maggie's opposite feeling. On the contrary, only in discovering the fact of the adultery—of Charlotte's claim on the Prince—does Maggie confront the full extent of her own need for him.[9] The Princess awakens at once to the imagination of others and of herself, and her heightened awareness finally leads not to self-denial and renunciation but to a passionate, if hidden, act of self-assertion. In *The Golden Bowl*, full consciousness and conscience overlap, but they do not coincide. And much of the moral disquiet which this novel arouses in us stems from just this uneasy conjunction.

For the moral comfort of its readers at least, there is a sense in which *The Golden Bowl* thus gives us a heroine who knows not too little but too much. If the Princess is so equivocal a heroine, the very intensity of her awareness helps, ironically, to make her so: in the second half of the novel, it is in large part Maggie's own imagination of consequences which keeps before us the possibility of the others' pain—and it is her consciousness of self which makes immediate to us the fact of her own deceit. For unlike Kate and Charlotte, her predecessors in the art of verbal manipulation, Maggie is granted by her creator a private language which sometimes calls her public words directly into question. Kate and Charlotte may prove liars, but even privately they themselves do not acknowledge such a possibility: they seduce us as well as their lovers by the strong conviction with which they assert their interpretations of events. When Charlotte pronounces the Ververs "beatifically" happy (23, III, v, p. 310), we may find the complacency of her remark troubling, but we have no way of being sure that Charlotte does not—consciously at least—believe in the Ververs' beatitude. And Charlotte's apparent faith tempts our own. But when Maggie and her stepmother confront one another in the drawing-room at Fawns, and the Princess herself attests to her blissful state ("You must take it from me that I've never at any moment fancied I could suffer by you. . . . You must take it from me that I've never thought of you but as beautiful, wonderful and good"), we know that Maggie lies—and we know it so clearly because she herself does: "The right, the right—yes, it took this extraordinary form of humbugging, as she had called it, to the end. It was only a question of not by a hair's breadth deflecting into the truth" (24, V, ii, pp. 250–51).

We might wish to protest, of course, that "this extraordinary form of humbugging" is all too ordinary a form of conversation in the world of James's late fiction—that if the Princess of *The Golden Bowl* finally rules with hypocrisy and lies, she has merely learned the appropriate language of her kingdom. After all, it is Charlotte whose verbal dexterity has first attracted us, and in the two crucial dialogues with her stepmother, Maggie may be said simply to match her, evasion for evasion, lie for lie. In the drawing-room at evening, the adulterous Charlotte establishes the fiction of her complete innocence, and Maggie, now grown deeply suspicious, nonetheless responds with a declaration of perfect trust:

> "I'm aware of no point whatever at which I may have failed you," said Charlotte; "nor of any at which I may have failed any one in whom I can suppose you sufficiently interested to care. If I've been guilty of some fault I've committed it all unconsciously, and am only anxious to hear from you honestly about it. But if I've been mistaken as to what I speak

of—the difference, more and more marked, as I've thought, in all your manner to me—why obviously so much the better. No form of correction received from you could give me greater satisfaction. . . ."
" 'If' you've been mistaken, you say?—and the Princess but barely faltered. "You *have* been mistaken."

(24, V, ii, pp. 248–49)

And in the garden at noon, Charlotte brazenly pretends that she remains in control of her own fate, while the Princess lies so that the other woman's saving fiction may have the semblance of truth. "I want, strange as it may seem to you," Charlotte declares, "to *keep* the man I've married. And to do so I see I must act":

"You want to take my father *from* me?"
The sharp successful almost primitive wail in it made Charlotte turn, and this movement attested for the Princess the felicity of her deceit. Something in her throbbed as it had throbbed the night she stood in the drawing-room and denied that she had suffered. She was ready to lie again if her companion would but give her the opening. Then she should know she had done all.

(24, V, v, pp. 315–16)

While we may feel that the humbugging in these scenes is mutual, that so much of Jamesian conversation is in fact humbugging, only in Maggie Verver does James make this consciousness explicit. We have no direct access to what Charlotte is feeling here: her sudden declaration of love for Adam and American City may be a simple lie, yet it may also represent a glorious self-delusion—a delusion so deeply willed that it has become, in a manner of speaking, the truth. But we cannot escape the fact that in these encounters the Princess is a conscious hypocrite, one who delights in "the felicity of her deceit." Attracted as we are by the "serenities and dignities and decencies" with which Maggie Verver hopes to people her world (24, V, ii, p. 236), we remain uncomfortably aware that Maggie's dignity is in part deception, her serenity a lie.

Yet if the Princess is a heroine who disturbs us by knowing too much, there is another sense, paradoxically, in which her consciousness proves inadequate to the world in which she rules—a sense in which we feel ourselves wanting to know more than she does, and are made uneasy by our desire. At her final parting from her beloved father, Maggie consoles herself with the thoughts that Adam shares in her celebration of Charlotte's "value": "If Maggie had desired at so late an hour some last conclusive comfortable category to place him in for dismissal, she might have found it here in its all coming back to his ability to rest upon high values. Somehow, when all was said, and with the memory of her gifts, her variety, her power, so much remained of Charlotte's!" (24, VI, iii, p. 365). It is a consolation which we as readers can only take on faith; Maggie may or may not have a "last conclusive comfortable category" in which to place Adam "for dismissal"—even her desire for such a category is at most hypothetical—but our own last terms can be neither so conclusive nor so comfortable. Despite the glimpse into his consciousness which the first half of the novel affords, Adam Verver remains for us essentially a mystery, a man whose "unfathomable heart" (24, V, v, p. 305) may stand as a sign of all that the Princess—and perhaps even James himself—ultimately chooses not to confront.

For all his accumulated millions, the little man may simply be, as Fanny Assingham says, "stupid." "Yet on the other hand," she characteristically adds, "he may be sublime: sublimer even than Maggie herself. He may in fact have already been. But we shall never know" (24, IV, vii, p. 135). Comic as Fanny's habitual self-contradictions may seem, her bewilderment mirrors our own: what Adam Verver really "knows"—of the adultery and betrayal, of the radically flawed structure of his life, of his daughter's own painful awakening—remains to the end profoundly obscure. And we are baffled in part because Maggie wills herself to be; despite Fanny's assertion that "She'll know—about her father; everything. Everything" (p. 136), the Princess chooses, only half-consciously, to evade the truth about him. Immediately before her second confrontation with Charlotte, Maggie steps quietly into the nursery to visit the sleeping Principino, and finds her father, "the prime protector of his dreams," installed beside him:

> . . . her father sat there with as little motion—with head thrown back and supported, with eyes apparently closed, with the fine foot that was so apt to betray nervousness at peace upon the other knee, with the unfathomable heart folded in the constant flawless freshness of the white waistcoat that could always receive in its armholes the firm prehensile thumbs. . . . She looked over her fan, the top of which was pressed against her face, long enough to wonder if her father really slept or if, aware of her, he only kept consciously quiet. Did his eyes truly fix her between lids partly open, and was she to take this—his forbearance from any question—only as a sign that everything was left to her? She at all events for a minute watched his immobility—then, as if once more renewing her total submission, returned without a sound to her own quarters.
>
> (24, V, v, pp. 305–6)

Like some oriental deity in western dress, Adam Verver sits inscrutable. In his mysterious immobility he may, like the deity, know and understand all—or he may simply have fallen asleep. Maggie wonders, and then returns to her rooms in silence; she makes no attempt to determine the real state of her father's consciousness. She prefers to leave the enigma of Adam Verver undisturbed, to worship, but not to question him too closely.

When the little millionaire proposes to return with Charlotte to American City, we may choose to believe that he is fully conscious of why such exile is necessary, that he has a "certainty" as strong as Maggie's own about the true state of affairs (24, V, iii, p. 268). But it is Maggie herself, after all, who has first given Adam his cue: "You don't claim, I suppose, that my natural course, once you had set up for yourself, would have been to ship you back to American City?" she demands—to which Adam responds, "Do you know, Mag, what you make me wish when you talk that way? . . . You regularly make me wish I *had* shipped back to American City. . . . Do you know that if we *should* ship it would serve you quite right? . . . And if you say much more we will ship" (24, V, iii, pp. 270–71). Only Adam's eyes—"the light at the heart of which he couldn't blind"—seem to Maggie a revelation of some hidden knowledge (p. 268); no direct words are spoken. "They were avoiding the serious, standing off anxiously from the real, and they fell again and again, as if to disguise their precaution itself, into the tone of the time that came back to them from their other talk, when they had shared together this same refuge" (p. 257). The innocent Electra bond has been shattered (Maggie confesses that she loves her husband "in the most abysmal and unutterable way of all" [p. 262]), but father and daughter, seated on their old garden bench at Fawns, still adhere to the tone of their incestuously Edenic past. Talking with her father, once her most intimate ally, has become for Maggie an exercise in opacity and evasion little different from talking with Charlotte herself.

For to confront her father directly is a risk which the Princess cannot bear to take: it is as if she feared that knowing the truth about him might paralyze her entirely, might make all action and choice impossible. Rather than dare the knowledge of his bewilderment or pain, she thus chooses to act on the hypothesis that he is "all right"—and that somehow he mysteriously sanctions all she does. Her belief that Adam has his own "idea," an idea, which magically redeems her "sacrifice" of him, must attest for us more to the power of Maggie's will than to that of her intelligence. The talk in which Adam's plan is made manifest ends not with explanation, but with vision:

> With which, his glasses still fixed on her, his hands in his pockets, his hat pushed back, his legs a little apart, he seemed to plant or to square himself for a kind of assurance it had occurred to him he might as well treat her to, in default of other things, before they changed their subject. It had the effect for her of a reminder—a reminder of all he was, of all he had done, of all, above and beyond his being her perfect little father, she might take him as representing, take him as having quite eminently, in the eyes of two hemispheres, been capable of, and as therefore wishing, not—was it?—illegitimately, to call her attention to. The "successful" benficent person, the beautiful bountiful original dauntlessly wilful great citizen, the consummate collector and infallible high authority he had been and still was—these things struck her on the spot as making up for him in a wonderful way a character she must take into account in dealing with him either for pity or for envy. He positively, under the impression, seemed to loom larger than life for her. . . . Before she knew it she was lifted aloft by the consciousness that he was simply a great and

deep and high little man, and that to love him with tenderness was not to be distinguished a whit from loving him with pride. It came to her, all strangely, as a sudden, an immense relief. The sense that he wasn't a failure, and could never be, purged their predicament of every meanness—made it as if they had really emerged, in their transmuted union, to smile almost without pain. It was like a new confidence, and after another instant she knew even still better why. Wasn't it because now also, on his side, he was thinking of her as his daughter, was *trying* her, during these mute seconds, as the child of his blood? Oh then if she wan't with her little conscious passion the child of any weakness, what was she but strong enough too? It swelled in her fairly; it raised her higher, higher: she wasn't in that case a failure either—hadn't been, but the contrary; his strength was her strength, her pride was his, and they were decent and competent together.

(24, V, iii, pp. 272–75)

Though the grounds for all this beatitude are at best obscure, Maggie's response is not a question, but a declaration of faith: "I believe in you more than any one" (p. 275). With "his inscrutable incalculable energy" (p. 273), Adam Verver has become for his daughter not only a man to love and to trust; but a being to worship—and the necessary ground of her faith in herself.

If the Princess makes of her wealthy father a virtual deity, though, hers is a leap of faith which few readers of *The Golden Bowl* have been inspired to follow. Little millionaires make dubious gods—especially little millionaires who betray a passion for collecting people as well as things.[10] Father and daughter may part on a recognition of Charlotte's "value," but the Ververs' sense of values seems to take its measure as much from the gold standard as from a human one:

"It's all right, eh?"

"Oh my dear—rather!"

He had applied the question to the great fact of the picture, as she had spoken for the picture in reply, but it was as if their words for an instant afterwards symbolised another truth, so that they looked about at everything else to give them this extension. She had passed her arm into his, and the other objects in the room, the other pictures, the sofas, the chairs, the tables, the cabinets, the "important" pieces, supreme in their way, stood out, round them, consciously, for recognition and applause. Their eyes moved together from piece to piece, taking in the whole nobleness—quite as if for him to measure the wisdom of old ideas. The two noble persons seated in conversation and at tea fell thus into the splendid effect and the general harmony: Mrs. Verver and the Prince fairly "placed" themselves, however unwittingly, as high expressions of the kind of human furniture required aesthetically by such a scene. The fusion of their presence with the decorative elements, their contribution of the triumph of selection, was complete and admirable; though to a lingering view, a view more penetrating than the occasion really demanded, they also might have figured as concrete attestations of a rare power of

purchase. There was much indeed in the tone in which Adam Verver spoke again, and who shall say where his thought stopped? *"Le compte y est. You've got some good things."*
Maggie met it afresh—"Ah don't they look well?"

(24, VI, iii, pp. 259–60)

In a novel whose central symbol is itself a collector's item, a novel in which the Prince and Charlotte too choose vehicles of gold for the tenor of love, we might almost take the language of this scene as purely emblematic—no more sinister in its implications than Spenser's calling his beloved's breasts "two golden apples of vnualewd price."[11] Even the Ververs' "rare power of purchase," after all, may carry a redemptive as well as an economic force.[12] But as they stand in this room so densely filled with precious objects, a room in which Charlotte and the Prince blur disturbingly into sofas, cabinets, and chairs, the Ververs' triumph may seem not so much a transcendence of the material as a surrender to it. "The note of possession and control"—that note which Maggie hears in her father's voice as he pronounces his last words upon his wife (24, VI, iii, p. 365)—rings ominously in our ears: it is a note more worthy of a Gilbert Osmond than of a beneficent god. Though to Maggie "it was all she might have wished" (p. 365), James's readers have rarely felt themselves equally satisfied.

Adam Verver is at once a moral and an intellectual mystery: the Princess's arbitrary faith is a magnificent affirmation, but the grounds on which it rests remain for us both suspect and obscure. Denied access to the sort of knowledge which would make judgment possible, we become, in our bewilderment, strangely like the Prince himself—a man radically cut off from the terms and values of a familiar world and forced to confront the limits of his powers of translation. "Find out for yourself!" Maggie has challenged him (24, IV, x, p. 203), but about his opaque little father-in-law, the Prince can find out nothing:

> Nothing however had reached him; nothing he could at all conveniently reckon with had disengaged itself for him even from the announcement, sufficiently sudden, of the final secession of their companions. Charlotte was in pain, Charlotte was in torment, but he himself had given her reason enough for that; and, in respect to the rest of the whole matter of her obligation to follow her husband, that personage and she, Maggie, had so shuffled away every link between consequence and cause that the intention remained, like some famous poetic line in a dead language, subject to varieties of interpretation.
>
> (24, VI, ii, pp. 344–45)

Like the baffled Prince, readers of the novel are apt to feel themselves exiles in a world whose language is virtually untranslatable: if the ending of *The Golden Bowl* has indeed remained "like some poetic line in a dead language, subject to varieties of interpretation," it is because in the Ververs, James has so obscured the links between cause and consequence, motive and act, that the full meaning of their final gestures must remain impenetrably ambiguous. For Maggie's is a triumph of that Jamesian logic which conquers by defying the seeming contradictions of language and of fact, which from the intractable conditions of human life verbally wills a harmonious resolution.

When the carriage containing Adam and Charlotte has finally rolled out of sight, and the Principino has been spirited away with the accommodating Miss Bogle, Maggie turns at last to the husband she has won. Dreading lest he shatter the serenity of this moment with a direct confession, she seeks from him instead some echo of her own language, some final acknowledgment of the resolution she has willed:

> "Isn't she too splendid?" she simply said, offering it to explain and to finish.
> "Oh splendid!" With which he came over to her.
> "That's our help, you see," she added—to point further her moral.
>
> (24,VI, iii, p. 368)

But the Prince cannot necessarily meet her on the ground she has chosen; he can only acknowledge the limitations of his own vision:

> He tried, too clearly, to please her—to meet her in her own way; but with the result only that, close to her, her face kept before him, his hands holding her shoulders, his whole act enclosing her, he presently echoed: " 'See'? I see nothing but *you*." And the truth of it had with this force after a moment so strangely lighted his eyes that as for pity and dread of them she buried her own in his breast.
>
> (pp. 368–69)

The Prince speaks here the language of a devoted husband but his words have an ominous sound. For in this impassioned declaration of love we may also hear a confession of failure—and the sign of an irremediable division between husband and wife. Reunited though they finally are, Prince and Princess do not speak the same language, nor see in the drama they have enacted the same "moral." Maggie offers her verdict on Charlotte "to explain and to finish," but the tension between her question and her husband's response is a reminder of all those tensions which continually hover in the spaces between the novel's words, of all that unease which no talk of Charlotte's splendor can magically dispel. The long-awaited embrace of the Princess and her Prince has the appearance of a comic resolution, but in its "pity and dread" are tragic tones.[13]

And though we as readers necessarily see further than the bewildered Prince, there is a sense in which we share at the end in his problem of vision. Like him, we may find ourselves unable to meet Maggie in her own way, to "see" what she seems to: the Princess's language holds out the promise of harmony restored, a world magically transformed, but a full sense of that harmony continues to elude us. Too much seems suppressed or evaded; too many disturbing questions remain. With its marriages reaffirmed and its couples neatly paired off, the ending of *The Golden Bowl* superficially resembles the closed structure of comedy; but what we really witness here is less a closed fiction than a character struggling to will such a fiction. We are confined so closely to Maggie's point of view in the second half of the novel that we are moved intensely to identify with her, yet we may also find our very confinement stifling. Denied a means of clearly distinguishing the social world of the novel from Maggie's invention of it, we cannot directly confirm or deny her language, cannot simply read the ending of *The Golden Bowl* either as comedy or as irony. Rather, we find ourselves once again curiously like the baffled Prince—able to see clearly, at this end, nothing but Maggie Verver herself.

Indeed, how deeply James's own vision penetrates at the novel's close is a troubling and much vexed question. A recent critic complains that toward the end of *The Golden Bowl* James himself grows "coy": when we are told that "to a lingering view, a view more penetrating than the occasion really demanded," Charlotte and the Prince "also might have figured as concrete attestations of a rare power of purchase" (24, VI, iii, p. 360), it is the novelist, Philip Weinstein argues, who shrinks back from that more penetrating view, who finally refuses to count the cost of Maggie Verver's empire.[14] But that characteristic blurring between novelist and characters which the late style effects makes all such distinctions uncertain at best: is it really James who coyly dodges the issues here, or is it simply the Ververs who thus console themselves? Whatever its source, there is no question but that this tranquil parting depends for its very existence on the avoidance of all lingering looks, all probing questions and doubts. Indeed the occasion only exists by virtue of the careful averting of four pairs of eyes: "To do such an hour justice would have been in some degree to question its grounds—which was why they remained in fine, the four of them, in the upper air, united through the firmest abstention from pressure" (p. 361). Not only Maggie and her father, but Charlotte and the Prince as well, seem to conspire in the fiction that their novelistic lives must have this closed ending: "that strange accepted finality of relation, as from couple to couple, which almost escaped an awkwardness only by not attempting a gloss" (p. 361).

As it dramatizes the superb tranquility of this resolution, the novel nearly seduces us into the belief that all this peace is in fact real; by concluding *The Golden Bowl* with the Princess's victory, James makes the shape of his fictional world coincide closely with the shape his heroine has imposed upon it. There is no novelistic time or space, even if there were psychological possibility, for the Prince to begin in turn to play a doubting Densher to Maggie's triumphant Kate. But if it is to James as novelist that we wish finally to ascribe all this passion for closure, this willful suppression of the open ending, it is also to James as novelist that we must attribute the openness which stubbornly persists, the doubts which make themselves felt in their very negation. Though at times *The Golden Bowl* may seem to hover between ambiguity and mere obscurity, between complexity and deep confusions, it derives its power to haunt us precisely from this tension between the reality which its characters will into being and the irreducible "facts" which never wholly vanish—between our delight in Maggie Verver's triumph and our painful if suppressed awareness of its necessary price. Even those readers who have felt compelled to bring that suppressed awareness to the surface, and to conclude that the cost of Maggie's victory has been too great, are indirectly witness to that haunting power.

And if *The Golden Bowl* reaches its moving conclusion only by seeming to foreclose discussion and suppress disturbing questions, the unfinished *Ivory Tower* may stand as evidence that for James himself the hidden questions characteristically surfaced once again. James's last completed novel may close with the apparent triumph of American "innocence" and American capital, but in *The Ivory Tower* the American struggle for wealth has become an overtly sinister enterprise—an "awful game of grab" (25, I, ii, p. 35). Abel Gaw, the wizened old capitalist who appears "like a ruffled hawk . . . with his beak, which had pecked so many hearts out, visibly sharper than ever" (25, I, i, p. 6) has nothing of Adam Verver's mysterious appeal; even Mr. Betterman, the rich benefactor with the name worthy of Bunyan, has only come to realize on his deathbed the "poison" of his life (25, II, ii, p. 112). In the hero of his novel, a young American who returns to his native land after having lived virtually all his life in Europe, James sends a sensitive and cultivated surrogate on the journey which Adam Verver and Charlotte Stant were about to make at the close of *The Golden Bowl*—and in the Newport of *The Ivory Tower*, Graham Fielder confronts an American City as disturbing as any the reader may have imagined in store for Charlotte. James himself had returned to America in 1904, only to find his beloved Newport "now blighted with ugly uses," a mere breeding-ground for white elephants."[15] Even as the buried implications of a metaphor so often emerge in the movement of James's late prose, even as Graham Fielder's own images "find . . . him out, however he might have tried to hide from them" (25, IV, i, pp. 252–53), so the sinister possibilities in all the Ververs' talk of wealth and purchase rise dramatically to the surface of *The Ivory Tower*.

And it is from just those sinister possibilities, "the black and merciless things that are behind the great possessions,"[16] that Fielder shrinks—making the ivory tower both a hiding-place for Gaw's ominous letter and a fit talisman for himself. Refusing to denounce Horton Vint's apparent swindle, willing to sacrifice his newly acquired inheritance, the hero of James's preliminary sketch for the novel more closely resembles the dovelike Milly Theale than the combative Princess of *The Golden Bowl*. Indeed, James's notes project for Graham Fielder no such victory as Maggie's: *The Ivory Tower* was to have concluded, like so many Jamesian novels before it, in renunciation. But *The Ivory Tower* we actually possess ends abruptly in mid-sentence—a novel even more drastically open-ended than any James had intended to write. James abandoned his last novel in August 1914: "With the outbreak of the war," wrote Percy Lubbock, "Henry James found he could no longer work upon a fiction supposed to represent contemporary or recent life."[17] Whatever the conjunction of personal and public history which led to that final broken sentence—and to James's abortive return to the equally unfinished *Sense of the Past*—the sequence of events is peculiarly suggestive. Maggie Verver's victory preserves the civilized forms of her world and the closed shape of her novel, but beneath the surface of these lingering nineteenth-century fictions, imposed at such tremendous cost, we feel an almost unbearable strain. That *The Golden Bowl* was to have been followed by a novel which questioned in turn the very basis of those civilized forms has something of the rhythm of a Jamesian paragraph writ large—its suppressed implications, only faintly adumbrated at first, emerging at last with inexorable force. But that the magnificent if uneasy conclusion of *The Golden Bowl* should in fact have been followed by the broken shape of *The Ivory Tower* and the outbreak of the First World War makes for a more disturbing, though equally compelling metaphor.

Unlike poems, whose existence is so intensely a matter of their language, novels seem to have a reality apart from the words that compose them: reading fiction, we succumb to the illusion that its characters and events have an independent existence to which the words on the page merely point. Rarely is this more dramatically true than in our encounters with the late James, where what is evaded and denied by the words we actually read nonetheless compels our fascinated attention. What the characters refuse to talk about, what they refuse even to think, becomes for us—especially in retrospect—the real substance of James's fiction. But the actual experience of reading the late James is still less emotionally tidy than we usually recall. For even as we are consistently drawn "behind" the words on the page to the narrative they conceal, the words themselves exert on us their own fascinations. Few novels demand more persistently that we translate them, yet few novels feel so relentlessly verbal, even so untranslatable. The melodramatic events we decipher, the social and moral questions those events arouse, are perhaps what remain with us longest, but they do not alone shape experience as we read. The metaphors which develop out of taboo may move us as deeply as the feelings those metaphors conceal: the fictions Jamesian characters imagine and the fictions they speak have, in the immediacy of our reading, a power of their own. Indeed the more susceptible we are to the reading of any novel—the more we characteristically surrender to the realities that words create—the more emotionally rich, if sometimes disquieting, our reading of the late James must be.

Notes

1. Henry James, *The Notebooks of Henry James*, ed. F. O. Matthiessen and Kenneth B. Murdock (1947; rpt. New York: George Braziller, 1955), p. 18: "The obvious criticism of course will be that it *[The Portrait of a lady]* is not finished—that I have not seen the heroine to the end of her situation—that I have left her *en l'air.*—This is both true and false. The *whole* of anything is never told; you can only take what groups together. What I have done has that unity—it groups together. It is complete in itself—and the rest may be taken up or not, later."

2. See chapter 1, note 2, for references to the critical debate surrounding this novel. I owe a particular debt to Philip Weinstein, whose acute chapter on *The Golden Bowl* (*Henry James and the Requirements of the Imagination*, pp. 165–201) has several obvious points of connection with my own. I too am concerned by much of what troubles him in this novel, though my sense of what is crucial in the reading of it is finally quite different. But even where I disagree with him, I have found his argument stimulating.

3. The sense in which Maisie "loves" Sir Claude—the degree of sexual passion in her feeling for him—remains, like so much else in *What Maisie Knew*, rather ambiguous. Certainly we feel that by the end of the novel Maisie has left her childhood behind her. Accused of destroying her moral sense, Sir Claude responds, . . . "On the contrary, I think I've produced life" (11, xxxi, p. 354).

4. Sallie Sears, *The Negative Imagination*, p. 56; for the argument that Maggie exercises a redemptive love, see, for example, Laurence Holland, *The Expense of Vision*, pp. 377–407; and Dorothea Krook, *The Ordeal of Consciousness*, pp. 232–324, especially pp. 240–79.

5. Sallie Sears argues that the two-part structure of the novel thus divides our sympathy. See *The Negative Imagination*, pp. 173–83.

6. Charles Samuels is also struck by the implications of this passage, and is more just to Maggie here than most recent commentators. See *The Ambiguity of Henry James*, p. 216.

7. Philip Weinstein, *Henry James and the Requirements of the Imagination*, p. 185.

8. George Eliot, *The Mill on the Floss*, Riverside Edition, ed. Gordon Haight (1860; rpt. Boston: Houghton Mifflin, 1961), VI, xiii, p. 410. All subsequent references are to this edition.

9. Of course Charlotte's claims on Amerigo are in no sense as socially legitimate as Lucy's on Stephen Guest. Part of Maggie Verver's strength—as well, perhaps, as the modern reader's distrust of her—comes from the conventional righteousness of her position: she is the married woman recovering her own. But it is not simply the form of her marriage which the Princess struggles to save.

10. Matthiessen's objection may stand as representative: "There is not enough discrimination between Mr. Verver's property and his human acquisitions." See "James and the Plastic Arts," *Kenyon Review* 5 (1943): 546.

11. Those metaphorical apples rest in a silver dish, lavishly placed in turn on "a goodly table of pure yrory." Transformed by his metaphor, Spenser's beloved might make a valuable addition to Mr. Verver's collection. See Sonnet LXXVII ("Was it a dreame, or did I see it playne"), in *The Minor Poems*, II, ed. Charles Grosvenor Osgood and Henry Gibbons Lotspeich (Baltimore: Johns Hopkins Press, 1947), p. 227.

12. See Dorothea Krook, *The Ordeal of Consciousness*, p. 322. Her two chapters on *The Golden Bowl* constitute a very thorough account of the ambiguities surrounding Adam Verver and his daughter's triumph.

13. Several critics have touched on the suggestion of tragedy in these final lines. See especially R. P. Blackmur's Introduction to the Dell Laurel *Golden Bowl* (New York: 1963), pp. 5–13; and Dorothea Krook's response to Blackmur in *The Ordeal of Consciousness*, pp. 317–24.

14. *Henry James and the Requirements of the Imagination*, p. 194.

15. *The American Scene* (1907; rpt. Bloomington, Ind.: Indiana University Press, 1968), pp. 223–24.

16. Henry James, "Notes for *The Ivory Tower*," 25, p. 295.

17. Preface to *The Ivory Tower*, 25, p. v.

A New Reading of Henry James's "The Jolly Corner"
Daniel Mark Fogel*

> They [Henry James's ghosts] have their origin within us. They are present whenever the significant overflows our powers of expressing it; whenever the ordinary appears ringed by the strange. The baffling things that are left over—the frightening ones that persist—these are the emotions that he takes, embodies, makes consoling and companionable.
>
> —Virginia Woolf[1]

Although readers agree that "The Jolly Corner" stands among the three or four finest short fictions of Henry James, and though the story has been accorded more critical commentary than any of the tales, excepting only *The Turn of the Screw* and "The Beast in the Jungle," the central issues of interpretation remain largely unresolved. Is Brydon redeemed by his ordeal in the house on the jolly corner, delivered from the solitude of his egotism into the saving community of human love with Alice Staverton, or is "the essential point Brydon's inability to change," Brydon's "much vaunted awakening love for Alice . . . simply a shift from a bare acknowledgment of her existence as a friend who will tirelessly listen to his talk of himself to a complete dependence on her as a buffer to shield him from having to face the harsh facts of his life"?[2] Is the tale about Brydon's (and Henry James's) reconciliation with America, or is it "anti-American with a vengeance"?[3] Does the apparition that Brydon stalks in the house of his childhood represent the self that might have been had he remained in America, or does it represent his actual, present selfhood, what he has become during his thirty-three years of expatriation in Europe, or are there in fact two ghosts in the house, one embodying the Brydon who might have been, the other the Brydon who is?[4] In his preface to the volume of the New York Edition containing the tale, Henry James seems to suggest that criticism of "The Jolly Corner" may do no more than increase our bafflement over such questions—these are far from the only ones, as we shall see—for he himself says very little about the story, remarking that "Spencer Brydon's adventure however is one of those finished fantasies that, achieving success or not, speak best even to the critical sense for them-

*This essay was written specifically for this volume and is published by permission of the uthor.

selves—which I leave it to do."⁵ Nevertheless, close reading of the hitherto virtually unnoticed germ for "The Jolly Corner" in James's Notebooks, along with a simple but until now overlooked arithmetical calculation, opens the way to a new reading that will resolve, insofar as is possible, the principal controversies surrounding the tale.

In an editor's note on "The Jolly Corner" in 1953, Leon Edel remarked that "[t]here is no note in the notebooks devoted to the story."⁶ In 1962, however, in a footnote attempting to show that the idea of "The Jolly Corner" might have predated the composition of *The Ambassadors*, Dorothea Krook observed that "the important entry about the too-late theme dated 5th February 1895 mentions as a possible story something very similar to that of *The Jolly Corner*."⁷ Finally, in 1976, Ellen Tremper also noted the connection between the Notebook entry of 5 February 1895 and "The Jolly Corner," devoting to it a single sentence: "With very few changes—principally, the man's wanting to recover his dead or other self not for the joy of it but to discover what it was to have been, and his losing consciousness instead of dying—we see the skeleton of what was to become, eleven and one-half years later, 'The Jolly Corner.' "⁸ Neither Krook nor Tremper seems to have realized the potential usefulness of this discovery for developing a new reading of James's tale. Here in its entirety is the passage from *The Notebooks of Henry James:*

> There comes back to me, *a propos* of it [the possible germ of a tale— "The Beast in the Jungle"—"in the idea of *Too late*"], and as vaguely and crookedly hooking itself on to it, somehow, that concetto that I have jotted down in another notebook—that of the little tragedy of the man who has renounced his ambition, the dream of his youth, his genius, talent, vocation—with all the honour and glory it might have brought him: sold it, bartered it, exchanged it for something very different and inferior, but mercenary and worldly. I've only to write these few words, however, to see that the 2 ideas have nothing to do with each other. They are different stories. What I fancied in this last mentioned was that this Dead Self of the poor man's lives for him still in some indirect way, in the sympathy, the fidelity (the relation of some kind) of another. I tried to give a hint in my former note, of what this vicarious self, as it were, might amount to. It will require returning to; and what I wanted not to let slip altogether was simply some reminder of the beauty, the little tragedy, attached perhaps to the situation of the man of genius who, in some accursed hour of his youth, has bartered away the fondest vision of that youth and lives ever afterward in the shadow of the bitterness of the regret. My other little note contained the fancy of his *recovering* a little of the lost joy, of the Dead Self, in his intercourse with some person, some woman, who knows what that self was, in whom it still lives a little. This intercourse is his real life. But I think I said there was a banality in that; that, practically, the little situation will have often enough been treated; and that therefore the thing could, probably, only take a form as the story, not of the man, but of the woman herself. It's *the woman's sense of what might <have been>* in him that arrives at the intensity. (The link

of connection between the foregoing and this was simply my little feeling
that they each dealt with might-have-beens.) *She is his Dead Self: he is
alive in her and dead in himself*—that is something like the little formula
I seemed to *entrevoir*. He himself, the man, must, *in* the tale, also materially die—die in the flesh as he had died long ago in the spirit, the *right*
one. Then it is that his lost treasure revives most—no longer *contrarié*
by his material existence, existence in his false self, his wrong one.—But
I fear there isn't much in it: it would take a deuce of a deal of following
up.[9]

One notes immediately that there are more differences between the
idea sketched here and "The Jolly Corner" than Krook and Tremper suggest. Yet they are undoubtedly right in taking this notebook passage to be
the germ of Spencer Brydon's adventure. James's misgivings about the idea
he was sketching in his notebook perhaps help to explain the transforma-
tions the germ underwent as it turned into the finished story. James worries that the situation is banal. After all, the idea that a man's best self, long
betrayed by him, might live on in a woman who loves him is a stock theme
of nineteenth-century literature. To rescue such an overused idea might indeed "take a deuce of a deal of following up." I would propose, however,
that James's stroke of genius, in order to rescue the idea from banality, was
to make it Brydon's "worst self," not his "best," that lives "in the sympathy,
the fidelity (the relation of some kind)"—in the words of the note—of Alice
Staverton! The "worst self" lives in her; it is dead, or rather, perhaps, latent in Brydon. She suggests its existence to him. She sees it, knows it,
and loves it when it is still only the dimmest, vaguest of stirrings within
him. By her suggestions and by her steadfast, upholding sympathy she aims
and arms him for his encounter with his alter ego, the alternately worthy
and repulsive beast awaiting him at the jolly corner.

There is more suggested for our reading of the story in the notebook
entry; but we can see already that Alice's part may be more major, more
effective, more critical to Brydon's fortunes, than has been suggested in almost all of the critical literature. Though I do not agree with Floyd Stovall's
two-ghost reading, or with his idea that the ghost at the bottom of the stairs
is simply Brydon's "false or European self," I think he is right in his emphasis on Alice's importance when he says that the power to reject the false
self came to Brydon "not from himself so much as from Alice Staverton,
who had been having psychic communication with his buried self and was
now beginning to revive it."[10] To make this more emphatic, we might add
that the ghost would not have revived, nor would Brydon have encountered it, without Alice's agency. Seen in this light, Brydon's statement to
Alice (after he awakens, cradled in her lap, from the swoon into which he
fell when the apparition at last advanced upon him) that "You brought me
literally to life" applies broadly to her role throughout the story and not
just to her presiding over his return to consciousness.[11]

We can find textual support for this view of Alice's active role at numerous points in the text. I will mention only a few. It is Alice, first of all, who starts Brydon thinking about his dormant abilities when she suggests that "[i]f he had but stayed at home he would have discovered his genius in time really to start some new variety of awful architectural hare and run it till it burrowed in a goldmine" (JC, 440–41). These words remain with Brydon "for the small silver ring they had sounded over the queerest and deepest of his own lately most disguised and most muffled vibrations" (JC, 441). At the end of the first of the three sections of the tale, Alice tells Brydon that she has already seen his alter ego twice; the spectre materializes for her long before it appears to him. Alice, moreover, is only apparently absent from the long second section of the tale during which Brydon stalks his other self throughout the rooms and passages of the house on the jolly corner. It is one of the many ironies associated with the blindness of Brydon's egotism that he thinks to himself, regarding his nightly visits to the house, that "even Alice Staverton, who was moreover a well of discretion, didn't quite fully imagine" (JC, 454). For of course she does; as she tells him in section three, "I've known, all along . . . that you've been coming" (JC, 482). Whenever Brydon enters the house of his childhood alone—or ostensibly alone, as he thinks himself—the past, "that mystical other world that might have flourished for him had he not, for weal or woe, abandoned it," awakens for him with a sound effect: "This effect was the dim reverberating tinkle as of some far-off bell . . ." (JC, 455). The alert reader will recognize this bell as Alice's, the representative of the past (as we shall see shortly), "the dim reverberating tinkle" in section two of the story a reiteration of the "small silver ring" she had sounded for him with the hint of his repressed potential in section one.

Henry James refers in the notebook entry to his protagonist's "Dead Self." Yet "Dead Self" is something of a misnomer since the identity so denominated lives on in the projected heroine of the germinal tale outlined in the note. One source of the confusion and disagreement among critics of "The Jolly Corner" is precisely the proliferation of terms applied to the apparition. Are we dealing with a "Dead Self" as opposed to a "Living Self"? Or a "False Self" as opposed to a "True One"? Or an "American Self" (whether true or false, dead or alive) as opposed to a Europeanized one? Or a Doppelgänger or double or alter ego? I have introduced the term "worst self" by design into the present discussion because it seems to me to dispel some of the difficulties the other labels for the spectre inevitably create. First, the worst self can easily be conceived of as embodying *both* Brydon's unrealized potentials for development (what he might have been had he remained in America) and some of his actual traits, developed in the course of his European expatriation, particularly his egotism and blindness to all but his own concerns. Second, the concept of a worst self necessitates that we introduce the concept of a "best self," one that, like the "worst self," has only been partially realized in Brydon's life: the Europeanized dilletante who comes back to New York after thirty-three years abroad is no more the best self than he is the worst. When Brydon asks Alice if she believes that he is "as good as I might ever have been," she replies emphatically: "Oh no! Far from it" (JC, 451). It is implicit in the story, then, that Alice knows the best self as well as the worst, though it is the worst self that she revives in her dream visions for Brydon's eventual confrontation. The best self, like the worst, represents some aspects of Brydon that have at most lain dormant and some that have in fact developed within him. Third, it is above all important to keep in mind that while the worst and best selves represent extremes (almost, we might say, Platonic ideals) of negative and positive development, what is wanted in the end is some kind of transaction or mediation between these extremes. Brydon recoils from the rapacity, ruthlessness, and ravage that he reads (and that we are surely meant to read too) in the face of the spectre, from what he takes to be "evil, odious, blatant, vulgar," but he himself has need, in his relation with Alice, of the power for feeling that the ghost also embodies, "the roused passion of a life larger than his own" (JC, 477). At the same time, the ghost, before its final courageous advance, is shamed by Brydon, covering its face with its raised hands "as for dark deprecation," for, though Brydon is typically egotistical and, of course, wrong in supposing midway through the encounter with the worst self that he himself is the best ("the achieved, the enjoyed, the triumphant life"), he does possess valuable traits that are at most dormant in his alter ego, particularly his taste, his sensibility, his heightened consciousness for shades and nuances, for discrimination (JC, 475–76). Indeed, one way of putting the central thematic question in "The Jolly Corner" might be summed up in this question: Can power be purchased without the loss of sensibility?[12]

Before returning to the notebook entry, I want to set forth the little bit of arithmetic promised at the outset of this essay. Henry James first drafted "The Jolly Corner" in 1906.[13] The story was originally published in December, 1908, in the inaugural issue of *The English Review*. It appeared in its final form in 1909 in volume 17 of the New York Edition of *The Novels and Tales of Henry James*. The first paragraph of the story itself seems to stress numerology: we learn that Brydon has been away from America for thirty-three years, that he was twenty-three when he left, and that he is presently fifty-six. Now, the biographical parallels between Henry James and Spencer Brydon have been widely noted: the central one is that both return to their New York birthplaces after long sojourns in Europe.[14] Cushing Strout has wisely pointed out the pitfalls of equating author and character, remarking that "Spencer Brydon and Henry James cannot be merged."[15] Strout's own comment on the numerology of "The Jolly Corner" unintentionally illustrates the danger of such equations: "Freud, with his interest in the psychological significance of numbers, would surely not have been surprised to discover that the hero of James's story, also an expatriate returning to America after thirty-three years, had left when he was twenty-three and returned when he was fifty-six, thus exactly reversing the digits in his creator's case."[16] Strout's point on the reversal of numbers is quite brilliant, but he is misleading when he says that Brydon *also* returns after thirty-three years. Henry James's adult residence in Europe began in late 1875; his return may be calculated as having occurred twenty-nine years later, in 1904, or, if his two trips home in 1883 when his parents died are taken into account, as having occurred after an absence of somewhat less than twenty-one years. James was not an expatriate of thirty-three years. Why, then, did he choose thirty-three years as the period of Brydon's absence? Here is the simple calculation, or, rather, two calculations. First, subtract thirty-three from the date of first publication of "The Jolly Corner," December, 1908, and the result is 1875, within a month of James's actual departure for Europe in November of that year. Second, subtract thirty-three from the date of the publication of the story in its final, durable and enduring book form, 1909, and the result is a signal year in American history, 1876.[17]

Embedded with a sort of Joycean or Nabokovian cunning in the numbers provided at the beginning of "The Jolly Corner," then, is a clear clue that this is the second of Henry James's Centennial stories, following "An International Episode" (1878–79), which is structured, as Adeline R. Tintner has shown, by covert references to 1876 and to 1776 as well.[18] Thus, Brydon's apostasy in having left his native land—in having abjured what James called "one's supreme relation . . . to one's own country"—is heightened by his having begun his expatriation during the Centennial year. Since no one has noticed this Centennial aspect of "The Jolly Corner" before, no one has pointed out what seems to follow logically from it regarding the values embodied in Alice Staverton. It is a commonplace in the commentaries, of course, that Alice embodies the virtues of an old New York for which Henry James himself nostalgically yearned when he saw, in 1904, how it had been swept away during his long absence. Here is a key description of Alice that appears early in the tale:

> His old friend lived with one maid and herself dusted her relics and trimmed her lamps and polished her silver; she stood off, in the awful modern crush, when she could, but she sallied forth and did battle when the challenge was really to "spirit," the spirit she after all confessed to, proudly and a little shyly, as to that of the better time, that of *their* common, their quite far-away and antediluvian social period and order. She made use of the street-cars when need be, the terrible things that people scrambled for as the panic-stricken at sea scramble for the boats; she affronted, inscrutably, under stress, all the public concussions and ordeals; and yet, with that slim mystifying grace of her appearance, which defied you to say if she were a fair young woman who looked older through trouble, or a fine smooth older one who looked young through successful indifference; with her precious reference, above all, to memories and histories into which he could enter, she was as exquisite for him as some pale pressed flower (a rarity to begin with), and, failing other sweetnesses, she

was a sufficient reward of his effort. They had communities of knowledge, "their" knowledge (this discriminating possessive was always on her lips) of presences of the other age, presences all overlaid, in his case, by the experience of a man and the freedom of a wanderer, overlaid by pleasure, by infidelity, by passages of life that were strange and dim to her, just by "Europe" in short, but still unobscured, still exposed and cherished, under that pious visitation of the spirit from which she had never been diverted.

(JC, 439–40)

Three times in these three sentences, James uses the word *spirit*, and it would seem fainthearted not to suggest, after our Centennial calculation, that the "pious visitation of the spirit from which she had never been diverted" is the "Spirit of '76," a spirit that Alice has preserved for them both.

I have already clarified one of the cruxes of the tale mentioned at the beginning of this essay in suggesting that the division among critics about whether the apparition is Brydon as he is or Brydon as he might have been can be resolved by identifying the ghost as a worst self that includes aspects of the actual and of the subjunctive Brydon. Now that we can see Alice Staverton as a mature version of Bessie Alden, the heroine of "An International Episode," embodying the "Spirit of '76" in her quiet pride and independence, as well as in her ability to sally forth and do battle "when the challenge was really to 'spirit,' " we are ready to address another of those cruxes: insofar as Brydon's reconciliation is with Alice Staverton, who represents the best American spirit, the tale is not at all, in Bewley's words again, "anti-American with a vengeance." But, just as the spectre represents Spencer Brydon's worst self, it also represents the most destructive potentials of American national identity, for it has succumbed to "the rank money-passion," has been "hammered so hard and made so keen" by its conditions, and has been cruelly marked by the violence of the American lust for power—the apparition's missing fingers, "reduced to stumps, as if accidentally shot away" (JC, 449, 476). Brydon, then, accepts the best in his American identity when he is reborn to reciprocal love with Alice, even as he rejects the worst in the national character in his revulsion from the spectre. Alice knows the brutal conditions of the American marketplace, and by her knowledge she is able to bring Brydon's worst self to life. But her greatest independence is her freedom from those conditions, a freedom that allows her to envision Brydon's best self as well. Identification of Alice, finally, as a kind of avatar of the "Spirit of '76," is resonant with her address, Irving Place, for, as Jesse Bier points out, the street name associates her with the first great American teller of tales, and Spencer Brydon's amazement at the changes in America during his time away perhaps has some resonance with the amazement of Rip Van Winkle on his return.[19] We might observe, moreover, the additional resonance of Washington Irving with Alice as "Spirit of '76" in view of Irving's having been born in the

year of the British surrender, 1783, and of his having been named for the
general who received that surrender, George Washington.

To return briefly to the notebook entry of 5 February 1895, one recalls
that James supposes that his protagonist will recover "a little of the lost joy,
of the Dead Self, in his intercourse with some person, some woman."
When, however, James transformed the germ by making the "Dead Self"
the worst, and not the best, projection of his hero's identity, he deprived
the spectre of any joy whatsoever. As Alice says, "He has been unhappy,
he has been ravaged" and "he's grim, he's worn." Moreover, as Brydon observes at the last, "He has a million a year. . . . But he hasn't you" (JC,
485). To reread the notebook entry in the light of the finished tale, we
might indeed say that "lost joy" is no less proper to the Dead or worst self
than to Brydon at the time of his return to America. Brydon does at last
recover the joy, for all, so to speak, of his associated identities, in his triumphant possession of Alice.

At the end of the notebook entry, James proposes that his hero "must,
in the tale, also materially die" and that "[t]hen it is that his lost treasure
revives most." Tremper is right, of course, that Brydon loses consciousness
instead of dying, but James stresses again and again that his is a symbolic
death and rebirth. When he comes to—comes to himself (in one of the significant puns in the tale [JC, 483])—he knows "that Alice Staverton had for
a long unspeakable moment not doubted he was dead."

> "It must have been that I *was*." He made it out as she held him. "Yes—
> I can only have died. You brought me literally to life."
>
> (JC, 480)

The "interminable grey passage," the "dark other end of his tunnel," may
be taken, then, as a symbolic birth canal (JC, 479). The language of the
finished story, furthermore, closely echoes James's notebook description of
the revival of the hero's "lost treasure." At the end of the second section
of the tale, the apparition appears "as some black-vizored sentinel guarding
a treasure" (JC, 475). Thus, too, in Brydon's "rich return to consciousness"
in the first paragraph of the third section, he feels that he has been left
"with a treasure of intelligence waiting all round him for quiet appropria-
tion" (JC, 478). Similarly, in the next paragraph, Brydon likens himself to
"a man who has gone to sleep on some news of a great inheritance, and
then, after dreaming it away, after profaning it with matters strange to it,
has waked up again to serenity of certitude and has only to lie and watch
it grow" (JC, 479).[20]

There remains one final crux of interpretation to dispel, if we may.
That is, can we read the conclusion of the tale as fully affirmative? To what
extent must we credit complaints like that of Allen Stein, who is not alone
in being troubled by Brydon's seeming denial of any identity with the apparition? Noting that Buitenhuis sees Brydon as triumphant despite his apparent failure to accept the spectre as his own, Stein says trenchantly,

"One finds it hard to accept this thesis, which seems to assume that for James a real moral victory or a spiritual renewal can come without an awareness on the individual's part of his shortcomings, yet this is what the traditional reading of 'The Jolly Corner' would have us believe."[21] Nevertheless, we can, for several reasons, affirm that there is a real moral victory at the end of the tale.

I have said that the apparition is Brydon's worst self and also that he himself, in his present actuality, is not the best self—far from it, in Alice's words. Even so, despite his initial John Marcher-like egotism, Brydon is better than the worst self, and not merely, as might seem in this apparently circular statement, by definition. In terms of the general Jamesian ethos, his hunger for an expanding consciousness, the very appetite for perception that makes him seek his alternative self so steadfastly and at such manifest risk, is superior to the mere "rank money passion" and appetite for power of the worst self. The telling point here, I think, is that the worst self would not have sought to discover his alternative identity and thus would have remained tragically incomplete and alone, for the worst self seeks only material goods, not the goods of consciousness. The worst self also, as I have observed, has lost his joy, but only the Europeanized Brydon, capable of conceiving of and exploring, in the back rooms of the old house, the hidden depths of his own mind, could recover that joy—recover it, as it were, for them both.

I would argue, furthermore, that Brydon's denial of identity with the spectre is only momentary. Since the alter ego strikes Brydon as "evil, odious, blatant, vulgar," it is only natural that he at first denies that the beast is a part of him. (Of course it is; it must be; the tale would be pointless otherwise; and Virginia Woolf is surely right when she says, in the passage I have taken as my epigraph, that James's ghosts "have their origin within us," as they do also, for example, in *The Turn of the Screw*.) "There's somebody," Brydon says, "an awful beast; whom I brought, too horribly, to bay. But it's not me," and a little later he repeats his denial: "But this brute, with his awful face—this brute's a black stranger. He's none of *me*, even as I *might* have been" (JC, 482, 483). Yet Brydon never denies the black stranger again. He accepts, indeed, almost immediately, that he, Spencer Brydon, appeared to Alice as *it:*

> But she kept the clearness that was like the breath of infallibility. "Isn't the whole point that you'd have been different?"
> He almost scowled for it. "As different as *that*—?"
> Her look again was more beautiful to him than the things of this world. "Haven't you exactly wanted to know *how* different. So this morning," she said, "you appeared to me."
> "Like *him?*"
> "A black stranger!"
> "Then how did you know it was I?"
>
> (JC, 483–84)[22]

Alice replies that she knew not only because of the way her imagination had worked but also " 'because you somehow wanted me. He seemed to tell me of that. So why,' she strangely smiled, 'shouldn't I like him?' " Brydon does not attack Alice's assertion that she knew *it* was *him*, and he does not question that *it* communicated to Alice *his own* desire for her. He is only amazed, in the ensuing dialogue, though perhaps secretly reassured as well, that Alice likes (or could have liked) "that horror," and that she accepts and pities *it*. At the climax of their final dialogue, when Alice's vision of him is confirmed as identical to his vision of *it* because of the details she provides of "[h]is great convex pince-nez" and of "his poor right hand," Brydon only winces, "whether for his proved identity or for his lost fingers" (JC, 484–85).

It is simply wrong, then, to assert that Brydon holds fast to his initial denial of any connection between himself and the apparition. Besides, he does not need any more explicit an acknowledgment of the apparition's relation to himself in order to meet Professor Stein's criterion that he show an awareness of his own shortcomings. Surely, he does so—and not, like John Marcher in "The Beast in the Jungle," too late—by repairing his earlier error with Alice Staverton, by opening himself up to her love and by offering his love to her. The effects on Brydon of his confrontation with the "black stranger" are complex: his obsession with his alternative life is over; he has exorcised the base elements in his own character embodied in the spectral vision of his worst self, particularly his isolating egotism; and at the same time he has absorbed something of the apparition's potency, its capacity for passional life, so that his final gesture, recorded in the last five words of the story, is active and manly: "he drew her to his breast" (JC, 485). The words that Miss Staverton murmurs just before he does so—"And he isn't—no, he isn't—*you!*"—are not, then, a mercifully false reassurance to a Brydon unable to face himself; rather, they are an affirmation that in having faced himself Brydon has indeed been reborn into a new life as a new man. Alice's underlying message entails a shift in tense: the apparition was you, both as you might have been and as you were, but he is not you now. Loving and beloved, Spencer Brydon enjoys at last a blessed state the beauty of which the black stranger had never tasted and could never taste.

I have not tried to cover every aspect of "The Jolly Corner" in this new reading of James's great story. For example, so far as sources are concerned, there are numerous analogues in James's art and life (including his notes for *The Sense of the Past* and his famous dream of the Louvre) that are amply treated by other commentators.[23] My aim, however, has been to develop new material—chiefly the notebook entry of 5 February 1895 and the hitherto undetected Centennial theme of the tale—in an attempt to resolve the principal problems of interpretation in the critical literature. In addition, the present essay has implications for reading other work by Henry James. Our reading of "The Jolly Corner" may remind us, for example, that Henry James was always of several minds about his native land, so that we see the American national identity at once celebrated, satirized, and condemned again and again, beginning with such early works as *The American*, "Daisy Miller," and *The Portrait of a Lady*. Students of James may also be alerted by the foregoing argument to the necessity of reading the notebooks carefully and afresh; it is a mistake to rely on authorities like Matthiessen and Murdock, the editors of the 1947 *Notebooks of Henry James*, who missed the connection that Krook and Tremper detected between James's 1895 note and "The Jolly Corner."[24] So far as James's creative process is concerned, my analysis of the transformation of the notebook germ into the finished story suggests the ingenuity James could muster to deflect the banal into the strikingly original. In the light of recent studies of *The Turn of the Screw* and "The Beast in the Jungle," the cunning with which James encoded the Centennial theme into "The Jolly Corner" seems more and more typical of his late work, where signs and symbols operate with a Modernist or even post-Modernist complexity.[25] The Centennial theme makes "The Jolly Corner" virtually the apotheosis of Henry James's Americano-European legend, a gorgeous, powerful fusion of James's intense interest in our national character and of his equally intense devotion to exploring the dark corridors and shifting vistas of consciousness.

Notes

1. "Henry James' Ghost Stories," *Times Literary Supplement* 20 (22 December 1921):850.

2. Allen F. Stein, "The Beast in 'The Jolly Corner': Spencer Brydon's Ironic Rebirth," *Studies in Short Fiction* 11 (1974):62–63. For a representative judgment of the excellent literary quality of "The Jolly Corner," see Krishna Baldev Vaid, *Technique in the Tales of Henry James* (Cambridge, Mass.: Harvard University Press, 1964), 247. The majority of commentators read the tale as redemptive: typical of affirmative readings are Jesse Bier's "Henry James's 'The Jolly Corner': The Writer's Fable and the Deeper Matter," *Arizona Quarterly* 35 (1979):321–34; J. Delbaere-Garant's "The Redeeming Form: Henry James's 'The Jolly Corner,' " *Revue des Langues Vivantes* 33 (1967):588–96; and Courtney Johnson's "Henry James's 'The Jolly Corner,' " *American Imago* 24 (1967):344–59. A sizeable minority of readers, however, see no salvation for Spencer Brydon: the most forceful exemplars of this view are Stein, in the essay cited above, and Joan Delfattore, in "The 'Other' Spencer Brydon," *Arizona Quarterly* 35 (1979):335–41. Edward Wagenknecht provides a useful overview of the critical debate in *The Tales of Henry James* (New York: Frederick Ungar, 1984), 155–60.

3. Marius Bewley, *The Complex Fate: Hawthorne, Henry James, and Some Other American Writers* (London: Chatto and Windus, 1952), 73. The most prominent of the numerous critics who see Brydon and James as discovering a new acceptance of America and of American identity is Leon Edel, who remarks at the end of his discussion of the tale, "All that he [James] did from this time on was intimately related to his American past" (*Henry James, The Master: 1901–1916* [Philadelphia: J. B. Lippincott, 1972], 317).

4. Representative of the more widespread view that the apparition is the Brydon who might have been are F. O. Matthiessen, in *Henry James: The Major Phase* (New York: Oxford

University Press, 1944), 136–37; Edel, in *Henry James, The Master*, 312–17; and Napier Witt and John Lucas, in their introduction to *Americans and Europe: Selected Tales of Henry James* (Boston: Houghton Mifflin, 1965), xix–xx. Quentin Anderson argues forcefully that the apparition is not the might-have-been Brydon but rather the Brydon-who-is, in *The American Henry James* (New Brunswick, N.J.: Rutgers University Press, 1957), 177–78. Raymond Thorberg ably develops Anderson's idea in "Terror Made Relevant: Henry James's Ghost Stories," *Dalhousie Review* 47 (1967):185–91. Floyd Stovall, in "Henry James's 'The Jolly Corner,' " *Nineteenth Century Fiction* 12 (1957):72–84, follows Anderson (drawing on earlier articles that Anderson incorporated in revised form into *The American Henry James*), but adds the twist that there are two ghosts in the tale, the one upstairs, who is the might-have-been Brydon, and the one downstairs, who is Brydon as he is. Pamela Jacobs Shelden, in "Jamesian Gothicism: The Haunted Castle of the Mind," *Studies in Literary Imagination* 7 (1974):121–34, follows Stovall in the two-ghost reading. The idea that there are two distinct apparitions is ingenious but finally unconvincing, chiefly—though not solely—because of the thin textual evidence offered in its support. For a good critique of Stovall and of some of the psychobiographical studies cited below, see Peter Buitenhuis's discussion (one of the best available on the tale) in *The Grasping Imagination: The American Writings of Henry James* (Toronto: University of Toronto Press, 1970), 210–21.

5. Preface to volume 17 of *The Novels and Tales of Henry James* (New York: Charles Scribner's Sons, 1909), xxiv.

6. *Henry James: Selected Fiction*, ed. Leon Edel (New York: E. P. Dutton, 1953), 584.

7. *The Ordeal of Consciousness in Henry James* (Cambridge: Cambridge University Press, 1962), 334n.

8. "Henry James's Altering Ego: An Examination of the Psychological Double in Three Tales," *Texas Quarterly* 19, no. 3 (1976):70.

9. *The Notebooks of Henry James*, ed. F. O. Matthiessen and Kenneth B. Murdock (New York: Oxford University Press, 1947), 183–84. See also James's earlier note, "that concetto I have jotted down in another notebook," in *Notebooks*, 143–44.

10. Stovall, "James's 'Jolly Corner,' " p. 83. Closest, perhaps, to my reading of Alice Staverton's active role is Edwin Honig's in "The Merciful Fraud in Three Stories by Henry James," *Tiger's Eye* 1, no. 9 (15 October, 1949):83–96. Speaking of all three stories ("The Jolly Corner," "The Beast in the Jungle," and "The Altar of the Dead"), Honig says, "The means by which this is done [discovering or rediscovering the value of the self in some other than its present form] involves an active communion with another person from whom the self elicits a disguise with which to enact the role of the ideally projected or mysteriously potential other self. The sympathetic person is a woman . . ." (84). Then, speaking specifically of "The Jolly Corner," Honig writes that "[n]o small part of the ritual the event [sic] of Brydon's 'rebirth' depends on the maternal-romantic role of Miss Staverton. For it is she, as the fruitful mother-substitute, who has induced the growth of Brydon's search through the dark womb of the past, the passages from which he emerges reborn" (86). Other commentators who lay more than usual importance on Alice's role are Courtney Johnson, Ernest Tuveson, in " 'The Jolly Corner': A Fable of Redemption," *Studies in Short Fiction* 12 (1975):271–80, and J. Delbaere-Garant. Thoroughly untenable, in my view, is the reading presented by John R. Byers, in "Alice Staverton's Redemption of Spencer Brydon in 'The Jolly Corner,' " *South Atlantic Review* 41, no. 2 (1976):90–99, an argument, to be sure, that Brydon is redeemed "through the determined efforts of Alice Staverton," but one that sees those efforts as consisting chiefly of Alice's lying every time she says she has seen the apparition; she has not seen the thing, says Byers, and in the end she just guesses that the ghost wears a pince-nez and has a right hand missing two fingers. Byers says that she guesses correctly about the hand because Brydon himself is missing two fingers on his right hand, an amputation that no other reader has ever detected and for which there is not a shred of presentable evidence.

11. Henry James, "The Jolly Corner," in *The Novels and Tales of Henry James*, vol. 17 New York: Charles Scribner's Sons, 1909), 480, hereafter cited parenthetically as JC.

12. Bier, "The Writer's Fable," p. 328, makes a similar point, as well as an astute comment on the title of the tale: "What James's title, 'The Jolly Corner,' tells us is that the protagonist seeks an ideal intersection of possibilities that are otherwise running in different directions. At a certain nexus might one not join high sensibility to an equal and opposite potency." Bier continues, incidentally, with the remark that "Familiar name symbolism in James is helpful in this regard. The hero, Spencer Brydon, has spent himself but, as Bride-on, he hopes for an assumption of force, with its sexual component, at last; and Miss Staverton will provide his support." More, perhaps, may be said about the names of the two principal characters. *Alice* derives at its root from the Greek word for truth, *alētheia*, which is consonant with Alice's part in leading Brydon toward new truths about himself and also with the infallibility attributed to her in the last scene of the story (JC, 483). *Staverton* suggests not only the staff that is Brydon's support, but also, perhaps, Alice's part in helping Brydon stave off the inner demon that she has also helped him summon. *Staverton* may also suggest Alice's staying in the town that Brydon, the prodigal son, had long forsaken. *Brydon* suggests to me not so much "Bride-on" as it does bridegroom, or the *don*, that is the gentleman or knight (like Don Quixote), destined for a bride, a meaning resonant with Brydon's image of himself as a figure from "an age of greater romance," proceeding on his ghostly quest "with a drawn sword" (JC, 464).

13. Edel, *Henry James, The Master*, 312–13.

14. Edel's account of the story in *Henry James, The Master*, of course, develops the psychobiographical materials. These are also heavily stressed in Saul Rosenzweig's famous essay "The Ghost of Henry James," in the *Partisan Review* 11 (1944):436–55. See, also, among other attempts to connect James's biography and "The Jolly Corner": Tremper's "Henry James's Altering Ego: An Examination of the Psychological Double in Three Tales"; Robert Rogers's "The Beast in Henry James," in *American Imago* 13 (1956):427–54; J. W. Schroeder's "The Mothers of Henry James," in *American Literature* 22 (1951):424–31; F. W. Dupee's *Henry James* (n.p.: William Sloane, 1951), 182–83; Manfred Mackenzie's "A Theory of Henry James's Psychology," in the *Yale Review* 63 (1974):347–71, and reprinted, much revised, in Mackenzie's *Communities of Honor and Love in Henry James* (Cambridge, Mass.: Harvard University Press, 1976); and Christof Wegelin, *The Image of Europe in Henry James* (Dallas: Southern Methodist University Press, 1958), 155–56.

15. "Psyche, Clio, and the Artist," in *New Directions in Psychohistory*, ed. Mel Albin (Lexington, Mass.: D. C. Heath, 1980), 108. Buitenhuis also stresses the pitfalls of reading the tale biographically (212), as does Stovall (84).

16. Strout, 106.

17. James must have thought until almost the last minute that the story would only be published in the 1909 volume. See Edel's note in *The Ghostly Tales of Henry James*, ed. Leon Edel (New Brunswick, N.J.: Rutgers University Press, 1948), 725, where it is explained that James expected that "The Jolly Corner" would be the only previously unpublished tale in the 1909 volume of the New York Edition: "He was assembling the ghost volume (vol. xvii) when the opportunity for publication came in Ford Madox Hueffer's newly founded *English Review* where the story appeared in December 1908."

18. "'An International Episode': A Centennial Essay on a Centennial Story," *Henry James Review* 1 (1979):24–56. Tintner discusses Henry James's interest in the Centennial celebration on 26–28.

19. Bier, "The Writer's Fable," 322–23. Washington Irving had a house on Irving Place, which was named after him (see Robert Shackleton, *The Book of New York* [Philadelphia: Penn Publishing Company, 1917], 22–23). Also, according to Leon Edel, Henry James remembered meeting Irving on the steamboat to Fort Hamilton (see *Henry James, The Untried Years: 1843–1870* [London: Rupert Hart-Davis, 1953], 106).

20. Brydon may be aptly likened here to the prodigal son in the parable. In "Universality in 'The Jolly Corner,'" in *Texas Studies in Language and Literature* 4 (1962):12–15, Wil-

liam A. Freedman points out allusions to other parables in Matthew 25; for example, Alice "trimmed her own lamps," like the wise virgins awaiting the bridegroom. Such scriptural allusions, as well as the motif of Brydon's being born again, lend considerable support, in my view, to affirmative readings of the conclusion of "The Jolly Corner."

21. Stein, "The Beast in 'The Jolly Corner,' " 63.

22. James's revision of this dialogue strongly reinforces the reading offered in the present essay. Where the New York Edition text of 1909 reads "But she kept the clearness that was like the breath of infallibility," the *English Review* text of December 1908 reads only "But she kept her clearness." Where the New York Edition text reads "Her look again was more beautiful to him than the things of this world," the *English Review* text reads "Her lucid look seemed to bathe him." James obviously intended to bestow a practically supernal authority upon Alice.

The changes James made between magazine publication in 1908 and New York Edition publication in 1909 call into question the widespread (and perhaps complacent) assumption of James scholars that James's revisions of the later works for his collected edition were minor. For example, a recent critic (Deborah Esch in "A Jamesian About-Face: Notes on 'The Jolly Corner,' " *ELH* 50 [1983]:587–605) remarks that "[i]n keeping with James's characteristic practice of revision, even this late tale underwent minor modification as it passed from the journal to volume 17 of the New York Edition. In most respects, however, the two versions are identical" (589). But my collation of the two texts of "The Jolly Corner" includes more than one hundred substantive variants (not counting the numerous changes entailed in James's having called Brydon's cleaning lady Muldoody in the first and Muldoon in the second version). Many apparently minor changes are in fact highly significant. For example, the Alice of 1908, in conversation with Brydon, refers to "that day of your bringing me" to the house on the jolly corner; the Alice of 1909 speaks of "that day of my going with you." This particular revision suggests that James intended, in the later version, to give increased emphasis to Alice's active role in the tale.

23. See especially the various commentaries by Leon Edel cited above.

24. As Professor Edel remarked some years ago (in his address at the inaugural meeting of the Henry James Society in 1979), one of the most pressing needs in James studies is for a new, authoritative edition of Henry James's notebooks.

25. See, for example, Donal O'Gorman, "Henry James's Reading of *The Turn of the Screw,*" *Henry James Review* 1 (1979–80):125–38, 228–56, and James Ellis, "The Archaeology of Ancient Rome: Sexual Metaphor in 'The Beast in the Jungle,' " *Henry James Review* 6 (1984):27–31.

INDEX